Advance Praise for

Activists, Advocates, and Agitators:
21st Century Justice-Oriented Teacher Activist Organization

"Don't just close your doors–talk to one another, support each other, and above all, organize! Here are the stories of teachers who did just that, in service of social justice, confronting the scourges of standardized testing and privatization."

—Anthony Cody, co-founder of the Network for Public Education and author of *The Educator and the Oligarch: A Teacher Challenges the Gates Foundation*

"Brianne Kramer's Activists, Advocates, and Agitators: 21st Century Justice-Oriented Teacher Activist Organizations *is one of the first books to guide educators and grassroots education activists on how to weave issues of social justice in the education workspace. Brianne takes readers on a journey by example. She presents some of the great education social justice grassroots organizations in the country. She presents readers with the work of Dr. Denisha Jones, a force in the Black Lives Matter at School and the important work of the Trinational Coalition in Defense of Public Education in discussing how the privatization of education is not inclusive to the U.S. She outlines the templates for organizing used by UCORE, the Red for Ed Movement, and Teacher Action Group (TAG). Brianne has written a must-read primer for anyone interested in elevating social justice in the education space and, more importantly, how to train teachers to do the work."*

—Marla Kilfoyle, NBCT Educator and Union Leader for 30 years and Former Executive Director of The Badass Teachers Association (2013-2018)

"Activists, Advocates, and Agitators *is a timely, necessary contribution. The book offers a rare diversity of perspectives by placing leading scholars, activists, and leaders in conversation with one another as they offer essential insights on the dynamic teacher activist organizations forwarding social justice in education. Developed through both on-the-ground experiences and dynamic analyses of recent activist efforts,* Activists, Advocates, and Agitators: 21st Century Justice-Oriented Teacher Activist Organizations *is essential reading for anyone concerned with understanding transformative action in schools and the groups on the forefront of these efforts."*

—Noah Karvelis, co-founder of the Arizona RedForEd movement

"This important new collection offers a timely and incisive investigation of teachers' work for collective social justice in and out of schools, with robust contributions from teachers, organizers, academics, and activists. This accessible and comprehensive volume highlight the struggles and successes of radical courage and organizing in neoliberal times. This is an essential book for anyone interested collective futures in education and teaching as a social act."

—Arlo Kempf, Associate Professor, Department of Curriculum, Teaching Learning, University of Toronto and Co-editor, Routledge book series: Critical Perspectives on Teachers' Work

"Essential reading for anybody interested in the present and future of teacher activism—and public education generally"

—Eric Blanc, author of *Red State Revolt: The Teachers Strike Wave and Working-Class Politics*

"Activists, Advocates, and Agitators: 21st Century Justice-Oriented Teacher Activist Organizations *is, at once, a primer, a historical recounting, a guide, an instiller of hope, and a call to continued actions to disrupt the dismantling of our public education system in the United States. The contributors include union activists, scholar activists, educators, and more who refuse to allow the manufactured crises in education to serve as covers for the perpetuation of racism, classism, power/control structures, and more that undermine the possibilities of a truly democratic system of education. In this volume, we witness the work of grassroots movements and actions, with some growing into larger groups, or even morphing into national movements—all focused on initiating actions that will lead to sustained changes and processes that will celebrate and respond to unique individuals, groups, and communities. In very direct responses to attacks on communities of educators and learners via mandates, legislation, policy, and habituated actions rooted in inequities, these inspiring stories will serve as points of origin for imagining and then acting upon ideas for a future that is decent, fair, just, tolerant, and open to the cultural, linguistic, ethnic, spiritual, and educative richness that is necessary for our very survival as a democratic country."*

—Rick Meyer, member the organizing committee of Uniting to Save Our Schools, a former elementary school teacher, and faculty emeritus at the University of New Mexico.

"Activists, Advocates, and Agitators: 21st Century Justice-Oriented Teacher Activist Organizations *is a clear demonstration of the power of educator activism through the growth and establishments of rank-and-file movements. As a former veteran teacher and 6 year Maryland State Education Association and National Education Association Board member, I understand first hand the importance of educator activism from the ground up through rank-and-file organizing and caucuses. Throughout my tenure as a union leader, I became more and more disillusioned with the NEA and AFT, realizing the intensely embedded bureaucratic structure and the unwavering dedication to democratic party with what seems like zero accountability demands. It was the CORE groups and other on-the-ground educator activism movements across the country described in this book that kept me inspired and motivated to keep up the fight for educational justice in my own state and county. Reading through each chapter reminded me of the pride I felt as a teacher watching educators across the country fight back against the incessant criminalization of Black, Indigenous, and brown students, anti-CRT legislation, and other racist policies and legislation. I felt the connection of the stories shared throughout this book to my own involvement in activism movements like Black Lives Matter at School, and how collective action and power can absolutely create change. I highly recommend this book to anyone in the education field, especially to Aspiring Educators seeking camaraderie and unity in union spaces."*

—Erika Strauss Chavarria, Former Teacher
and Former MSEA/NEA Director

"Brianne Kramer's edited volume brings together a range of organizer-scholars-educators to document, theorize, and illustrate the movement work on various fronts that collectively make up educator resistance movements today. In the composition of the volume, Kramer centers the perspectives and analyses of educators doing the work on the ground. This is what makes this book so crucial for understanding and making visible the work *of social justice education movements as it takes place over time and across diverse geographies. As the chapters demonstrate, these fronts include curricular movements for Mexican American studies and Black lives, teacher education, in the streets of George Floyd Square, in union halls and on the picket lines, in education workers' collective inquiry spaces, on the margins of teacher education, and so many more. Together, the chapters make visible how educators build power*

through networked relationships of solidarity within and across these fronts. Via their intellectual work in the book, Kramer and chapter authors also, importantly, contribute to nurturing this very relational solidarity. In the spirit of the book's aims, I think this text is best read collectively—gather your fellow activists, advocates, and agitators and read together!"

—Erin Dyke, Associate Professor of Curriculum Studies,
Oklahoma State University

"In this critical historical moment, where students, teachers, and communities committed to justice are under attack, I cannot think of a more important collection than Activists, Advocates, and Agitators: 21st Century Justice-Oriented Teacher Activist Organizations. *This book highlights just how powerful teachers can be, even in the face of political forces that make it dangerous to even teach the truth about power and oppression."*

—Wayne Au, Professor, University of Washington Bothell;
Editor, *Rethinking Schools*

Activists, Advocates, and Agitators

Published by Myers Education Press, LLC
P.O. Box 424, Gorham, ME 04038

Myers Education Press is an academic publisher specializing in books, e-books, and digital content in the field of education. All of our books are subjected to a rigorous peer review process and produced in compliance with the standards of the Council on Library and Information Resources.

Library of Congress Cataloging-in-Publication Data available from Library of Congress.

13-digit ISBN 978-1-9755-0563-9 (paperback)
13-digit ISBN 978-1-9755-0564-6 (library networkable e-edition)
13-digit ISBN 978-1-9755-0565-3 (consumer e-edition)

Printed in the United States of America.

All first editions printed on acid-free paper that meets the American National Standards Institute Z39-48 standard.

Books published by Myers Education Press may be purchased at special quantity discount rates for groups, workshops, training organizations, and classroom usage. Please call our customer service department at 1-800-232-0223 for details.

Cover design by Teresa LaGrange

Visit us on the web at **www.myersedpress.com** to browse our complete list of titles.

Activists, Advocates, and Agitators

21st Century Justice-Oriented Teacher Activist Organization

EDITED BY *Brianne Kramer*

Gorham, Maine

Dedication

This book is dedicated to my grandparents, who introduced me to unions and politics, creating a foundation for the work I center myself in today.

Table of Contents

Part 2: Teacher-Activist Organizations and Social Justice Unionism

Part 3: Opportunities for Preparing Preservice and Current Teachers

Acknowledgments

Activists, Advocates, and Agitators: 21st Century Justice-Oriented Teacher Activist Organizations has been a dream of mine since I researched the Badass Teachers Organization for my dissertation study. This book shaped into a resource even better than I could have ever imagined! It has been a privilege to put together an edited text that works to inform readers about 21st century teacher activist organizations and social justice unionism. This book is intended for anyone interested in educational movements, unions, and grassroots teacher activist organizations.

To the contributors: Thank you for being part of this text. The work your unions and organizations do have inspired so many nationally and beyond. I am forever grateful that you allowed the stories of your organizations to be shared here. For the researchers who contributed their important research regarding these social movements, thank you for sharing your work in this book.

Special thanks to the entire team at Myers Education Press. Your support and mentorship in making this book a reality is extremely appreciated.

I would also like to thank my family, who were supportive during the development of my second book. It is no easy feat to create an edited text, but with the encouragement at home, it made the process move much more smoothly. Thank you Jason, Ava, and Emerson.

Finally, I would like to thank my grandparents: Edmund, Evelyn, Jerry, and Mary Lou. This book is dedicated to all of you. It means the world to me that both of my grandfathers are still present on this earth to see this text finished. The lessons I learned during my youth from each of you have continued to impact me through today.

Part 1:
Why and How Teachers Organize

CHAPTER 1

The Need for Teacher Activism and Organizing: An Introduction

Brianne Kramer

Introduction

I GREW UP in Northwest Ohio with blue-collar roots. My grandparents were foundational in beginning my understanding of activism, advocacy, and politics. My maternal grandfather worked for the railroad, retiring after many decades of service. He was part of the Brotherhood of Locomotive Engineers and Trainmen (BLET) and served the union in various roles. I grew up raised on stories about his time in the union—the times he won against "the boss man," being part of an amicus brief filed, the brotherhood established between BLET members, and the day-to-day challenges in organizing to preserve workers' rights and dignity. My paternal grandfather, who spent most of his life as a farmer, also participated in political advocacy by becoming elected as a Township Trustee during my childhood. I remember being in awe that my grandfather's name appeared on campaign materials! No one I knew had ever run for office or seemed that politically engaged to serve the public, so this was a new and exciting possibility. Both of these men, through their service and advocacy in different ways, impressed upon me the importance of action—both through a union and civic involvement.

Both of my grandmothers were examples of what I would define as strong women, and although they would not have defined themselves as feminists, I hold them in high esteem as my earliest feminist role models because they both exemplified strength and perseverance in different ways. My maternal grandmother was a stay-at-home parent to seven children, working hard to run a household during my grandfather's time away for his job on the railroad. My paternal grandmother raised three children and ran a household, while also taking time to work in certain areas on the farm or at a local factory, as needed. After my grandfather retired from farming, my paternal grandmother worked at the County Clerk of Courts office as a Title Clerk. Both of my grandmothers showed me that women were important contributors, regardless of the places they occupied. Later in my life, my grandmothers were extremely supportive as I entered the workforce, became a parent, and chose to further my education by enrolling in a PhD program. They never questioned my decisions along the way and were wonderful champions for my accomplishments, truly making me feel as if I could achieve anything I set out to.

I share these early experiences in order to provide context for the beginning of how I became aware of unions and political advocacy. I began as an outspoken child and teenager, retaining this quality into adulthood. Although I did not have the opportunity to take part in activism, as it is broadly defined, I did not shy away from asking the hard questions to those in power in the spaces I occupied. A chance encounter in July 2014 would bring activism to the forefront of my life and changed how I thought about activism and organizing.

In a blog post on June 13, 2014, the founders of the Badass Teachers Association (BATs), Dr. Mark Naison and Priscilla Sanstead, shared there would be a celebration for BATs' first anniversary and a march planned at the U.S. Department of Education on July 28th (Naison & Sanstead, 2014). Despite this announcement, and the fact that many from the greater educational community planned to attend, I had no idea that this group even existed . . . until the day of their march. In my dissertation, I detailed my first impressions of what I found that day:

> Protest songs, signs, and individuals chanting and singing along with the people leading the crowd greeted me as I walked up to the Federal Department of Education on July 28, 2014. I was in Washington D.C. for a vacation when I decided to stop by the Department of Education during an afternoon of sightseeing. I was not expecting a large protest to be occurring on a quiet Monday afternoon in the city. Children ran around the courtyard wearing

t-shirts with phrases such as "I am not a test score," while many of the adults held various signs protesting the Common Core State Standards and increased teacher accountability. A graveyard consisting of cardboard tombstones listed elective courses such as visual art, choir, band, and physical education placed in front of a large banner with a black bat symbol in the middle. Numerous speakers stood on a small stage and presented issues in their communities. The crowd responded with applause and cheers when the speakers asserted their visions for democratic public education and also responded with hisses and jeers when the speakers shared the problems that public schools were faced with. In between speakers, a small band of men and women led the crowd in various protest songs, such as "Solidarity Forever" and "We Shall Overcome." I was in disbelief that teachers and parents had banded together to create such a large protest, and, as I quickly learned, a newer grassroots teacher activist organization with a radical name. As I spoke to those members in attendance, I learned that the Badass Teachers Association (BATs) had just marked the organization's first anniversary. The members seemed very dedicated to this group, many traveling to the nation's capital from various parts of the country despite the primary engagement of the group occurring on a Facebook page. Everyone present shared the same goal—to draw attention to issues in public education, such as the Common Core State Standards. Many members of the group felt the issues they were experiencing within their school districts were exacerbated by changes in content standards and increased accountability for teachers, students, and school districts put into action by Arne Duncan, the Secretary of Education at that time. I was only able to stay at the protest for two hours, but as I walked away, I joined the national Facebook page. After checking the national page later that evening, I learned several members of the leadership team secured a meeting with the Secretary of Education and several other important individuals within the Department of Education. During this meeting, the BAT leaders proposed their vision of democratic public schools that support all students and families. Due to the

> conversations within the Facebook site, I spent much of the next several days reading all I could about this new group, cementing my commitment to the mission and vision of the organization. This was the type of group I never could have imagined, but now after being a part of the Badass Teachers Association for three years, I could not imagine a world where this teacher activist organization did not exist. (Kramer, 2017)

It has now been 10 years since I first learned about BATs, and the network of Teacher Activist Groups (TAG) has continued to grow. Some larger teachers' unions have also centered their activism around social justice organizing. Much of this teacher activism has sprung out of the need to challenge these horrific neoliberal reforms that have plagued education since the 1980s. Giroux (2013) defined neoliberalism as:

> not merely an economic doctrine that prioritizes buying and selling, makes the supermarket and mall the temples of public life, and defines the obligations of citizenship in strictly consumerist terms. It is also a mode of pedagogy and a set of social arrangements that uses education to win consent, produce consumer-based notions of agency, and militarize reason in the service of war, profits, power, and violence while simultaneously instrumentalizing all forms of knowledge." (p. 459)

While teacher activism is not solely a 21st century phenomenon, there are many things that have changed in the way teachers and public education supporters are activating, organizing, and protesting. Furthermore, increasing legislative attacks and issues that stemmed from the pandemic have also necessitated the type of organizing we have witnessed in this century.

21st Century Teacher Activism

The new century found unions beginning to mobilize using social justice organizing, while many new teacher activist groups sprung up from grassroots organizing efforts. The new ways of mobilizing public school supporters were necessary as increased accountability measures put increased pressures on teachers who were forced to teach to more stringent standards and use standardized tests and materials. Once President Barack Obama took office, many educators were hopeful his administration would issue new education legislation to eliminate No Child Left Behind. That hope quickly fizzled as Obama introduced the Race to the Top program, which required states to compete for grant funds by following specific guidelines that paved the way for further neoliberal reform (Kramer, 2017). Because of this disappointment, educators began to organize around a variety of local, state, and federal issues in education. During this time, we saw teachers unions strengthen and organize within community contexts focusing on larger social justice issues, while numerous grassroots organizations sprang up as individuals and separate networks combined forces in order to build a larger movement. Whether union or grassroots organization, they held many similarities. Stark et al. (2022) identified several cultural processes of contemporary education movements: centering ethical principles, using new technologies, and engaging in networks. Each organization featured in this text utilizes these processes, and, collectively, the development of these areas during 21st century organizing is further discussed in this chapter.

Social Justice Unionism

The build to the social justice unionism we see today began with a few specific movements. The Bargaining for the Common Good (BCG) movement was utilized in Chicago in 2012, as educators went on strike for 10 days, demanding smaller class sizes, facility improvements, and other demands that went further than the typical 'bread-and-butter' issues that unions tended to focus on previously (McCartin et al., 2020). BCG also focused on getting the community represented in the demands the unions were bargaining for and used bargaining as a longer-term strategy instead of a short-term fix for specific issues (McCartin et al., 2020). St. Paul, Seattle, and Los Angeles teachers unions also embraced the ideas behind BCG in their campaigns (McCartin et al., 2020). This movement led up to #RedforEd, which began in 2018.

Social justice unionism has been taken up and furthered by several larger teachers' unions and caucuses across the country. The first social justice–oriented caucus was formed in the Chicago Teachers Union in 2008, with the formation of the Caucus of Rank-and-File Educators (CORE) (Asselin, 2022; Stark et al., 2022). The Movement of Rank-and-File Educators (MORE) of New York's United Federation of Teachers (UFT) formed in 2012, while the Caucus of Working Educators in Philadelphia (WE) formed in 2014 (Asselin, 2022; Riley, 2015). In Canada, Ontario Education Workers United (OEWU) was formed in 2019 with members across several of Ontario's teachers unions (Bocking, 2022; Maton, 2022). Each of these caucuses were crucial in pushing their larger unions to adopt more social justice–focused demands centered on the needs of the greater community.

Social Media and Virtual Organizing

Another large change for organizing in the 21st century was the advent of social media. Once individuals began to better understand the possibilities of how groups could form and utilize social media for various actions, campaigns, and general organizing, several groups developed online and found that space to be an important home for their organizations. Tarlau (2023) found movements that utilized social media helped to "reinvigorate the labor movements" and increased members' participation in union infrastructure (p. 837). Many members of the Badass Teachers Association found social media to be a democratizing factor, allowing people to participate in organizing and activism without being located in a specific area or even having to leave their home (Kramer, 2017, 2023). Many of the group's successful campaigns originated from and were situated in the online space, despite some leaders not initially seeing the possibilities that existed for organizing on the internet (Kramer, 2023).

West Virginia teacher, Jay O'Neal founded West Virginia Teachers United on Facebook in 2017, but after about 6 weeks without much movement on the page, he renamed the group WV Public Employees United, in order to be inclusive of all public sector workers who would fall under the proposed changes to public workers' health insurance (Tarlau, 2023). Teacher, Justin Endicott's impassioned plea for teachers to unite in a live-streamed video during a low-attended demonstration brought more attention to the group and began the wave of organizing efforts that led to the 2018 WV Teachers strike (Tarlau, 2023). In 2020, West Virginia again organized using a secret Facebook group, Teachers TOGETHER, in order to share information about COVID-19 transmission data, legislative happenings, and the move to return to in-person learning (Howell & Schmitzer, 2022). Howell and Schmitzer (2022) also found several overt functions of the use of social media as an organizing tool, including mapping the worker community, gathering and sharing information, exchanging or generating tactics, creating a free space for members' voices, empowering members, and entertaining members. Covert functions of social media organizing groups are creating connections to the wider labor movement, creating intersections between the personal and professional, and reimagining the good teacher subjectivity (Howell & Schmitzer, 2022). Karvelis (2022) shared how one Arizona #RedforEd organizer started in the movement by seeing a Facebook event posted by other educators and then volunteered time to become a moderator for the Facebook group, Arizona Educators United (AEU). AEU had nine administrators running the group initially, leading to their first #RedforEd event on March 7, 2018 with over 20,000 people interested in attending, and later went a step further in creating an Action Network database from the social media group (Tarlau, 2023). In Oklahoma, teacher Alberto Morejon created the Facebook group Oklahoma Teacher Walkout—The Time is Now!, providing a space for educators and supporters to aid in local organizing (Krutka et al., 2018; Tarlau, 2023). While many educators participated in both these social media groups and the teachers unions, the social media groups were successful in rallying a variety of supporters who could not join the union because they were not a teacher or educational support professional (ESP), but rather, were community members who wanted to support these educational movements.

#RedforEd and Wildcat Strikes

The other large change seen during this time was educators began to organize and strike in traditionally 'red' states with Right-to-Work (RTW) laws that prevented collective bargaining rights. This was unprecedented during this time, as the majority of teachers strikes happened in states with collective bargaining rights where teachers may not have been risking their livelihood to walk out of their classrooms in the ways their RTW state counterparts were. The 2018 West Virginia teachers strike resulted in teachers from all 55 counties of the state organizing at the state capitol, effectively shutting down schools for days (Blanc, 2020; McCartin et al., 2020). Oklahoma and Arizona followed later in spring 2018, with North Carolina, Kentucky, and Colorado teachers walking out for one day (Blanc, 2020; McCartin et al., 2020). This larger movement was called #RedforEd and later was seen in more Democratic cities like Chicago and Los Angeles in 2019 (Blanc, 2020; McCartin et al., 2020). #RedforEd was a pivotal time for grassroots and union organizing that showcased the possibilities of a larger movement.

The Current Climate for Educators

The pandemic ushered in many changes for education; however, it also became a catalyst for right-wing groups to utilize the momentum of 'parents' rights' groups surrounding pandemic issues like mask mandates and school building closures to take up manufactured concern about critical race theory being taught in K-12 classrooms and 'sensitive/pornographic material' in classroom materials and library books. These right-wing supported and corporate-funded groups, like Moms for Liberty, worked with conservative think tanks and state legislatures to support bills that sought for teachers to publish their course lesson plans for the year, created policies censoring books primarily with LGBTQ+ and BIPOC characters, and passed anti-CRT and anti-DEI legislation that effectively stripped P-16 education of important diversity and inclusion work that had been built upon since the 1970s (Kramer & Jones, 2024). Florida's HB 241 created a Parents' Bill of Rights, preventing the state from mandating certain health care or educational requirements, as a reaction to the mask mandates several school districts tried to implement during the 2021–2022 school year (Blount et al., 2022). This was the beginning of the wedge issue the pandemic created, bridging the gap between those issues and the agendas right-wing groups were pushing.

These attacks are not new, spanning decades in education and surrounding various previous topics like homeschooling, book bans, imposition of religious values, opposition to comprehensive sex education, LGBTQ+ inclusive materials, and the erosion of the nuclear family (Caruso, 2022; Eichner, 2023; Kramer & Jones, 2024; Nossel, 2022). The individuals, conservative think tanks, and right-wing groups who have been central in these attacks are the American Legislative Exchange Council, the Christian Coalition, Of the People, Charles Koch, Rupert Murdoch, Democrats for Education Reform, and Michael P. Ferris (Caruso, 2022; Cunningham, 2023; Eichner, 2023; Nossel, 2022). The groups and individuals in this current movement are Moms for Liberty, the Parental Rights Foundation, No Left Turn in Education, Parents Defending Education, Charles Koch Institute, Walton Family Foundation, Vela Education Fund, the Leadership Institute, Turning Point USA, Heritage Action for America, the Heritage Foundation, the Manhattan Institute, Edward Blum, and Christopher Rufo (Cunningham, 2023; Kramer & Jones, 2024; Nossel, 2022, Ravitch, 2013; Williams, 2022). The result of the push from these conservative groups and individuals is policy that has been developed in order to either control or chill educators inclusion of BIPOC and LGBTQ+ students and historically factual incidents in the curriculum (Baêta & Meehan, 2023). Teaching topics or books focused on health and wellbeing, socio-emotional learning, grief and death, violence and physical abuse, race and racism, and LGBTQ+ themes have been labeled 'divisive,' so the curriculum has been challenged or books containing these issues have been consistently challenged or banned (Meehan & Friedman, 2023). PEN America found, in their 2-year study from July 2021 to July 2023, 5,894 instances where book bans were put into place in 41 states, totalling 247 school districts (Baêta & Meehan, 2023). Additionally, CRT Forward (2023) found that since 2021 there have been 783 local, state, or federal anti-CRT measures passed or put into place nationwide. All of these attacks on educators have left many turning to their unions or other grassroots groups for help on pushing back on these issues or for education on how to teach subversively in order to provide an equitable educational environment for all students. Other educators have decided to leave the profession entirely, citing the pandemic and political issues as two reasons, setting the United States up for the possibility of a continued churn of vacancies in schools across the nation (Barnum, 2023). It is imperative that teachers join unions and other grassroots teacher activist organizations in order to find solidarity to fight back against these issues in education and work to build better schools and communities for all students and their families.

Introduction to the Text

The book is organized in three parts. The first part of the book, "Why and How Teachers Organize," provides a look at why teachers choose to organize and the events that have spurred them to action. The second part of the book, "Teacher-Activist Organizations and Social Justice Unionism," focuses on specific teachers unions and activist organizations, and the third part of the book, "Opportunities for Preparing Preservice and Current Teachers," provides some ideas to better engage preservice and current educators into activism within their own classrooms and organizations.

Part 1 contains five chapters. Chapter 2, "Why Do Teachers Engage in Justice-Oriented Activism?: Reflections from Philadelphia's Teacher-Activists," is framed using historical and contemporary accounts of how educators have engaged in political activism in their profession and communities in order to examine Philadelphia teachers' engagement with TAG. Overall, the chapter provides important understandings as to how teacher-activists can be supported based on their experiences personally and professionally. Chapter 3, "Transformative Teacher Activism: A Political and Educational Awakening," provides a detailed case study using Giroux's (2011, 2013) framework of transformative intellectuals to detail the creation of KY120 United and share how members pushed back on former Governor Matt Bevin's anti-teacher rhetoric, paving the way for the historic election of Governor Andy Beshear. The TAG's focus centered in the larger ideas of the #RedforEd movement that developed across several 'red' states in 2018. Chapter 4, "'We can join together to help fix it': UCORE and the Movement for Social Justice Unionism," focuses on the history of social justice caucuses in the United States who make up United Caucuses of Rank-and-File Educators (UCORE). These caucuses are rooted in social justice unionism, which consists of rank-and-file members organizing from the bottom-up to best represent the demands of their profession and the students and communities they serve. Taken from an original 5-year ethnographic study, the chapter highlights how UCORE has furthered social justice unionism as part of a larger social movement. Chapter 5, "The Crossfires of Hate," provides a comprehensive history of various Chicano/a/x movements in education that have led to the most recent movements to uphold Mexican American Studies in the Tucson Unified School District (TUSD). The key lessons that can be taken out of the historical and present-day attacks on Chicano/a/x curriculum and programming is that student walkouts and protests have worked in the past to preserve students' rights to learn their own history and culture, so new social movements must work to challenge these bans and other laws utilizing the parameters set forth in the legislative language itself.

Part 2 contains eight chapters. Chapter 6, "We Refuse to be Blamed: The Badass Teachers Association," details the inception and growth of BATs, a national teacher-activist organization. BATs has most recently organized surrounding issues of school safety in regards to school shootings and the COVID-19 pandemic. Chapter 7, "The Movement and the Mayor," highlights the important win of Chicago Mayor Brandon Johnson and the challenges that come next. Johnson, a former teacher in Chicago Public Schools (CPS) and an organizer for the Chicago Teachers Union (CTU), was elected after two other attempts to get candidates who would represent CPS and CTU's needs best in office. Chapter 8, "So We Stand: Minneapolis Federation of Teachers," was written from a conversation I had with the Minneapolis Federation of Teachers' President and First Vice President. Their candid chapter chronicles this time period, the importance of their new union contracts, and what the union was planning next at the time of publication.

Chapter 9, "Black Lives Matter at School and the Ongoing Pursuit of Educational Justice for Black Lives," focuses on denouncing the institution of public schooling due to the harm the educational system has done to Black students, which is used to frame many understandings leading up to the overall discussion of the Black Lives Matter at School (BLMAS) movement. Overall, this movement focuses on teaching truth, which is necessary given all the challenges to curriculum and education in today's political climate. Chapter 10, "National Educators United (NEU): Collective Action Outside of Formal Union Spaces," was created from a conversation between NEU leaders and me. The group rose in prominence and membership during the first year of the pandemic due to many educators trying to find spaces for information about the virus and its perceived impact on classrooms. Throughout the chapter, leadership members discuss the moments during their movement that meant the most to them and held the largest organizing possibility.

Chapter 11, "NYCoRE's Inquiry-to-Action Groups: Developing Political Education Toward Liberatory Futures in Education," shares the history of the

New York Collective of Radical Educators (NYCoRE) and their development of the Inquiry to Action Groups (ItAG). The organization's central work lies in creating a space for radical educators, developing and offering critical professional development, and linking educators to various actions. The chapter provides more detail as to the creation and execution of the ItAG, especially as they have changed over the time of the organization's rise. Chapter 12, "Privatization Doesn't Stop at Borders: The Trinational Coalition in Defense of Public Education," shares a history of the creation and growth of the Trinational Coalition, which has existed for 30 years. Unions from Mexico, Canada, and the United States have participated in the Coalition since its inception, and the organization has created a biannual conference that allows attendees to take part in public school tours in the conference host city, sessions, workshops, and issue-based discussions. The words of long-term members and newer members share more about the growth of the organization into the present day. Chapter 13, "USOS: Our Part in the Struggle to Save the Public's Schools," tells the story of the individuals who came from other organizing spaces to create Uniting to Save Our Schools. The overarching belief in the organization was that literacy serves to liberate. This chapter shares important detailed history chronicling the growth and actions of the organization.

This book would not be complete without a discussion of engaging preservice and current teachers in organizing and action. Part 3 provides some ideas for how teachers can get engaged. Chapter 14, "Aspiring Educators as Aspiring Organizers and Activists: A Blueprint for Action," focuses on one Aspiring Educators (AE) chapter at Northern Arizona University and the faculty, students, and organizers who have worked to begin the chapter and continue to recruit students to take part in it. The chapter concludes with plans for ongoing action and further examination of how they want to continue to utilize social justice unionism. Chapter 15, "Reframing Curricular Opportunities to Nurture and Sustain Critical Consciousness," provides strategies educators can use to create or redefine their curriculum using Curricular Critical Reflection to move into Instructional Critical Action, which utilizes Freire's critical consciousness concept. The chapter contributes an excellent how-to model for teachers who want to be more purposeful in creating or redesigning curriculum rooted in social justice models.

Together, this collection represents what it means to organize for justice. This is the book I have been waiting to see come to fruition since I finished my dissertation study on the Badass Teachers Association. I aim for you to find it informative and inspiring on your own activism journey.

References

Asselin, C. (2022). Fighting racism through teacher union democratization: Activist educators in social justice caucuses in New York City and Philadelphia. *Critical Education, 13*(3), 44–62. http://ojs.library.ubc.ca/index.php/criticaled/article/view/186566

Baêta, S., & Meehan, K. (2023). *Spineless shelves: Two years of book banning* [Data summary]. PEN America: The Freedom to Write. https://pen.org/spineless-shelves/

Barnum, M. (2023, March 6). 'I just found myself struggling to keep up': Number of teachers quitting hits new high. *USA TODAY*. https://www.usatoday.com/story/news/education/2023/03/06/more-teachers-quitting-than-usual-driven-stress-politics-data-shows/11390639002/

Blanc, E. (2020). The Red for Ed movement, two years in. *New Labor Forum, 29*(3), 66–73. https://newlaborforum.cuny.edu/2020/10/03/the-red-for-ed-movement-two-years-in/#:~:text=In%20late%20February%202018%2C%20teachers,labor%20may%20have%20finally%20arrived.

Blount, H., Figg, M., Finke, A., Gilbert, C., O'Connell, M., Minya, N., Neeranjan, K., & Rodriguez, A. (2022). *COVID aftermath: The impact of the pandemic on Florida's public school students.* [White paper, Gator Team Child Juvenile Law Clinic]. UF Law Scholarship Repository. https://scholarship.law.ufl.edu/gator-team-child/2

Bocking, P. (2022). 'No cuts to education': The story of a protest movement. *Critical Education, 13*(4), 20–41. http://ojs.library.ubc.ca/index.php/criticaled/article/view/186603

Caruso, C. (2022, March 9). *The parental rights' movement is history repeating itself.* Dame. https://www.damemagazine.com/2022/03/09/the-parental-rights-movement-is-history-repeating-itself/

CRT Forward. (2023, December 10). *Interactive map.* UCLA School of Law Critical Race Studies Program. https://crtforward.law.ucla.edu/map/

Cunningham, M. T. (2023). *Merchants of deception: Parent props and their funders.* Network for Public Education. https://networkforpubliceducation.org/wp-content/uploads/2023/01/Merchants-of-Deception.pdf?fbclid=IwAR2wWJKZSEk1T8to3qoNXxYJe4UgooQ_nnowZjLc8HKzr4i-LMrPOPp3DzI

Eichner, M. (2023). Free-market family policy and the new parental rights laws. *North Carolina Law Review, (101)*5, 1305-1350. https://ssron.com/abstract=4421480

Giroux, H. A. (2011). Teachers as transformative intellectuals. In E. B. Hilty (Ed.), *Thinking about schools: A foundations of education reader* (pp. 183–189). Westview Press.

Giroux, H. (2013). Neoliberalism's war against teachers in dark times. *Cultural Studies-Critical Methodologies, 13*(6), 458–468. https://doi.org/10.1177/1532708613503769

Howell, C. D., & Schmitzer, C. (2022). Online and on the picket line: West Virginia teachers' use of an online community to organize. *Critical Education, 13*(2), 59–76. http://ojs.library.ubc.ca/index.php/criticaled/article/view/186613

Karvelis, N. (2022). Rural organizing, institutionalization, and "getting back": An interview with #RedForEd organizer Vanessa Arredondo. *Critical Education, 13*(2), 96–102. http://ojs.library.ubc.ca/index.php/criticaled/article/view/186550

Kramer, B. (2017). *A case study on leadership members in a teacher activist group: "The fight for public education is a fight for democracy"* [Doctoral dissertation, University of Toledo]. OhioLINK Electronic Theses and Dissertations Center. http://rave.ohiolink.edu/etdc/view?acc_num=toledo1513284001679202

Kramer, B. (2023). Being "Badass:" Identity of a teacher activist organization. *International Journal of Political Activism and Engagement, 10*(1), 1–12. DOI: 10.4018/IJPAE.315602

Kramer, B., & Jones, D. (2024). A new framework to dismantle public schools: How legislators and right-wing groups used the pandemic as a wedge issue to control school curriculum and policy. In Y. Medina & E. J. Blair (Eds.), *Social foundations of education reader: Critical essays on teaching, learning, and leading* (2nd ed.). Peter Lang.

Krutka, D. G., Asino, T. I., & Haselwood, S. (2018). Editorial: Eight lessons on networked teacher activism from #OklaEd and the #OklaEdWalkout. *Contemporary Issues in Technology and Teacher Education, 18*(2), 379–391.

Maton, R. (2022). 'We're ready to fight': The story of a protest movement. *Critical Education, 13*(4), 42–49. http://ojs.library.ubc.ca/index.php/criticaled/article/view/186603

McCartin, J. A., Sneiderman, M., & BP-Weeks, M. (2020). Combustible convergence: Bargaining for the common good and the #RedforEd uprisings of 2018. *Labor Studies Journal, 45*(1), 97–113. DOI: 10.1177/0160449X20901643

Meehan, K., & Friedman, J. (2023, April 20). *Banned in the USA: State laws supercharge book suppression in schools.* PEN America: The freedom to write. https://pen.org/report/banned-in-the-usa-state-laws-supercharge-book-suppression-in-schools/

Naison, M., & Sanstead, P. (2014, June 13). *Happy Birthday BATs!* Badass Teacher Association. https://badassteachers.blogspot.com/search?updated-max=2014-06-19T18:38:00-04:00&max-results=7&reverse-paginate=true&start=14&by-date=false

Nossel, S. (2022, September 20). Parents should have a voice in their kids' education but we have gone too far. *Time*. https://time.com/6215119/parents-rights-education-gone-too-far/

Ravitch, D. (2013). *Reign of error: The hoax of the privatization movement and the danger to America's public schools.* Alfred A. Knopf.

Riley, K. (2015). Reading for change: Social justice unionism book groups as an organizing tool. *PennGSE Perspectives on Urban Education, (12)*1. http://www.urbanedjournal.org/archive/volume-12-issue-1-spring-2015/reading-change-social-justice-unionism-bookgroups-organizing

Stark, L.W., Dyke, E., & Maton, R. (2022). Afterword: Reflections on contemporary educator movements. *Critical Education, 13*(4), 50–57. http://ojs.library.ubc.ca/index.php/criticaled/article/view/186729

Tarlau, R. (2023). Networked movements and bureaucratic unions: The structure of the 2018 #RedForEd teachers' strikes. *ILR Review, 76*(5), 833–863. DOI: 10.1177/00197939231189200

Williams, P. (2022, October 31). The right-wing mothers fueling the school board wars. *The New Yorker*. https://www.newyorker.com/magazine/2022/11/07/the-right-wing-mothers-fuelling-the-school-board-wars

CHAPTER 2

Why Do Teachers Engage in Justice-Oriented Activism?: Reflections from Philadelphia's Teacher-Activists

Dana Morrison

An essential question that must be explored in any inquiry of teacher activism is the question of *why*. Why do teachers, in addition to their numerous personal and professional responsibilities, take on the time- and energy-intensive work of justice-oriented activism? As demonstrated in the literature, modern teacher-activists are often motivated by deeply held beliefs about social, racial, economic, and educational justice (Marshall & Anderson, 2008; Montaño et al., 2002; Picower, 2012; Urrieta, 2010). More importantly, these beliefs foundationally shape their understanding of what it means to be a teacher. In their qualitative study of five teacher-activists, for example, Montaño et al. (2002) found that participants' definitions of a "good" teacher stretched beyond the walls of the classroom. Confronted by daily inequities, the teachers saw the issues that plagued their schools as embedded in broader issues of social injustice (e.g., systemic racism and class inequality), which led them to develop an expanded notion of teachers' work that included "participation in a collective project for change" (p. 272). As stated by one of the study's participants, "you cannot be a social justice teacher and *not* be an activist" (p. 272, emphasis added).

As the chapters of this book demonstrate, teachers in the 21st century are facing a myriad of increasing injustices that impact their students, their schools, and their work. Legislative efforts to ban critical race theory and LGBTQ+ positive curriculum and books, unsafe return-to-work plans during a global pandemic, increased high-stakes standardized testing and accountability schemes, work intensification, and stagnant wages have all contributed to low teacher morale and high teacher turnover. Amidst these struggles, however, teacher activism has provided a gleam of hope. Whether advocating for more diverse curricula, more school funding, safe work conditions, or better pay, teachers across the country have been increasingly engaging in activism, and winning. In 2018 and 2019, teacher activism took the form of massive work stoppages with 373,000 teachers in 2018 and 264,000 teachers in 2019 going on strike (Bureau of Labor Statistics, n.d.). In 2020, sparked by the COVID-19 pandemic and the racial justice uprisings after the murder of George Floyd, teachers began engaging in activism to demand health safety measures and anti-racist curriculum. Much of the conservative reactionism we now see is due in large part to the successful activism of teachers, parents, and students during this time.

As state legislatures and courts become further sequestered by these conservative forces, only a genuine movement of people can counteract the backlash. Thus, efforts like those detailed above are needed now more than ever, and understanding why teachers have engaged in such work is essential for continued movement building. First, understanding why can provide essential insights that might be utilized in developing *new* teacher-activists. Particularly for teacher educators and current teachers in activist organizations, identifying common motivations that have spurred teachers to activism holds tremendous promise for bringing more teachers in and growing the movement. Second, however, activism is tough, draining, and often disappointing work. Teacher-activists are routinely required to push through today's losses and fight for a better tomorrow. Answering the question of *why* teachers engage anyway holds important insights into how communities can support and sustain teacher-activists.

This chapter will begin with a review of the historical and contemporary literature that provides insight into why teachers engage in activism. From the earliest days of the profession in the United States, educators have taken up political activism to seek change in their work, their schools, and their communities. This literature review will highlight important findings from scholars who have documented this activism past to present.

Next, this chapter will detail important insights derived from interviews conducted with ten Philadelphia teachers who were members of various justice-oriented activist organizations in the city. Derived from research completed for my dissertation,[1] I will share key findings that illuminate why this group of teachers took on activism, what motivated them to get involved, and motivated them to stay involved. More specifically, I will highlight the ways in which their engagement was driven by a variety of personal and professional influences.

I will conclude the chapter with reflections on what these findings can contribute to a developing movement of teacher activism. For those who believe teacher activism can be a key mechanism for saving our schools, these insights can help us bring educators together in a project of collective social change.

Literature Review: Why Do Teachers Engage in Justice-Oriented Activism?

In their edited collection of research on activist educators, Marshall and Anderson (2008) note that teacher-activists face many challenges that stem from the fact that "education is often imagined as an apolitical enterprise" (p. 1). In this vision of education, teachers are expected "to maintain a respectful distance from hot-button issues and significant political and social movements" (p. 1). This belief often informs the "professional culture" of teaching so that when educators venture "too close" to the political world, their actions carry significant professional risks, such as threats to their career mobility, job security, and professional credibility. This environment often pressures teachers—particularly socially and economically marginalized educators (Legrand, 2008; Williams, 2008)—to avoid political activism altogether (Marshall & Anderson, 2008). In spite of this reality, teachers have continued to participate in political activism not merely in spite of their profession, but in many cases *because* of their profession.

A Brief History of Teacher Activism

As members of a profession long associated with social equality, justice, and democracy, teachers have often been drawn to change-seeking movements throughout history. Prominent abolitionists such as Lucretia Mott, Abbie Hopper Gibbons, Maria Chapman, and the Grimké sisters were teachers, as were nearly half of the feminist abolitionists of the time (Clifford, 2014, p. 295). These women wrote essays, made speeches, arranged local meetings, and created organizations in support of the abolition of slavery.

In addition to their engagement in the Black liberation struggle, teachers were also prominently involved in the movement for women's suffrage (Clifford, 2014; Mead, 2006; Rousmaniere, 2005). As explained by Rousmaniere (2005), "many of the earliest women's rights activists in the nineteenth century had been schoolteachers who had perfected their public speaking skills by standing in front of classrooms" (p. 127). It was these women teachers, often economically independent and highly literate, who "made up the bulk of suffrage supporters and activists through the turn of the century" (p. 127).

In the years leading up to and following emancipation, Black teachers from across the country were critical in the creation of schools for freed people (Butchart, 2010). Black teachers who taught secretly before 1861, continued and even expanded their work. As documented by Butchart (2010), "with the collapse of the Confederacy in 1865, black teachers accelerated the pace of school creation across the South, opening no fewer than *400 new schools* from North Carolina to Texas, Missouri to Florida, in one year" (p. 22, emphasis added).

In addition to these engagements, teachers became key players in early labor and school reform movements, creating thousands of local teachers associations and solidifying nationwide unions like the National Education Association (NEA) and the American Federation of Teachers (AFT). They took up work around pensions and pay, but also teacher autonomy and the gender disparity of the profession. Some of the earliest teacher union activists, for example, fought what Margaret Haley (1904), Vice President of the burgeoning Chicago Federation of Teachers, called the "factoryizing" of education. In Haley's words, these policies framed the teacher as a mere factory hand, whose duty it was "to carry out mechanically and unquestioningly the ideas and orders of those clothed with the authority of position." While Haley became the public face of many of these fights, she "was rarely alone in this work; she was usually supported by a mass of teachers who did much of the footwork and office labor of this grassroots political organization" (Rousmaniere, 2005, p. 57).

With early teacher unions and associations racially segregated, Black teachers who were members of state and national Black teachers associations (e.g., American Teachers Association, or ATA) sought to resist racial oppression within public schooling. As noted by Houchen (2020), Black teachers associations routinely fought "inequality in school facilities and length of school terms, second class curricula, unequal teacher salaries, insufficient school supplies, and paltry transportation" (p. 267). In many southern states, such as Florida, Black teacher activism during the Jim Crow era contributed to watershed civil rights cases, such as when the Florida State Teachers Association (FSTA) took up the fight for integrating higher education in the state via *Virgil Hawkins v. Florida Board of Control (1957)*. The FSTA financially supported the legal process and advised the plaintiff and the broader community throughout the proceedings (Houchen, 2020, p. 277).

Examples such as these showcase the long tradition of activism within the teaching profession driven by personal and professional commitments to freedom, universal human rights, and democracy. Teacher-activists in these early years were commonly motivated by injustices connected to their identities as women and/or people of color. And despite the risks that came with such political engagement, these educators expressed their commitments clearly in their activities, publications, and speeches. As stated by FTSA President, Edward D. Davis, it was the role of the teacher, particularly the role of the Black teacher, to "fight consistently for freedom in America" (Houchen, 2020, p. 275). The historical literature makes clear that Davis' sentiment was one that commonly animated teachers across the country to engage in justice-oriented activism.

Contemporary Literature Review of Teacher Activism

With this long history of activism in the profession, contemporary researchers have turned their attention to the factors that motivate modern teachers to engage politically. Much like previous teacher-activists, current educators have often been driven to activism because of injustices related to their personal experiences as marginalized people. In Keith Catone's (2016) work, *The Pedagogy of Teacher Activism*, for example, we are provided with in-depth histories of four educators engaged in various forms of justice-oriented work. One teacher in particular, a self-identified queer woman named Rosie, noted that much of her commitment was due to her experiences with systemic discrimination as a youth. Her involvement in a subgroup of the New York Caucus of Rank and File Educators (NYCoRE), NYQueer, was explicitly connected to this goal. Rosie's engagement was motivated by wanting to "combat homophobia and transphobia in schools" because she had witnessed them herself growing up (Catone, 2016, p. 38).

In a similar vein, Luis Urrieta's (2010) ethnographic work with Chicana/o activist educators echoed this finding, noting that the primary factor motivating the teachers to engage in activism was their identity within the Chicana/o community. As explained by Urrieta (2010), participants "referred to joining *la causa* (the cause) in an attempt to empower themselves and their communities" (p. 73). For these educators, it was their personal relationship to and experiences within a historically oppressed community that motivated them to organize.

In addition to these personal factors that incited educators to engage in activism, research has shown that teacher-activists are also often motivated by their professional experiences in unequal school settings. Montaño et al. (2002), for example, found that teacher-activists were incited by the tangible injustices experienced by their students due to poverty and systemic racism. The participants of the study expressed repeatedly that their students were "the reason and reference for their engagement" in organizing outside of the classroom. As articulated by Montaño et al. (2002), the teachers' motivations were rooted in the immediate needs of inner-city students, particularly the students in their own classrooms, who gave their struggle meaning and urgency (p. 272).

For many teacher-activists, this type of political work then becomes an essential component of who they are as educators. In Picower's (2012) inquiry with nine teacher-activists, for example, participants expressed that engaging in activism outside of the classroom was an important part of being a teacher. In fact, for many of the educators, struggling for justice was embedded in their professional identity. As articulated by Picower (2012) the teachers' engagement in activism "was not a conscious choice that the teachers made—rather it was a fundamental part of who they were" (p. 565). Because of this, they felt their calling was to reconcile their visions of justice with what was happening in the world and become teacher-activists (p. 565).

With these deeply personal and professional motivations, it is not surprising that researchers have also found teacher activism to be a critical lifeline for educators. As demonstrated in the literature, teachers often engage in activist work because of the emotional and professional support activist networks provide. As noted by Stern and Brown (2016), for example, teachers located their engagement in activism as a "therapeutic antidote" to their feelings of professional depression. In school environments rife with stressors, participants turned to various activist organizations to find educators with similar understandings, values, and goals for education. This form of support was a professional life saver for many of the teachers. As expressed by Lou, a high school history teacher, "there's no way I would have kept going" (Stern & Brown, 2016, p. 347) without finding community in the organizations he joined.

Much of this support comes from the outlet of having a road map for change within a community. As expressed by teacher-organizer, Kelley:

> anytime you do any kind of organizing work you are putting yourself in a position to be working toward solutions and that, in and of itself, is empowering. You're not in a victim mode. [Instead it is] these things are wrong, how are we going to fix it? You're involved with a network of teachers and identifying problems and solutions. (Stern & Brown, 2016, pp. 349–350)

Picower (2012) similarly found that working with like-minded educators was essential for teachers sustainability. As explained by Picower (2012) engaging in activist efforts "provided them with knowledge, motivation, strength…and the ability to keep going in the face of adversity" (p. 570). This proved to be essential, particularly as educators took on activism that went against the grain of mainstream policies. "Rather than always feeling like an outsider, working in a group of allies helped teacher-activists "normalize" their stance and their work" (Picower, 2012, p. 570).

Reflections from Philadelphia's Teacher-Activists

These findings and more were on my mind as I engaged with ten teacher-activists in Philadelphia for my dissertation work. I began this research by contacting teachers I met at various education-focused community events in the city. I also reached out to several activist groups whose work sought change around issues of educational, racial, or social justice. After conducting qualitative narrative interviews with ten teachers from seven different organizations, I asked four of the teachers to collaborate more closely. In the following months, I worked and learned alongside these four educators, conducting additional interviews, engaging in observations, and participating in the activist work they took up.

Our earliest conversations centered on their activist origin stories, particularly where, when, and how they got involved in justice-oriented work. This discussion helped to uncover their *why,* what specifically motivated them to get involved at the outset, as well as what kept them involved several years (or decades) in. Through these conversations, teachers expressed a variety of personal and professional motivations for their activist engagement that can help us better understand how to increase and sustain teacher activism in the modern era.

The Personal

As we explored what brought the teachers to focus on issues of justice and change, they often recounted stories that centered the importance of their personal experiences. For many of the educators, their families, their education, and their identities were noted as motivations for their justice-oriented activism. Several of the participants shared stories about family members who directly discussed topics like fairness, inequality, race, and class as meaningful in their development toward a justice orientation.

Chris, a high school humanities teacher, for example, recounted his mother's consistent discussion about her own political activism when detailing his concern with racial and economic justice:

> I think it was something that I was always brought up to think about. My mom grew up in Virginia in the 1950s . . . so she was sort of around segregated schools and went into activism and organizing. So, like she always sort of had those conversations about race and important issues with us growing up. (Chris, personal communication, August 1, 2017)

It was this initial introduction that Chris used to frame his subsequent journey into anti-racist work as a white high school teacher and activist. This work culminated with the formation of a group that would bear the acronym BAR WE, short for *Building Anti-Racist White Educators,* of which Chris was a founding member.

Created in conjunction with the Philadelphia Teacher's Action Group (TAG) and the Caucus of Working Educators (WE), BAR WE was envisioned as a space for white-identifying teachers to develop an explicitly anti-racist stance as professionals. Chris and the other educators who created BAR WE met routinely to learn, reflect, and take action on school policies, curricula, and even their own biases as white educators. In the years following my conversations with Chris, BAR WE took on national outreach, providing learning materials that educators across the country could use to become anti-racist white educators.

While additional life experiences were shared as motivations for Chris' organizing, the initial centering of his mother's own anti-racist perspective and activism highlights the role that family can play in framing the grassroots work taken up by educators. In fact, family members conscious discussion of social and political issues was a meaningful theme not only for Chris, but for several of the teachers in the study.

In addition to the impact of their families, the teachers also recounted a variety of personal educational experiences that were framed as important motivations for their commitment to justice and transformation. Zack, a white high school Spanish teacher, for example, articulated his attendance at both a progressive public school and a justice-focused Jewish after-school program as formative in his activism. Zack's experience in this program was grounded in what he described as a radical Eastern European working-class tradition, something he spoke about as having shaped his view of social and political struggles.

Several other teachers also recounted stories of educational experiences that were meaningful in their development as activists. While they noted that justice-centered classroom curricula were important in spurring them to activism, the teachers often spoke most impactfully about educational experiences that extended beyond the classroom. Samantha, for example, a white middle school math educator, detailed a particularly meaningful educational experience that played a key role in her identification as a grassroots organizer. She explained how she spent a large portion of her senior year in college in Zimbabwe and South Africa exploring women's liberation struggles, and that this experience was formative in her subsequent commitment to grassroots work. As she reflected on speaking with dozens of women on this trip, she recounted,

> [those experiences] made me realize that stuff that happens at a local level is . . . the building blocks of everything else and is the most meaningful. And those are the kernels of where the world

> change happens, everything is built off of that, if you don't have that nothing is to come . . . there is no above without below. (Samantha, personal communication, July 17, 2017).

As highlighted by Samantha's narrative, these direct experiences through a study abroad solidified her future commitment to on-the-ground political organizing. It was this portion of Samantha's narrative that most clearly connected with her current activism as a founding member of WE, a social justice caucus within the Philadelphia Federation of Teachers (PFT). Her belief that "there is no above without below" resounds throughout WE's platform, "when we organize, we harness the power of millions of people (teachers, students, parents, citizens) who care about Philadelphia's schools. When we organize, we build the power we need to make real change" (Caucus of Working Educators, 2024 , para. 1).

Stories like Samantha's highlight the true possibility of critical approaches to education, whereby teachers engage students as potential agents of social change. This means incorporating curricula and experiential opportunities that shine a light on injustice and show students the possibility of social transformation. Yet, while educators at all levels will find comfort in the promise that their practices can have a genuine impact on students, it is important to note that not all of the teachers' educational experiences were positive. Some of the teachers recounted significant stories of injustice and discrimination in their education that connected to their subsequent activism as teachers.

Jesse, a white, veteran early grades educator of over 30 years, for example, recalled pushing against the gendered practices of her school as a main motivation for her activism as an educator. She identified herself as a having been a young feminist and recounted becoming a "radical leader in the 6th grade" as she "got the rules changed about girls having to wear dresses." For many young people, school is the first step beyond the family and thus often their first experience with the social politics of the larger world. Inequality, sexism, and racism connected to their identities were underlying themes within the stories that highlighted the teachers' direct experiences with injustice in their schooling.

Perhaps the most salient example of such experiences came from Isaac, a Black African American history teacher at the high school level. In our conversation, Isaac recounted an experience with a teacher who made racist remarks about his speech impediment in front of the class. After sharing this discrimination with his parents, the teacher was made to apologize, but the impact stayed with him. As knowledge of the situation spread, his school's librarian reached out to Isaac to give him her original copy of the *Autobiography of Malcolm X*. As Isaac remembered, he and his mom read it that year and by the next, he was wearing Malcolm X hats and kids were calling him [Isaac] X (Isaac, personal communication, July 25, 2017).

Isaac became, in his words, a "voracious reader, going out of [his] way to read biographies trying to get to the deeper root of why people function the way they function" (Isaac, personal communication, July 25, 2017). Yet, his experiences with a largely white teaching population and Eurocentric curriculum led him to describe his schooling experience as "dehumanizing." It was because of these experiences, however, that he wanted to become an activist teacher in Philadelphia. He found teaching to be a synthesis of his love for learning and his "total disgust" with what happens in schools.

This context deeply motivated Isaac's work on the National Black Lives Matter Week of Action organized by the Racial Justice Committee of WE. Inspired by 2,000 Seattle teachers who coordinated a Black Lives Matter day in the Fall of 2016, Isaac and other Philly teachers organized a week of action in January 2017. Educators across the city collected curricular resources, developed lesson plans, and organized community events centered on the thirteen guiding principles of Black Lives Matter (Jones & Hagopian, 2020; Morrison & Porter-Webb, 2019).

In 2018, the week went national, with educators from over 20 cities coordinating local activities and putting forth collective demands. These national demands were informed by each city's working group and included the call for public schools to 1) end zero tolerance policies and replace them with restorative practices, 2) mandate Black history and ethnic studies in their curriculums, and 3) hire more Black teachers. It was the last two demands that resounded in Isaac's stories of his unjust educational experiences, where he recounted struggling in schools that didn't understand his experience and didn't provide him with a meaningful curriculum.

The Professional

As I explored the teachers' motivations for engaging in their activist organizations, they often expressed sentiments that connected to their roles and experiences as professional educators. One common theme, for example, was the inciting impact that unjust professional environments had on their motivation to get involved in grassroots work. In particular, their professional experiences were characterized by many of the issues that educators across the country have faced in the modern era: dwindling autonomy, high stakes standardized testing, austerity and cutbacks, school closures, and more.

In our discussions about the teachers' engagement in justice-oriented organizations, several recounted very tangible professional experiences that spurred them to take up work seeking transformative change. Philadelphia's massive budget cuts and school closures, for example, were common motivations that the teachers identified for joining activist groups. As explained by Leah, a white middle school math teacher, for example, she first got involved when she moved to the city and became aware of the devastating budget cuts that occurred in 2010 and 2011. Similarly, Isaac spoke about experiencing the closure of the historic high school in which he planned to have a lifelong career.

Nearly all the teachers, in fact, expressed the direct connection between the current problematic conditions of their professional lives and their motivation to get involved. When I asked Peter, a Black high school social studies teacher, for example, why he engaged in political work, he explained,

> Well, for one it clearly affects me. I mean with teaching obviously my life is a lot worse if I have forty kids in the class as opposed to twenty. So, I mean that whole range of things, like the building conditions I work in, conditions of the student's life. It definitely has a direct impact on me. (Peter, personal communication, August 1, 2017)

Other participants shared specific stories of their involvement being spurred by their experiences with failed reforms and negative working conditions. This was particularly evident in the narrative shared by Jackie, a white, retired early grades teacher, who worked in the district until 2013. Spurred to grassroots work by the increasingly oppressive reforms she experienced at the end of her career, Jackie's frustration with the environment of the district was evident. She recounted the following story about her initial engagement in the Alliance for Philadelphia Public Schools (APPS):

> I started independently . . . I was not a "joining" kind of person and independently I started questioning and pushing back. I started like registering to speak at a [school reform commission] meetings when I had no idea what they were. I was petrified and was like by myself like there was nobody else . . . then one of the founding members of APPS approached me after the meeting and was like "that was awesome!" here is my card . . . . and I ended up joining APPS." (Jackie, personal communication, August 7, 2017)

APPS operates with the expressed goal of holding the then school reform commission (and now the school board) accountable for its decisions. Led by parents, community members, and current and retired school staff, APPS works to "assure that the public is present" when issues regarding the district are discussed. As stated on the APPS official website, members work to "prevent true stakeholders from being pushed aside by private organizations who meet in secret to decide crucial issues including principal training, which schools receive additional funding, and school closures" (APPS, n.d.). For Jackie, the work that APPS took on in exposing the decisions being made by the commission was an essential task to sustaining a system of public education as budgets were being slashed and over 30 schools closed in the 2011–2013 school years.

In addition to these stories of unjust professional environments, the teachers also articulated the role of activist organizations in their growth and sustainment as justice-oriented educators. By connecting the participants with like-minded teachers, these organizations facilitated the sharing of curricular resources as well as the development of skills that translated into their classrooms. Many of the teachers, for example, expressed motivation for their involvement that centered on what their grassroots organizations brought to them as educators. This was particularly emphasized by the participants involved in TAG Philly.

As stated on the TAG website, the organization is "a member of the Network of Teacher Activist Groups, a national coalition of grassroots teacher organizing groups" that work "to build an education movement for liberation, locally and nationally, through shared analysis, political education, mutual support and learning, and joint projects." TAG Philly, in particular, organized yearly Inquiry to Action Groups (iTAGs), a summer reading series, and a conference highlighting the work done within the community.

These activities were noted by many of the teachers as crucial in their growth as justice-oriented educators. For example, when I asked Chris why he got involved with TAG, he explained, "I think in some way it's really like teacher-led professional development, but obviously through a social justice lens . . . the type of thing that I didn't get much early in my career" (Chris, personal communication, August 1, 2017). As explained by Isaac, these meetings were organized "to create a situation where teachers can actually improve their practice and their professional knowledge while at the same time being somewhat experimental with what they're talking about and what to do and how they're dealing with it" (Isaac, personal communication, November 29, 2017).

This experimental atmosphere is a key aspect in the development of what author and educator Jay Gillen (2014) has called "crawl spaces," sites where individuals can "rehearse, plan, and try on personas that might later be used in the public arena" (p. 131). As stated by Gillen (2014), a crawl space is "a place to crawl until you can walk" (p. 131). Particularly for justice-oriented educators working on openly critical approaches to education, these crawl spaces can be essential. As noted in the above literature review, justice-oriented educators frequently meet challenges spurred by the ideological orthodoxy that teachers should be apolitical. Whether it is a dearth of curricular resources, mandates for scripted instruction, or "environments characterized by fear, compliance, and pressure to conform" (Picower, 2011, p. 1112), these educators face significant obstacles. For the teachers I spoke with, their engagement in activist organizations was often motivated by a search for communities that could help them overcome these professional obstacles.

As I explored the teachers' motivations for engaging in grassroots organizations, they also frequently noted the role their activist community played in facilitating relationships with others. In fact, nearly all of the participants detailed the importance of building connections to others in their rationales for engaging in their organizations. The various benefits of these relationships were at the center of their narratives. They joined to learn more about other teachers, students, and schools, to find a sense of camaraderie, and to feel supported in their work both inside and outside of the classroom. Importantly, these educators weren't simply looking for friends to spend time with, they sought out other educators who had a similar focus on seeking change and who would understand them.

As explained by Leah, for example, it was essential for justice-oriented teachers to find events outside of their school where they are "feeling listened to and they have a community of some kind that they are connected to" (Leah, personal communication, November 30, 2017). Discussing an event organized in the wake of the Charlottesville protests, Leah explained that such activities play an important role in connecting people, and making them "feel hopeful" and ready to take on justice-oriented activism. In the unjust environments in which they found themselves, having spaces to be hopeful was essential to maintaining their identities not only as activists, but as educators.

Reflections

Understanding why teachers engage in justice-oriented activism provides important reflections that can be used to both develop and sustain teacher-activists. For those who believe in the power of teacher activism, identifying motivations that have spurred teachers to take up such political work can help bring in more teachers and expand existing movements. Likewise, understanding why teachers engage in activism can show us how to best support and sustain teachers already taking on these complex efforts. The examples above demonstrate that teacher-activists are often moved to activism by a variety of personal and professional reasons. Thus, whether it be because of conversations with family members, justice-oriented education, or a search for like-minded colleagues, educators in the 21st century have continued in the long tradition of participating in the time and energy intensive work of activism.

As a teacher educator, I would first like to draw attention to the role that educational experiences played in the teachers' narratives. Whether it was through direct integration of justice-oriented content into their schools' curriculum or the structuring of experiential learning opportunities and community work, the participants consistently recounted aspects of their schooling that informed their engagement in various activist organizations. The teachers of this study articulated not only specific curricular decisions made by their schools and teachers as factors in their commitment to social transformation, but they also detailed the ways in which justice-oriented experiential learning opportunities shaped them into future activists. Even Isaac's traumatic experience with a teacher's racism was buttressed by his recounting of the school librarian, who ultimately opened his eyes to a vision of social change that influenced him for decades to come. These findings demonstrate the promise—and responsibility—that educators hold for structuring justice-centered educational experiences that open up opportunities for students to become active agents in their learning and their lives.

Adding to the emerging research detailing the ways in which activist groups support educators (Picower, 2012; Riley & Solic, 2017; Stern & Brown, 2016), the teachers of this inquiry frequently discussed their motivation to connect with other teachers who shared similar values and commitments to social change. Whether looking for a sense of camaraderie, curricular support, or just someone who understood their values, the teachers' engagement in activist organizations was often sparked by a desire to connect with like-minded others in the profession.

Particularly for educators currently in activist organizations, these findings highlight practices that can help bring in more teacher-activists and sustain them in the process. One consistent motivation from the participants was their search for a community that could provide them with educational opportunities to become better justice-oriented teachers. Book groups, inquiry groups, and local conferences where teachers could workshop their skills drew many of the teacher-activists in this study to their organizations. Likewise, the teachers routinely created public curricula, lesson plans, and class activities for issues they were working on (e.g., the Black Lives Matter at School Week of Action).

These educational opportunities not only supported the participants as teachers, helping them enhance their classroom practices, but they also became spaces where the educators could identify and learn about their unjust work environments. For these teacher-activists, it was essential to have a space where they could collectively study their current contexts in order to do something about them. Having an organization to help facilitate this "power-structure analysis," as termed by McAlevey (2016), can provide activists with the support needed to develop a thorough lay of the land, informing not only where they should focus their attention, but also what strategies might be most effective when seeking transformation in the present environment. These opportunities, to use Leah's phrasing, can provide teachers with the ability to "feel hopeful" in a context rife with injustices. Particularly for early-career educators or those hesitant to get involved, organizations that provide learning opportunities inextricably linked to action can undermine common feelings of apathy, overwhelm, loneliness, and helplessness.

Conclusion

With the ongoing assault of right-wing politics in schools and society, teacher activism in recent years has offered some of the most hopeful possibilities for just social change. The findings highlighted in this chapter present critical reflections on how we might develop and support teacher-activists in this project. Teacher educators, organization leadership, or even individual teachers trying to spark change in their communities can learn from the motivations of contemporary teacher-activists and engage in practices that grow and sustain them. Thus, for those who believe teacher activism to be a key mechanism for social transformation in the 21st century, learning about *the why* behind teacher activism is as essential as the activism itself.

References

Alliance for Philadelphia Public Schools (APPS). (n.d.). *About*. https://appsphilly.net/about/

Bureau of Labor Statistics. (n.d.). *Work stoppages involving 1,000 or more workers, 1993-Present [Detailed monthly listing]*. Retrieved from https://www.bls.gov/web/wkstp/monthly-listing.htm

Butchart, R. E. (2010). *Schooling the freed people: Teaching, learning, and the struggle for black freedom, 1861-1876*. University of North Carolina Press.

Catone, K. C. (2016). *The pedagogy of teacher activism: Four portraits of becoming and being teacher activists*. Harvard University.

Caucus of Working Educators. (2024, February 18). *Our platform*. Caucus of Working Educators. https://www.workingeducators.org/our_platform

Clifford, G. J. (2014). *Those good Gertrudes: A social history of women teachers in America*. Johns Hopkins University Press.

Gillen, J. (2014). *Educating for insurgency: The roles of young people in schools of poverty.* Ak Press.

Haley, M. A. (1904). Why teachers should organize. *The Journal of Education, 60*(13), 215–222.

Houchen, D. F. (2020). An "organized body of intelligent agents," Black teacher activism during de jure segregation: A historical case study of the Florida state teachers' association. *Journal of Negro Education, 89*(3), 267–281. https://www.jstor.org/stable/10.7709/jnegroeducation.89.3.0267

Jones, D., & Hagopian, J. (2020). *An uprising for educational justice: Black Lives Matter at school.* Haymarket Books.

Legrand, A. (2008). Surprising ways to be an activist educator. In C. Marshall & A. Anderson (Eds.), *Activist educators: Breaking past limits* (pp. 91–106). Routledge.

Marshall, C., & Anderson, A. L. (Eds.). (2008). *Activist educators: Breaking past limits.* Routledge.

McAlevey, J. (2016). *No shortcuts: Organizing for power in the new gilded age.* Oxford University Press.

Mead, R. (2006). *How the vote was won: Woman suffrage in the western United States, 1868-1914.* NYU Press.

Montaño, T., Lopez-Torres, L., DeLissovoy, N., Pacheco, M., & Stillman, J. (2002). Teachers as activists: Teacher development and alternate sites of learning. *Equity & Excellence in Education, 35*(3), 265–275.

Morrison, D., & Porter-Webb, E. (2019). Building power through racial justice: Organizing the #BlackLivesMatterAtSchool Week of Action in K-12 and beyond. *Berkeley Review of Education, 9*(1). DOI: 10.5070/B89146431

Picower, B. (2011). Resisting compliance: Learning to teach for social justice in a neoliberal context. *Teachers College Record, 113*(5), 1105–1134.

Picower, B. (2012). Teacher activism: Enacting a vision for social justice. *Equity & Excellence in Education, 45*(4), 561–574.

Riley, K., & Solic, K. (2017). "Change happens beyond the comfort zone": Bringing undergraduate teacher-candidates into activist teacher communities. *Journal of Teacher Education, 68*(2), 179–192. https://doi.org/10.1177/0022487116687738

Rousmaniere, K. (2005). *Citizen teacher: The life and leadership of Margaret Haley.* SUNY Press.

Stern, M., & Brown, A. (2016). "It's 5: 30. I'm exhausted. And I have to go all the way to f*%#ing Fishtown.": Educator depression, activism, and finding (armed) love in a hopeless (neoliberal) place. *The Urban Review, 48*(2), 333–354. https://doi.org/10.1007/s11256-016-0357-x

Urrieta, L. (2010). *Working from within: Chicana and Chicano activist educators in whitestream schools.* University of Arizona Press.

Williams, A. (2008). The fight of their lives: African American activist educators. In C. Marshall & A. Anderson (Eds), *Activist educators: Breaking past limits* (pp. 31–50). Routledge.

Endnotes

1 Author's note: some of the following chapter has been taken directly from this publication:
Morrison, D. (2018). *Organized: an exploration of teachers' engagement in grassroots organizing* (Publication No. 13421182) [Doctoral dissertation, University of Delaware]. ProQuest Dissertations and Theses Global. University of Delaware. Please see the complete document for a full accounting of the findings discussed herein.

CHAPTER 3

Transformative Teacher Activism: A Political and Educational Awakening

Jennifer Sink McCloud

KENTUCKY TEACHER ACTIVISTS have been "waking up" (Pam, teacher participant) from neoliberal reform agendas. State-level legislation related to pensions, charter schools, and budget cuts motivated Kentucky teachers to mobilize from 2018 to 2020. Kentucky, a "right-to-work state," prohibits labor strikes and restricts teacher union power. However, like colleagues in other "right-to-work states" such as West Virginia and Arizona (Blanc, 2019), Kentucky teachers engaged in protest, which ultimately influenced legislation and the 2020 gubernatorial election. Just as importantly, participants in this qualitative study reimagined their roles as teachers solely relegated to a classroom and engaged as "transformative intellectuals" (Giroux, 2011, 2013a).

Neoliberal Education and Kentucky: Red for Ed

Neoliberalism, a logic of thought and practice, has driven education "reforms" for decades (Giroux, 2013a, 2013b; Hill & Kumar, 2009; Huckaby, 2019). Neoliberalism "values free-market economics . . . corporate language . . . surveillance, competitiveness, and rugged individualism" (Hurley & McCloud, 2017, p. 32). Privileging standardization and quantitative data, it conflates accountability with "accountancy" (Spooner, 2015). As Huckaby (2019) explains, while liberalism asks whether government or market intervention is necessary, neoliberalism asks "not what to touch or not touch, but how to touch" (p. 106). It reaches past economic markets to educational contexts, setting "conditions that would allow a certain sector to function as a market" (Huckaby, 2019, p. 106).

Neoliberalism is fraught with discourse that can appear benign but is belied by its means to reform, such as privatization and corporate involvement in public education, teacher control, and reduction of teaching and learning to standardized tests. Ravitch writes:

> The "reformers" say they want excellent education for all; they want great teachers; they want to "close the achievement gap"; they want innovation and effectiveness; they want the best of everything for everyone. They pursue these universally admired goals by privatizing education, lowering the qualifications for future teachers, replacing teachers with technology, increasing class sizes, endorsing for-profit organizations to manage schools, using carrots and sticks to motivate teachers, and elevating standardized test scores as the ultimate measure of education quality. (2013, p. 19)

Reducing knowledge and teaching to a property to be measured and controlled is a hallmark of neoliberal logic. One result is dehumanized teachers: "Depicted as the new 'welfare queens,' their labor and their care have been instrumentalized and infantilized; they have been fired *en masse* under calls for austerity; they have seen rollbacks in their pensions; and have been derided because they teach in 'government schools'" (Giroux, 2013a, p. 458). Neoliberalism has markedly shaped the U.S. educational landscape since No Child Left Behind with its implementation of standardized, high-stakes testing to measure school and teacher quality, as well as opening the door to privatization by allowing corporations and for-profit charters to take over schools that did not meet adequate yearly progress (Black, 2020; Ravitch, 2011, 2013, 2020). Race to the Top ushered in more competitive market framing and Common Core standards with close ties to technology, testing, and publishing markets (Huckaby, 2019; Ravitch, 2013). With No Child Left Behind, a bipartisan bill signed into law by George W. Bush, and Race to the Top, an Obama initiative, neoliberalism is not strictly confined to one political party. As Giroux argues, "politicians at the state and federal levels, irrespective of their political affiliation, advocate reforms that amount to selling off or giving away public schools to the apostles of casino capitalism" (2013a, p. 459). Huckaby argues constituents across party lines experience its effects:

> What's happening to education via neoliberal policy is not a liberal or conservative issue. . . . No Child Left Behind (NCLB) was a bipartisan initiative and its impact on students and families is nonpartisan. While poor communities and communities of color feel the brunt of neoliberal education reform, families in the shrinking middle class are not exempt. (2019, p. 4)

To combat some of these effects on teachers and students, teachers in states such as Oklahoma, West Virginia, Arizona, and Kentucky have pushed back on the negative impacts of decades of "reform." Red became the symbol for taking back public education.

Red for Ed: Resistance to Neoliberal Reforms

Red for Ed, largely a social media movement transcending state lines, has followers in politically red, blue, and purple states. With support from the National Educational Association (NEA), Red for Ed gained prominence in 2018 as a rallying cry for state-level teacher strikes and walkouts (Blanc, 2020). One central goal of Red for Ed, shared across states, is funding for public education without strings to privatization (Blanc, 2020; Walker, 2019). Even with flexibility for states to contextualize Red for Ed for their own needs, the message presents a critique of neoliberal reforms. Followers may not cite neoliberalism explicitly, but their demands for change are, nevertheless, grounded in a critique of neoliberal educational policies. For example, the California Teachers Association #RedforEd site defines quality education in terms opposed to neoliberal policies. They demand: "[S]maller class sizes, less testing and more teaching, stronger oversight and regulation of charter schools, competitive wages, and adequate funding" (California Teachers Association, n.d.). Unspoken in their definition of quality education is a challenge to the current neoliberal state of affairs—"smaller" implies existing large class sizes, "less testing" implies an abundance of testing, "stronger oversight" implies little to no oversight of charter schools, and "competitive wages and adequate funding" implies inadequate wages and funding. All of the above are critiques of neoliberal policies that shape public education nationwide, including Kentucky.

Kentucky Red for Ed: Research Study Context

Neoliberalism transcends political lines, yet 2017 to 2019 represented a simultaneous acceleration in the neoliberal agenda in Kentucky and transformation to a one-party dominated state. Kentucky had long been a red state in federal elections; however, there had not been a Republican governor in four decades until Matt Bevin won the gubernatorial election in 2015 (Robillard, 2015). By 2017, the Republican party controlled the Office of the Governor, the Kentucky House of Representatives, and Senate, leading to a wave of educational legislation. In 2017, the state legislature passed charter school legislation. That same year, Governor Bevin signed an executive order to change nine state education boards and councils, as well as gave the Office of the Governor more control in appointing school boards. In March 2018, the Senate passed Senate Bill 151 (SB151), which Bevin signed into law in April 2018. It proposed budget cuts, elimination of teacher positions, changes to retirement guidelines, and changes to the funding and allocation of the state pension system. Due in part to the 2008 recession, "itself brought on by neoliberal economics" (Douglas, 2014-15, p. 34), and state underfunding of the pension system across decades, the Kentucky pension system was one of the most under-funded in the nation (Associated Press, 2018). SB151 moved pensions from a state plan to a hybrid one, which encompassed neoliberal logic with its "commitment to minimize or dismantle state intervention in the economy, and to limit or eliminate the state's role in redistributing wealth" (Douglas, 2014-15, p. 35).

SB151 was a tipping point for teachers, and in 2018, resistance emerged. Attorney General Andy Beshear, Democrat, filed a lawsuit against the governor on grounds that SB151 failed to follow Senate process and had broken "inviolable" contracts (Loftus & Watkins, 2018). Bill proponents had substituted SB151 for a bill related to the sewage system that already held the number of required votes, so they did not follow the Constitutional requirement that votes on proposals must occur "three times over three separate days" (Associated Press, 2018).

Eight months later, the Kentucky Supreme Court agreed with Beshear's argument and struck down SB151 on constitutional grounds.

Meanwhile, while the issue was taken up in the courts, Kentucky teachers and public-school employees mobilized to action in March 2018. Like colleagues in other "right-to-work" states, teachers organized several "sick-outs" by coordinating calling in sick *en masse* to force districts to close (Blanc, 2019). With many wearing red or Red for Ed shirts, nearly 8,000 teachers and other supporters showed up at the state capitol in Frankfort to protest SB151 on March 28, 2018. Over 30 school districts closed (Associated Press, 2018). Teachers mobilized through social media. On March 27, 2018, the day SB151 passed the General Assembly, a Fayette County school district employee started KY120 United, a Facebook page to organize teachers and public education employees across the state. The post read: "Reach out to western Kentucky, eastern Kentucky, southern Kentucky, northern Kentucky, central Kentucky. Unify under one message" (Yoo, 2018).

Representing the number of districts in Kentucky, KY120 United was a significant source of information on SB151 and bills in 2019. In 2019, House Bill 525 proposed to restructure the board charged with oversight of teacher pensions, including reducing the number of seats held by representatives from the Kentucky Education Association (KEA). House Bill 205 also proposed providing tax credits for scholarships to private schools (Theissen, 2019).

Echoing spring 2018, teachers in eight districts across Kentucky organized "sick-outs" so they could protest HB 525 at the capitol in February 2019. On March 3, 2019, KY120 United posted a statement called "Lines in the Sand," where they outlined their statement of action:

> We . . . are prepared to strike for the betterment of our state, the survival of our communities, and the economic security of our families if the Kentucky General Assembly does any of the following:
>
> - Attempts to provide scholarship tax credits for private schools, thus reducing public monies available to public schools
> - Attempts to create a funding mechanism for Charter Schools, thus reducing public monies available to community public schools

> - Attempts to reduce Defined Benefit Pension benefits to public employees
> - Attempts to remove new/future school employees from the inviolable contract
> - Attempts to reduce salaries of public employees
>
> These are our lines in the sand. Enough is enough. (KY120 United, 2019)

KY120 United later became an organizing and educational tool for the 2019 gubernatorial election. It had grown to such influence that several primary candidate hopefuls sat down with members for interviews posted on the Facebook page. After the primary, Matt Bevin ran as the Republican incumbent and Attorney General Andy Beshear, who had filed suit against SB151, ran as the Democratic candidate. KY120 United created videos on each candidate's educational platforms. They canvassed for Beshear, who ran on a pro-teacher platform. In November 2019, Beshear won by 5,000 votes, in large part due to teacher support (Blanc, 2020). In his acceptance speech, Beshear thanked teachers and invited several KY120 United leaders to the after-party. Beshear acknowledged their protest days at the capitol:

> I'll never forget the first couple of years that I was in office as your attorney general were . . . hard. . . . But I put on that armor and stepped up to the front line . . . until 12,000 reinforcements came to the capitol. To our educators, I know so many of you worked hard on this campaign. And I appreciate every single hour that each of you . . . spent knocking on doors. . . . To our educators, this is your victory. From now on, the doors of your state capitol will always be opened. We will treat each other with dignity and respect, and we will honor our commitments to our public servants. (Beshear, 2019)

Kentucky teachers and school employees had effectively joined Red for Ed. While the Kentucky story demonstrates tremendous political agency and influence, teacher activists experienced attacks along the way. Kentucky teachers were "too readily and far too pervasively . . . relegated to zones of humiliation and denigration" (Giroux, 2013a, p. 458), so much so that Beshear acknowledged their "courage to stand up and fight against all the bullying and name calling" (Beshear, 2019). A major source of denigration was from Governor Bevin himself.

Political Bullying Against Kentucky Teacher Activism: 2018–2019

Governor Bevin maligned teachers in contradictory ways. On the first day of protest in March 2018, Bevin framed teachers as lazy and uncommitted. He described them as "hanging out" and "taking the day off" (Van Sant, 2018). He stated: "I'm offended that people so cavalierly, and so flippantly, disregarded what's truly best for children" (Van Sant, 2018). When teachers booed during an open session, Bevin stated: "That's the kind of thug mentality that's being dealt with" (Sonka, 2018).

After calling teachers thugs, a polemical term with racist implications, Bevin turned to the contradictory trope of teacher as caregiver, even savior: "I guarantee you somewhere in Kentucky today, a child was sexually assaulted that was left at home because there was nobody there to watch them. . . . Children were harmed—some physically, some sexually . . .—because they were vulnerable and left alone" (Horton, 2018, para. 2). Because of teacher and public backlash for blaming teachers for child abuse, Bevin apologized, claiming his intent was to highlight "unintended consequences of shutting schools," even as he provided no evidence of abuse (Stelloh, 2018).

In April 2019, rhetoric ratcheted to action when the State Labor Department subpoenaed school districts for the names of teachers who had called in sick in February 2019 in protest of HB 525. In an April 2019 re-election event at a Rotary Club, Bevin again blamed teachers for a child being harmed due to a "sick-out" day, despite his former apology. A young boy accidentally shot his seven-year-old sister because of an improperly stored gun in the home. Bevin stated:

> One thing you almost didn't hear anything about while we had people pretending to be sick when they weren't sick and leaving kids

> unattended to or in situations that they should not have been in—a little girl was shot, 7 years old, by another kid. Because they were somewhere that they weren't intended and because a parent didn't have any option, put them in a situation so that they could go to work, it left these kids in a compromised situation where they encountered a gun and there was not enough awareness. (McLaren & Bailey, 2019)

Research Study: Kentucky Teacher Activists

The successes of teacher mobilization and Bevin's response demonstrated teachers' power to affect change (and draw ire). Bevin's critiques revealed something deeper about dominant conceptualizations about the roles teachers perform and what teaching entails. To understand why teachers mobilized and how they made sense of his critiques, I interviewed six public school teachers active in supporting the protests of 2018–2019. Press reports and KY120 United posts also served as data sources. I interviewed each participant[1] in spring 2019 and spring 2020. Participants identified as white women with 2 to 15 years of teaching experience at the elementary, middle, and high school levels. Four participants were active in KY120 United by creating site content or by coordinating events. Cross-case coding revealed themes across the audio recorded interviews (Mayan, 2009). Analysis included critical analysis of discourse, with emphasis on how discourse constructs individuals in particular ways (Davies, 2000; Foucault, 1975/1995; Hall, 1997). Henry Giroux's "transformative intellectuals" (2011, 2013a) provided the analytical framework.

Analysis

Participants developed a "critical consciousness" (Freire, 1970, 1998) whereby they saw their existing conditions through new eyes and sought to change them. Paulo Freire (1998) warned: "[T]here is . . . an immobilizing ideology of fatalism, . . . which insists that we can do nothing to change the march of social-historical and cultural reality because that is how the world is anyway. . . . The most contemporary version of such fatalism is neoliberalism" (p. 26). Participants resisted fatalism by engaging as transformative intellectuals (Giroux, 2011, 2013b). According to Giroux (2011), teachers who act as transformative intellectuals:

1. Acknowledge teacher work as intellectual work, "as opposed to defining it in purely instrumental or technical terms" (p. 186);
2. Identify the ideologies and epistemologies, as well as the practical conditions that shape their work. They take their understanding of these conditions and assess whether they are "conditions necessary for teachings to function as intellectuals" (p. 186);
3. Assert the "role teachers play in producing and legitimating various political, economic, and social interests through the pedagogies they endorse and utilize" (p. 186);
4. Participate in debates surrounding their work and acknowledge the public school as a site of democracy, rather than primarily a bureaucracy (p.184).

Participants acted as "transformative intellectuals" (Giroux, 2011, 2013a) by: 1) recognizing how the neoliberal agenda controls their work and representation, as well as obscures teaching as intellectual (Giroux, 2011, p. 193; Aronowitz & Giroux, 1985) and 2) articulating a consciousness that teaching requires civic action.

In the words of Pam, teachers "[were] waking up" to the neoliberal, fatalistic culture of survival. They fought not only for pensions and funding, but for the opportunity to create a school space where agency, critical thought, and hope are nurtured. As one sign at a rally read, teachers demanded that legislators "[H]elp our schools ~~survive~~ THRIVE." Participants pushed back on Governor Bevin's framing of their activism and teaching. Pam: "So, what am I? Lazy, a thug, or supposed to be preventing kids from getting assaulted or shot?" Annette: "I don't think you can reason with the things that [Bevin] says because what he's basically saying is, 'You guys are so important that when you're not in work, kids aren't safe, but you're just a bunch of lazy thugs?'" For all participants, Bevin's characterizations galvanized their involvement rather than curtailed it. His political bullying helped wake them up.

Neoliberal Agenda Obscures Teaching as "Intellectual Work"

Participants acknowledged how increased class sizes and data-driven decision making, earmarks of neoliberal reform (Giroux, 2011, 2013a), limit their role as intellectuals (Giroux, 2013b). They recognized the influence of "big money" in policies affecting their everyday work, as well as ideologies shaping reforms (Giroux, 2011). They stated this recognition as the rationale for supporting protests of bills that limit teaching conditions.

Olivia lamented data-driven processes that dehumanize her students:

> [We're] thinking of children as numbers instead of as children. It's progressively gotten more data-driven and data-driven. You sit in a meeting and project the document with all of the data. And you go to one specific column of an assessment, and you go down that column, and you pick out the number, and then arrow over to look at the kid. That's where it really started sinking in with me. . . . To sit there and have other people who have not worked with my children go down and pull out a number and THEN arrow over to the kid—the children have become numbers. That operation there is so backwards.

Monica linked budget cuts to increasing class sizes, while pointing out the hypocrisy of investing in charter schools instead. She stated: "I mean, I thought over 25 [in a class] was a lot 15 years ago and now I'm like, 'Please don't be over 35.' And we've asked for more resources, we've asked for smaller class sizes, and we haven't gotten money for it, but yet, there's money for charter schools?"

Olivia and Monica critiqued how extreme data-driven decisions, coupled with increased class sizes, restrict their teaching. These conditions confined them to "managing and implementing curricula programs rather than developing or critically appropriating curricula to fit specific pedagogical concerns" (Giroux, 2011, p. 184). Such conditions limit teachers' ability to use their expertise regarding effective pedagogies. Oliva and Monica engaged as transformative intellectuals seeking to assert their roles "in producing and legitimating various political, economic, and social interests through the pedagogies they endorse and utilize" (Giroux, 2011, p. 186).

All participants connected school practices and legislation to "big money." They identified 2018–2019 education bills as pursuing a "privatization" agenda rather than working within the existing public education structure to allocate more resources and improve conditions (Giroux, 2013a). Reflecting on a district that had allocated thousands of dollars to turn an elementary school into a charter school, Pam stated: "They want to privatize education. They don't give two rips about these kids. And when you privatize something and make people have to pay money for it, then you automatically eliminate all of the kids who are poor." Olivia shared her concern about charter schools:

> The idea of charter schools is to use public money for . . . certain groups of students. And inevitably . . . that would just further increase the gap between lower class and upper class people and families. So realistically, I would love to hear [Bevin] answer what would happen to those students, right? If they don't have public education, how are they going to get an education?

Participants critiqued the ways charter schools hurt students with learning disabilities, students in poverty, and students of color the most. Monica explained:

> [T]he most vulnerable kids are our lower socioeconomic kids and our minority kids and if you allow these things to happen and you're not funding public schools, you are sentencing them, basically, to end up in a prison. Same thing with our undocumented kids. . . . So I feel this has turned into almost a class warfare. It's a bunch of rich white people making decisions for poor people and minorities.

Monica explained how neoliberal political and economic structures limit teachers' agency. She said, "They made us "right-to-work" so they take away any of our collective bargaining."

Annette concurred:

> What makes me so mad about it is they use this premise of school choice for the Black children but [it's] systemic racism. So, they're using them for the exact thing that they're saying is going to help

> them, and they won't. I mean, those are the kids they're not going to have in their [charter] schools. They're not going to have any kids with IEPs in their school. It's all a plan [to] step by step dismantle it.

The participants all reflected on how legislative proposals—charter schools, pension cuts, public school budget cuts—emanated from larger agendas, both political and corporate. Annette, Pam, Monica, and Amy specifically named the influence of the American Legislative Exchange Council (ALEC) as particularly insidious. Bevin and a variety of state representatives had strong ties to ALEC—a national conservative group who drafts model legislation ranging from education, environment, labor, and health. Annette described Bevin's connections to ALEC and explained how Kentucky made up a larger movement of states pushing back on ALEC legislation. She stated,

> Bevin is just owned by Koch brothers and ALEC. . . . But we've stopped a lot of this, and it's because [KY120 United] has talked to and built relationships with some teachers in Arizona and Oklahoma and West Virginia. So, they got hit with these exact same bills before we did, so we were able to see them coming. So, I mean, we owe so much to KY120 because [it] was like, "Hey, y'all. This isn't good." I mean, it's a pure ALEC agenda every single thing. They're all just cookie-cutter [bills]. I mean, you can watch on the news, and everything that's happened—South Carolina and North Carolina are striking today, that's why I got on my red. So yeah. I mean, Bevin's just bought and paid for. . . . His only desire is to defund and kill public education.

Neoliberal Intersections with Gender

Participants reflected on the irony of Bevin claiming that teacher activism hurts children when his policies were doing harm. On the contrary, Monica equated her activism with caring for children:

> [I]f you say you care about the children, then what are you doing when you're affecting their education firsthand through all these

> various things with bigger class sizes, cutting classes? Kids are the ones being affected. . . . It's kind of ironic . . . for him to say that [we disregard what's best for children]. . . Because teachers doing this show that they're caring about the children. Whereas the state doing this shows that they really don't care about children. They just care about the money.

Bevin's concept of care demonstrated where neoliberalism capitalizes on sexism. Teachers have long been subjected to the "mother-teacher" role (Goldstein, 2014), which idealizes qualities of nurturing, care, and self-sacrifice. Yet, sacrificial behavior for the benefit of children has contributed to teachers "making do" with under-resourced teaching conditions. Prior to COVID-19, it meant teaching when unwell and not taking time off. Teachers calling in sick in order to protest and making demands shattered this sacrificial ideal, becoming fodder for Bevin's critique. Also drawing on Goldstein's (2014) research, Brown and Stern (2018) assert that teaching as historically "women's work" has created "a dialectical tension that both idealizes and vilifies teachers" (p. 179; Kumashiro, 2012). This tension was evident in Bevin's contrasting critiques (e.g., teachers as protectors from abuse one day and disregarding what's best for children the next). Neoliberalism undergirds this tension, as it capitalizes on individuals willing to make do with less within an oppressive status quo. Even a "neoliberal feminist is a subject that takes it upon herself to manage ongoing gender inequalities" (Scharff, 2019, p. 3), rather than dismantling inequalities. Neoliberalism intersects with sexism by rendering the systemic invisible or irrelevant, and instead celebrates how one overcomes the status quo of sexism (or classism, ageism, and racism) through individual hard work, strength of character, or grit (Douglas, 2014-15; Scharff, 2019).

Amy reflected on this intersection, explaining her frustration at how Bevin and supporters critiqued teacher activism in sexist ways:

> If we look at the historical trends in salary, in benefits, in the response to teachers when teachers ask for more pay, when we ask for professional development, [when] we ask to be treated like any other professional that has multiple degrees. Because this [has] for so long primarily been women's work and primarily been seen as something

> nurturing. Because it's been traditionally a woman-dominated field and because we're seen as nurturers and caregivers, we're not supposed to ask for things. We're just supposed to suck it up and do it because that's what we are. We're moms and women and are supposed to be nice and we're supposed to be polite. And I call bullshit on all of that. If I have one more person tell me that I really need to think of the kids instead of asking to be treated like a highly trained, highly educated professional, that's where I want to start throwing down because those are not mutually exclusive.

For Amy, teachers were "thinking of the kids" when asking for professional treatment so they could do their jobs well.

Naming ideologies that shape teacher roles means questioning the historically gendered notion that teaching requires self-sacrifice. Yet, the dominant narrative of teacher sacrifice prevails, and even teachers struggle to reject the narrative. Olivia initially wrestled with Bevin's comment about children being sexually assaulted. She said,

> I remember the first time reading it and thinking that he was absolutely right and that it's awful and horrible because he's right. There are those things happening . . . in our state to our children. But as time went on and you reflect more about that, well, . . . what are they exposed to on the weekends? What are they exposed to on breaks? What are they exposed to over the summer? So as time went on . . . this morphed into something completely different with me. Because it also made me feel like he has no idea what we would do if we did see our students exhibiting signs of physical and sexual abuse . . . It hit me like, "No. He's wrong." Because yes, that still might have happened, but . . . we have done our job in getting things reported and filed.

After grappling with Bevin's critique, Olivia concluded "sick-outs" did not endanger children. Annette, Monica, and Grace also identified Bevin's critiques as rooted in sexism, which demonstrated their ability to engage as transformative intellectuals in identifying both the ideologies of sexism and neoliberalism.

Articulation of a Growing Consciousness: Teaching Involves Civic Action

Participants acted as transformative intellectuals by recognizing the importance of participating in debates about their field and engaging in critical democracy (Freire, 1998; Giroux, 2011; Greene, 1995). Participants educated themselves on bills and larger political agendas that have driven reforms, such as charter schools. They analyzed how some reforms perpetuate racism, classism, and ableism. They read the work of Diane Ravitch. Three participants mentioned the documentary, *The Brainwashing of My Dad* (Senko, 2015), which explains the influence of talk radio and Fox News on right-wing personal and political discourse. KY120 led small groups and discussed these sources, analyzing Bevin's policies as right-wing thinking. They educated themselves on ALEC and its role in drafting legislation. In short, they realized how teaching connects with civic action.

Monica stated: "Teachers have to be politically active. They have to stay involved." Monica connected her participation in the protests with her role as a high school social studies teacher. She told her students why she called in sick and went to Frankfort. She educated them on the bills and shared her perspectives. She encouraged them to attend rallies at the Capitol to learn more. In 2018, several of her students came to the Capitol building and emailed her when they could not get inside. Already inside, Monica was livid that they were not allowed in. She stated:

> The students are like, 'We're the ones you're making decisions about. You have to talk to us and you have to give us a seat at the table and you have to let us come into these meetings.' When they came to Frankfort one time, [Capitol authorities] tried to lock the doors and lock everybody out and one of [the students] emailed me on their phone . . . and they were like, 'They're trying to lock us out,' and I'm like, 'What door are you at?' So, I go down there and I'm like, 'You are not allowed to lock these doors. This is a public building, these are my students, they're coming in here.'

Grace also shared the importance of educating on these matters. She said:

> The kids would ask about it. They'd say, "Why are teachers protesting?' And I would tell them. . . . I'd say, 'You know, these cuts to teacher positions are going to affect you. It's going to make your classes bigger, it's going to . . . affect what you do. . . . You should be aware that these are the decisions being made for you. Get involved.'

Both Monica and Grace acknowledged the "need to defend schools as institutions essential to maintaining and developing a critical democracy and also to defending teachers as transformative intellectuals who combine scholarly reflection and practice in the service of educating students to be thoughtful, active citizens" (Giroux, 2011, p. 184).

Annette worked with KY120 United to make videos to educate about the bills. She said:

> We got together . . . and started making educational videos about tax credits and all this stuff to put out to the public . . . . We made three so far. One was about the charters, one was about the vouchers —that was another thing we killed, those vouchers. We made just informational videos about—because the public just doesn't know, so. We did one, the kids held posters and dropped them. And then we did one where it was like a PowerPoint slideshow with facts. And we're probably going to make more. That's what we decided. This is what we do. Our classroom just got bigger. It just happens to be the entire state now.

When stating that their classroom just got bigger, Annette acted as a transformative intellectual by acknowledging teaching and the public school as a site of democracy, rather than primarily a bureaucracy (Giroux, 2011). Connecting teaching with larger social and political contexts extended her teaching beyond classroom walls and created agency. Pam further explained the importance of sending KY120 United representatives to open state committee meetings:

> We stayed very loud and made sure that to the best of our ability, we could educate the public. . . . [KY120] has retirees in every committee meeting. . . . Now you got eyes and ears on every single meeting.

> We had to learn the process of how these things go through, how many readings it takes, and what committees, where it moves from there. We became legislative experts.

In addition to becoming legislative experts, participants supported Beshear in the Gubernatorial election. Annette, Pam, and Monica were especially active in his campaign. Annette: "Last week, I did something so out of my realm. I had a 'meet and greet' for Andy Beshear and Jacqueline Coleman [Lieutenant Governor candidate]. And we were over at the local brewery, and they were there for—actually, two weeks before that, I got invited to lunch with Jacqueline Coleman. And I just wake up every day and I'm like, 'What?'" Annette was invited to the acceptance speech after-party in November 2019.

In 2020, three participants shared how KY120 United moved from protesting bills and being active in the gubernatorial campaign to working to ensure employee protection during the early days of COVID-19. Before schools went virtual, KY120 United pressured districts to provide masks and plastic barrier protections for elderly bus drivers and cafeteria staff.

Since COVID-19, KY120 United has maintained civic engagement as various "culture wars" have waged against public education. In 2022, the Kentucky legislature passed anti–critical race theory legislation that would have restricted how teachers teach about race had Governor Beshear not vetoed it (Henderson & Musa, 2022). When the anti-CRT legislation was presented in the House, KY120 United was one of several groups that gathered in the Capitol to protest, arguing that the legislation "would limit discussions of systemic racism in the state" (Web Staff, 2022). While the teacher gathering was much smaller than pension protests of 2018, KY120 United had maintained their organizing power to facilitate civic engagement on curricular matters, again maintaining their function as transformative public intellectuals. In 2023, the legislature passed anti-transgender legislation that gave staff power to deny using students' preferred pronouns (Associated Press, 2023). KY120 United condoned the legislation. They wrote: "Let us be clear—we will fight against and stand firmly opposed to ANY bill that bullies or singles out the students we serve or the teachers who serve them. We will also protect and defend our LGBTQ staff members from these disgusting and clearly politically motivated attacks" (Forward Kentucky, 2023). KY120 United remains involved in civic action.

Conclusion & Further Study

Participants transformed both the conditions of their teaching and named some of the underlying economic, political, and gender assumptions that led to these conditions. Their activism held many successes, such as how their political pressure, combined with the Office of the Attorney General, struck down SB151. They were essential in electing a pro-public education governor. They acted as transformative intellectuals by naming and challenging neoliberal ideologies directing school reform and enacting their teaching outside of classroom walls through civic action.

Participants like Amy, Grace, Monica, and Annette linked privatization to disparities related to race, class, and disability in educational contexts. Further study would illuminate how they responded to anti-CRT and anti-transgender legislation, as well as whether they have maintained involvement in KY120 United. Further study on the organizational structure of KY120 United through the lens of transformative intellectuals would establish knowledge on how to scale up those qualities at the organizational level.

In the meantime, participants engaged as intellectuals who effectively enacted change.

References

Aronowitz, S., & Giroux, H. (1985). Radical education and transformative intellectuals. *Canadian Journal of Political and Social Theory*, 9(3), 48-63.

Associated Press. (2018, December 13). *Kentucky court nixes pension law that prompted teacher protests*. NBC News. https://www.nbcnews.com/news/us-news/kentucky-court-nixes-pension-law-prompted-teacher-protests-n94749

Associated Press. (2023, February 17). *Kentucky Senate lets teachers decide on transgender pronouns*. WNKY. https://www.wnky.com/kentucky-senate-lets-teachers-decide-on-transgender-pronouns/

Beshear, A. (2019, November 6). *Acceptance Speech*. [Andy Beshear Governor Acceptance Speech]. Rev.com. https://www.rev.com/blog/transcripts/andy-beshear-kentucky-governor-acceptance-speech-transcript.

Black, D.W. (2020). *Schoolhouse burning: Public education and the assault on American democracy*. Hachette Book Group.

Blanc, E. (2019). *Red state revolt: The teachers' strikes and working-class politics*. Verso.

Blanc, E. (2020). The Red for Ed movement, two years in. *New Labor Forum, 29*(3), 66–73. https://newlaborforum.cuny.edu/2020/10/03/the-red-for-ed-movement-two-years-in/#:~:text=In%20late%20February%202018%2C%20teachers,labor%20may%20have%20finally%20arrived

Brown, A. E., & Stern, M. (2018). Teachers' work as women's work: Reflections on gender, activism, and solidarity in new teacher movements. *Feminist Formations, 30*(3), 172–197. DOI: 10.1353/ff.2018.0046

California Teachers Association. (n.d.). *We are #RedforEd.* Action Network. https://actionnetwork.org/petitions/redfored/

Davies, B. (2000). *A body of writing: 1990-1999.* Altamira.

Douglas, S. B. (2014-15). Still living with sexism (after all these years): How neoliberalism operates at the intersections of sexism and ageism. *Soundings: A Journal of Politics and Culture (58),* 34–43. https://www.muse.jhu.edu/article/565756

Forward Kentucky. (2023, February 8). *KY120 AFT statement on HB 173, an omnibus anti-trans bill.* Forward Kentucky. https://forwardky.com/ky120-aft-statement-on-hb-173/

Foucault, M. (1995). *Discipline and punish: The birth of the prison.* (A. Sheridan, Trans.). Random House. (Original work published 1975)

Freire, P. (1970). *Cultural action for freedom.* Harvard Educational Review.

Freire, P. (1998). *Pedagogy of freedom: Ethics, democracy, and civic courage.* Rowman & Littlefield Publishing.

Giroux, H. A. (2011). Teachers as transformative intellectuals. In E. B. Hilty (Ed.), *Thinking about schools: A foundations of education reader* (pp. 183–189). Westview Press.

Giroux, H. (2013a). Neoliberalism's war against teachers in dark times. *Cultural Studies-Critical Methodologies, 13*(6), 458–468. https://doi.org/10.1177/1532708613503769

Giroux, H. (2013b). *America's education deficit and the war on youth.* Monthly Review Press.

Goldstein, D. (2014). *The teacher wars: A history of America's most embattled profession.* Anchor Books.

Greene, M. (1995). *Releasing the imagination: Essays on education, the arts, and social change.* Jossey-Bass Publishers.

Hall, S. (1997). *Representation: Cultural representations and signifying practices.* Sage Publications.

Henderson, J., & Musa, A. (2022, April 7). *Kentucky governor vetoes bill incorporating 'anti-critical race theory,' calling it a step backward.* CNN. https://www.cnn.com/2022/04/07/us/kentucky-governor-vetoes-bill-anti-critical-race-theory/index.html

Hill, D., & Kumar, R. (2009). *Global neoliberalism and education and its consequences.* Routledge.

Horton, A. (2018, April 15). Kentucky governor apologizes for comments suggesting kids were sexually assaulted while teachers protested. *The Washington Post*. https://www.washingtonpost.com/news/education/wp/2018/04/14/kentucky-governor-claims-that-children-were-raped-used-drugs-while-teachers-protested/

Huckaby, M. F. (2019). *Researching resistance: Public education after neoliberalism*. Myers Education Press.

Hurley, A., & McCloud, J. (2017). Under the wheels of a juggernaut: Education programs in the midst of a moral quandary. *Philosophical Studies in Education, 48*, 30–44.

Kumashiro, K. (2012). *Bad teacher! How blaming teachers distorts the bigger picture*. Teachers College Press.

KY120 United. (2019, March 3). *Lines in the sand*. Medium. https://medium.com/@ky120united/lines-in-the-sand-43de3b77b2a2

Loftus, T., & Watkins, M. (2018, April 11). Kentucky attorney general challenges new pension-reform law, files suit against governor. *The Columbus Dispatch*. https://www.dispatch.com/story/news/politics/2018/04/11/teacher-public-employee-pension-reform-lawsuit/509421002/

Mayan, M. J. (2009). *Essentials of qualitative inquiry*. Left Coast Press, Inc.

McLaren, M., & Bailey, P. (2019, April 25). Gov. Matt Bevin: Kentucky teacher sickouts caused a 7-year-old to be shot. *Courier Journal*. https://www.courier-journal.com/story/news/education/2019/04/25/kentucky-teacher-sickouts-matt-bevin-child-shot-comment/3574640002/

Ravitch, D. (2011). *The death and life of the great American school system*. Basic Books.

Ravitch, D. (2013). *The reign of error: The hoax of the privatization movement and the danger to America's public schools*. Vintage.

Ravitch, D. (2020). *Slaying Goliath: The passionate resistance to privatization and the fight to save America's public schools*. Knopf.

Robillard, K. (2015, November 11). *Republican Bevin wins Kentucky governor's race*. Politico. https://www.politico.com/story/2015/11/kentucky-governor-race-matt-bevin-wins-215502

Scharff, C. (2019). Prepare her for sexism. *European Journal of Women's Studies, 27*(1), 3–8. https://doi.org/10.1177/1350506819885707

Senko, J. (Director). (2015). *The brainwashing of my dad* [Film]. Cinco Dedos Películas.

Sonka, J. (2018, March 21). *A day after apologizing for rhetoric, Bevin calls out "thug mentality" of teachers protesting pension bill*. Insider Louisville. http://www.insiderlouisville.com

Spooner, M. (2015). The deleterious personal and societal effects of the audit culture and a domesticated academy: Another way is possible. *International Review of Qualitative Research, 8*(2), 212–228. https://doi.org/10.1525/irqr.2015.8.2.212

Stelloh, T. (2018, April 15). *Kentucky governor apologizes after linking child abuse to teacher protests.* NBC News. https://www.nbcnews.com/news/education/kentucky-governor-apologizes-after-linking-child-abuse-teacher-protests-n866156

Theissen, T. (2019, March 9). *Teacher actions return to Kentucky.* Socialist Worker. https://socialistworker.org/2019/03/09/teacher-actions-return-to-kentucky

Van Sant, S. (2018, April 15). *Kentucky governor apologizes for comments on teachers' strike.* The Two-Way: Breaking News from NPR. https://www.npr.org/sections/the two-way/2018/04/15/602671694/kentucky-governor-apologizes-for-comments-on-teachers-strike.

Walker, T. (2019, May 24). *#RedforEd rallies step up pressure on lawmakers to take action on funding.* National Education Association. https://www.nea.org/advocating-for-change/new-from-nea/redfored-pressures-lawmakers-for-funding

Web Staff. (2022, January 13). *Kentucky students, teacher rally against anti-CRT bills Wednesday in Frankfort.* LEX18. https://www.lex18.com/news/kentucky-students-teachers-rally-against-anti-crt-bills-wednesday-in-frankfort

Yoo, S. (2018, March 31). *Teachers' 'Sick Out' inspired from single Facebook page.* Wave. https://www.wave3.com/story/37850577/teachers-sick-out-inspired-from-single-facebook-page/

Endnotes

1 All names are pseudonyms.

CHAPTER 4

"We can join together to help fix it": UCORE and the Movement for Social Justice Unionism

Lauren Ware Stark

Introduction

In September 2012, over 90% of the 26,000 members of the Chicago Teachers Union (CTU) voted to go on strike, mobilizing a sea of red that would occupy the city's streets for 7 days to demand "the schools Chicago students deserve" (Uetricht, 2014). This strike was the culmination of organizing by the Caucus of Rank-and-File Educators (CORE), a social justice caucus that had won the top executive positions in the CTU only 2 years earlier. This work stoppage represented a pivotal moment in the growth of a more militant and democratic model of unionism in the United States. Often discussed as social justice unionism, this model involves educators organizing from the bottom up to advance not only their own interests but also those of their students and communities. In social justice unions, members democratically build their collective power to advance justice by organizing, bargaining, and striking for the common good.

The influence of this model can be seen throughout the United States today, over 10 years after the groundbreaking 2012 Chicago teachers strike. In 2022, 135,380 U.S. educators participated in 73 work stoppages, representing over 60% of the stoppages tracked by the Cornell-ILR Labor Action Tracker (Kallas et al., 2022). Among these struggles, Columbus, Ohio teachers led a 4-day strike that secured heating, ventilation, and air conditioning improvements in school buildings; class size reductions; and improved access to art, music, and physical education for elementary students (Henry & Behrens, 2022). Seattle teachers led a 5-day strike that secured more equitable learning conditions in schools, pushing back against district proposals to reduce multilingual and special education services to students (Madeloni, 2022). Massachusetts educators in Malden and Haverhill led strikes advancing common good demands, including smaller class sizes; policies to diversify the teaching profession; initiatives to address housing insecurity among students; wage increases for paraprofessionals; and paid parental leave (Flannery, 2022; Madeloni, 2022).

Together, these struggles represent the ongoing influence of social justice unionism in educator labor organizations in the United States. Teachers unions are increasingly centering common good demands in bargaining, building solidarity with parents and students, and using open bargaining to bring stakeholders into the negotiation process. They are also, in many cases, using militant strategies to build and exercise power, up to and including strikes. Most significantly, for the purposes of this chapter, they are organizing from the ground up to push their unions toward a social justice unionist approach. Through social justice caucuses modeled after CORE and its successors, as well as grassroots networks modeled after statewide organizations in the Red for Ed movement, rank-and-file educators are both advocating for and practicing the principles of social justice unionism, driving a major shift in labor models from the ground up.

The national United Caucuses of Rank-and-File Educators (UCORE) network has played a significant role in this transformation, offering spaces for educators to share stories and gain insights from labor organizing in contexts across the United States and beyond. The UCORE network was officially formed in 2014, building on years of informal organizing among rank-and-file members in CORE and other caucuses. With the support of organizers in Labor Notes, a grassroots labor organization that publishes a newspaper with the same name, UCORE has hosted monthly virtual calls, biannual national conferences, and occasional regional and local gatherings that allow new and experienced educator organizers to build community and learn from each other's experiences. Using a horizontalist model that includes rotating facilitators, UCORE members employ popular education approaches that align with Freirean critical pedagogy to support collective learning between social justice caucuses (Stark,

2019). This network now includes over 40 caucuses and grassroots organizations, with organizers in emerging caucuses learning alongside organizers from caucuses that have been active in the network since its inception.

In this chapter, I discuss the history of UCORE, drawing on my movement ethnographic work within the network and its affiliated caucuses. In the 5 years leading up to the COVID-19 pandemic, I engaged in this network as an ethnographer and as a participant, first as a supporter traveling between multiple caucuses and then as a rank-and-file organizer and steering committee member in the Social Equity Educators caucus in Seattle. This included conducting over 45 oral history interviews, extensive document and social media analysis, and over 450 hours of participant observation, including documenting a participatory oral history of UCORE's founding in August 2015. In the first half of this chapter, I trace the history of UCORE, highlighting some of the ways in which this network has advanced both social justice unionism and contemporary educator movements. In the second half, I draw on this history and research on social justice unionism and educator social movements to argue that the network's work can be considered part of a decade-long social movement to advance social justice unionism within the United States.

Through its exploration of educator organizing in the UCORE network, this chapter contributes to this volume's discussion of how educators can challenge inequalities and advance justice through social movement organizations. It also provides a history of caucus organizing in the UCORE network that is relevant to practitioners, organizers, and educational historians. Likewise, it contributes to broader research in the fields of educational studies (Givan & Lang, 2020; Weiner, 2012) and social movement learning (Kuk & Tarlau, 2020; Niesz, 2021; Stark, 2023), including the growing body of research on social justice unionist organizing in the United States (Asselin, 2022; Dyke & Muckian Bates, 2019; Maton, 2022; Maton & Stark, 2021; Stark et al., 2022).

Teachers Unions and Struggles for Justice in the United States

The history of UCORE cannot be fully understood in isolation. Rather, it is crucial to see the ways in which this network and its caucuses have responded to pressing structural inequalities as they have advanced a more equitable vision for schools and society. Through this work, UCORE has built on and contributed to the history of educator organizing within and outside of teachers unions in the United States.

Since their inception in the late 19th century, educator unions have grappled with the structural inequalities that characterize life in the United States, with leftist educators organizing within or alongside major social movements. Critical educators in the nation's earliest teachers unions organized for fair salaries, progressive taxation, professional autonomy, and democratic governance of schools and unions (Murphy, 1990; Phelps, 2021; Rousmaniere, 2001). In doing so, they contributed to the burgeoning labor, progressive, and first-wave feminist movements. In the early 20th century, a militant minority of educators organized for radical social change, including New York's Teachers Union, which was targeted by anti-communist purges in 1941 but continued to organize for economic and racial justice until the mid-1960s (Taylor, 2010).

The nation's largest teachers unions and organizations had a complicated relationship with the Civil Rights Movement. While both the National Educators Association (NEA) and American Federation of Teachers (AFT) vocally supported efforts toward desegregation, the AFT-affiliated United Federation of Teachers (UFT) rejected efforts toward community control of schools for Black and Latinx families in New York City in the union's 1968 strike, with only a minority of educators breaking the picket line to stand alongside communities of color (Hagopian & Green, 2012; Kahlenberg, 2007; Winslow, 2010). In keeping with the history of the Civil Rights Movement as a whole, Black educator organizations in the pre-*Brown* South more significantly supported the movement through both their teaching and organizing (Baker, 2011; Loder-Jackson, 2015).

For much of the second half of the 20th century, teachers unions emphasized a model often known as business unionism, which emphasized advancing the economic interests of members through collective bargaining, grievances, and the provision of services such as insurance. A more militant unionism could be seen in some instances, however, with rank-and-file educators leading major strikes for labor rights and stronger contracts throughout the "long seventies" (Winslow, 2010). Moreover, while teachers unions did not develop major leftist caucuses similar to those in other labor sectors, educators developed groups focused on economic or racial justice in some urban teachers unions in Chicago and New York in the 1960s and 1970s (Brogan, 2016; Uetricht, 2014).

Toward the end of the century, educator unions continued to emphasize a business model, with an increasing emphasis on teacher professionalization. In many cases, union leaders supported the growing standards and accountability movement that characterized the last two decades of the century. Critical education scholars and leaders disavowed this movement, however, calling instead for progressive education and a return to the labor movement's militant roots. While the model of social movement unionism emerged in international labor circles, building on lessons from struggles in the global south, teacher organizers developed their own, related model of unionism: social justice unionism.

In the early 1990s, leftist educators articulated this vision in a range of venues, including conferences and progressive education journals and newsletters. Educators in the National Coalition of Education Activists (NCEA) met in 1994 to discuss this alternative form of teacher unionism, publishing a statement in *Rethinking Schools* that called on educators to organize democratically alongside parents, students, and community members for social justice in schools and society. While some educators put these principles into practice in their work as union organizers and leaders, this model found more fertile soil in a new form of grassroots educator organization: social justice caucuses.

Much like the leftist and reform caucuses of the 1960s and 1970s, social justice caucuses challenge the dominant norms of teachers unions and advanced progressive social causes. These caucuses are arguably unique, however, in their articulation and practice of social justice unionism. These caucuses focus on democratically advancing multiple forms of justice both within and through their unions, with the goal of using the institutional power of their union to advance justice in both schools and society. While many caucuses form to contest pressing and time-sensitive political challenges, such as school closures and other neoliberal reforms, they also address more longstanding structural inequalities, including racism and economic inequality.

The first social justice caucuses formed in the 1990s and early 2000s. Most notably, the Second Opinion caucus developed in Los Angeles in the 1990s, publishing a newsletter and organizing against neoliberal and racist school policies and reforms. Organizers in Second Opinion formed a new caucus, Progressive Educators for Action Caucus (PEAC) in the early 2000s, going on to win elected union positions as part of a joint slate in 2005. Organizers in this caucus would remain active in leftist educator circles in the decades to come, influencing the work of fellow organizers in California and across the country.

In this same period, educators throughout the United States faced an onslaught of harmful top-down educational reforms, including national policies such as No Child Left Behind and Race to the Top, as well as state- and district-specific reforms. These included standardized curricula and high-stakes tests; portfolio models of school reform, including closures and turnarounds; and performance models linking student test scores to teacher evaluations. While the leaders of the national teachers unions failed to condemn or effectively challenge these reforms, in some cases even welcoming them, rank-and-file educators considered how they might build the power necessary to defend and transform their schools and unions from the ground up.

Social justice caucuses like PEAC offered a model for bringing together like-minded educators to develop and put into practice an alternative vision for teacher unionism capable of standing up against neoliberal school reforms. In 2008, educators came together at several convenings, including the Tri-National Convention in Los Angeles and a "national gathering of reform teachers' caucuses" (Winslow, 2013). These conferences offered opportunities for leftist educators to share strategies and learn from each other's work, highlighting the potential for social justice caucuses to foster a movement for social justice unionism.

That same year, in part because of these conversations, the most influential social justice caucus, the CORE, formed in Chicago. The caucus brought together educators who were supporting the work of community organizers in the Kenwood Oakland Community Organization (KOCO), who were challenging racist school closures in the city. Organizers hosted a book club to study texts, including Naomi Klein's (2007) *The Shock Doctrine: The Rise of Disaster Capitalism*, which helped to develop a shared analysis of the ideologies underlying portfolio-based school reforms in the city. They also supported political education through campaigns and rallies, using an organizing model to build their collective power from the ground up. This enabled them to win the top elected positions in their union in 2010, shifting the entire labor organization to an organizing, social justice unionist model. This included developing organizing and research departments.

In the face of school closures and other neoliberal reforms, Seattle teachers developed their own social justice caucus, the Social Equality Educators, in

2009. Later called the Social Equity Educators, this caucus organized alongside community organizations including Educators, Students, and Parents for a Better Vision (ESP Vision) to challenge racism and neoliberal reforms in the city's schools. Educators in the caucus led the influential MAP boycott in 2013, which helped to ignite the National Opt-Out Movement against high-stakes tests in schools. While organizers in the caucus have won union board positions and nearly won the top officer positions of the union, much of their work has focused on leading grassroots campaigns and pushing their union toward a social justice unionist model.

In 2011, educators in CORE began reaching out to organizers in other contexts to see if they were interested in coming together to share insights from their practice. Over 200 educators from the United States, Canada, and Mexico came together for the National Conference to Fight Back for Public Education on July 6, 2011 to learn from each other's work (Brenner, 2011). While they did not yet consider developing a formal network, they continued to come together at the biannual conference of Labor Notes as well as other educator and labor gatherings.

Three new caucuses formed in this period: Oakland's Classroom Struggle, New Jersey's Newark Education Workers (NEW) (Owens, 2022), and New York City's Movement of Rank-and-File Educators (MORE) (Asselin, 2022; Bocking, 2020; Brogan, 2016). These caucuses built on insights from other caucuses, the ongoing Occupy movement, and the unique histories of struggles in their own contexts. At the same time, CORE continued to show what is possible with a social justice caucus taking the reins of a major teachers union: publishing the landmark, *The Schools Our Students Deserve,* and developing a complex organizing structure with Contract Action Teams at every school in their district. They used these teams and other tools to develop a series of escalating actions, leading up to the groundbreaking 2012 Chicago Teachers Strike.

UCORE and the Spread of the Social Justice Caucus Model

The 2012 Chicago Teachers Strike showed the potential for educators to transform their unions from the ground up into organizations capable of defending public education from privatization and ongoing systemic inequalities. Educators throughout the country reached out to see how they might be able to build a similar caucus and union model in their own contexts. They were, in turn, offered support and guidance, with some Chicago educators traveling to support burgeoning caucuses in cities across the United States. Four CORE leaders, Xian Barrett, Adam Heenan, Michelle Gunderson, and Debby Pope, met at Jackalope Coffee and Tea House in Chicago's Bridgeport neighborhood to discuss their shared work, opening a spreadsheet to develop a list of social justice unionist educators across the country. They took turns calling educators on this list, asking, "Would you like to do this work? Would you like to be part of national work? How are things going in your local? Would it help for you to know other people around the country?" (field notes, August 9, 2015).

These conversations laid the groundwork for the UCORE network. In 2013 and 2014, Labor Notes hosted two invitation-only meetings to bring together educators from the list compiled by Barrett, Gunderson, Heenan, and Pope. CORE organizers discussed the first meeting as a "conference for social justice unionism" (Winslow, 2013). At the second meeting, organized alongside the biannual UCORE conference, Al Ramirez of the CORE caucus made a motion to develop a formal network, and participants spent 12 hours democratically crafting the tenets of their collective work, which would be crafted into a formal mission statement by Educators for a Democratic Union (EDU) leader, Barbara Madeloni.

Through this mission statement, UCORE organizers articulated the network's shared commitment to the principles of social justice unionism, including advancing multiple forms of justice within schools and society:

> We are social justice educators and unionists committed to creating schools and workplaces that advance economic justice, racial justice, and democracy. We call for equitable public education as a human right. We assert that the workplace rights of educators are an essential element of public education and that the well-being of communities in which our children live is as much a part of our mission as the work we do in our schools.

Like the points of unity and mission statements developed by individual caucuses, this statement communicated the shared values and goals that inform organizers' work in a wide range of contexts across the United States.

A number of caucuses joined the network in the period of its formation. These include caucuses of educators engaged in major urban teachers unions such as Los Angeles's Union Power (UP), with roots in the legacy of radical educator organizing in PEAC and other caucuses, and Philadelphia's Caucus of Working Educators (WE) (Maton, 2015, 2018; Riley, 2015), with roots in progressive educator organizations, including Teacher Action Group (TAG). They also included statewide caucuses such as North Carolina's Organize 2020 (O2020) (Johnson, 2017), which developed in 2013 among educators engaged in the Moral Monday movement, and Massachusetts's EDU, building on movements against privatization and high-stakes testing in the state. Each of these caucuses would lead influential social justice unionist struggles in the years to come, with organizers in UP, O2020, and EDU winning executive leadership positions in their unions.

In the 3 years following the network's formation, organizers met once per year at a site hosted by a member caucus: Newark, NJ in 2015, Raleigh, NC in 2016, and Los Angeles, CA in 2017. Beginning in 2018, the network shifted toward biannual meetings, with UCORE gatherings on alternate years connected to the Labor Notes conference. Throughout this period, the network organized monthly national and steering committee Zoom calls, as well as regional meetings and meetups at national educator conferences. These meetings provided spaces for organizers in emerging, new, and established caucuses to share challenges and insights from their work, supporting collective learning and knowledge production (Stark, 2023). As a UCORE leader from Chicago noted while facilitating an oral history of the network at the Newark conference in 2015, "a movement is only as good as its ability to bring new people into the work," and UCORE organizers have committed themselves to building relationships with new organizers and caucuses as they develop across the United States and beyond.

The network continued to grow in the following years, supporting the growth and flourishing of a number of influential caucuses, including the Baltimore Movement of Rank-and-File Educators (BMORE), which organizers formed in 2017 before winning the top elected leadership positions in their union (Shiller & Caucus, 2019). Other affiliated caucuses formed in cities including Albuquerque, Boston, Denver, Portland, Racine, and San Francisco, as well as in states including Arizona, California, New Jersey, New York, Virginia, and West Virginia.

Social Justice Unionism and Social Movements

Educator organizers in this growing network have played significant roles in a number of educator social movements. They centered educational justice in the Occupy movement, as well as bringing strategies from that movement to educator struggles (Brogan, 2016; Picower, 2013; Schirmer, 2019). They also led struggles in the Opt Out movement, including campaigns against high-stakes testing. They further contributed to the development and growth of the Black Lives Matter at School movement, which developed in 2016 as a day of action in Seattle, expanded in 2017 to a week of action in Philadelphia, and grew into a significant national movement in the years to follow (Au & Hagopian, 2017; Jones & Hagopian, 2020; Stark, 2022). They also contributed to movements for immigrant rights in 2016 and 2017, organizing for sanctuary cities and schools and challenging attacks on immigrant and refugee students and their families.

Educators in the UCORE network also contributed to the Red for Ed movement, which represented a major labor upsurge and a testament to the potential for rank-and-file organizing for the common good (Blanc, 2019; Dyke et al., 2022; Dyke & Muckian Bates, 2019; Howell & Schmitzer, 2022). In many ways, statewide organizing in the Red for Ed movement built on the longstanding history of militant educator organizing, including the work of teachers in the "long seventies." However, educators in the statewide networks leading this work have since formed several social justice caucuses that more fully address multiple forms of justice. Most recently, educators in these caucuses and others in the UCORE network contributed to a movement for safe schools in the COVID-19 pandemic, pushing back against reactionary visions of school safety and arguing for accessible and inclusive working and learning environments (Stark et al., 2024).

Each of these struggles can be understood as examples of contemporary educator movements: networked social movements led by educators that advance multiple forms of justice from the ground up (Stark, 2019; Stark et al., 2022). Within these movements, organizers use both new and traditional organizing techniques to challenge longstanding structural inequalities as well as pressing policy debates. The UCORE network has played a pivotal role in connecting organizers in multiple social movements and struggles, building relationships and supporting learning and knowledge production among rank-and-file educators throughout the United States.

Crucially, for the purpose of this chapter, this network has also played a pivotal role in the development of a movement for social justice unionism within the United States. This movement aligns with major definitions of social movements as a "loose collectivity acting with some degree of organization, temporal continuity, and reliance on noninstitutional forms of action to promote or resist change in the group, society, or world order of which it is a part" (McAdam & Snow, 2010, p. 1). This movement is composed of a range of social movement organizations, including the UCORE network, its affiliated caucuses and statewide networks, and educator organizers influenced by their work throughout the country. It has been ongoing for over a decade, with influential members of the UCORE network educators organizing for social justice unionism in the first social justice caucuses.

Moreover, UCORE has advanced social justice unionism through a range of both institutional and noninstitutional forms of action. Organizers have advanced this movement through the institutional pathways of their unions, running slates of educators committed to transforming their unions into an organizing and social justice unionist model. In cities, including Baltimore, Boston, Chicago, and Los Angeles, as well as states including Massachusetts, educators in the UCORE network have been elected to the highest executive positions in their unions. They also frequently organize to speak at school board meetings and other formal institutional spaces for education governance. Moreover, in New York, Seattle, and other contexts, they have pushed their unions toward these models using other institutional strategies, including passing resolutions to shift the work of the union, as well as winning board positions. As the example of Philadelphia's Caucus of Working Educators shows, however, the process of running a grassroots electoral campaign can be transformative, even if a caucus' candidates aren't elected, growing the caucus' base and building educators' collective power from the ground up.

While these institutional forms of action are crucial, noninstitutional forms of action are arguably even more integral to the everyday work of organizations within the UCORE network and the broader movement for social justice unionism. Many caucuses grew out of grassroots protests against neoliberal school closures (Stark & Maton, 2019; Uetricht, 2014). They frequently host opportunities for nonformal education that build shared political analyses among organizers, including book groups, workshops, and conferences (Maton, 2018;

Riley, 2015; Stark, 2023). Through their campaigns, social justice caucuses, networks, and unions have organized a wide range of social actions, ranging from t-shirt days to protests to marches to sit-ins to strikes.

Whether in a noninstitutional wildcat or an institutionally sanctioned strike after lengthy arbitration, strikes represent the most visible tactics used by UCORE members in the movement for social justice unionism. Organizers generally use escalating tactics, building up to a strike, ranging from t-shirt days to petitions to protests (Bradbury et al., 2016). The 2012 Chicago teachers strike built on years of deep organizing and escalating tactics led by CORE and the CTU, including a research-based campaign for the "Schools Chicago Students Deserve," weekly red t-shirt days, mock strike votes, large rallies, and the development of a complex network of Contract Action Teams (Bradbury et al., 2014). Similarly, the 2019 Los Angeles teachers strike was organized over several years using a range of escalating tactics inspired by their Chicago siblings' work, including a campaign for the "Schools LA Students Deserve," protests organized alongside student activists in Students Deserve, and the development of a network of Contract Action Teams supporting building-based organizing conversations with every member of the union (Hagopian, 2019; Jaffe, 2019). By building their power over time and withholding their labor through a landmark strike, Los Angeles educators won major gains for their students and communities, including smaller class sizes; additional counselors, librarians, and nurses; limitations on standardized testing; an immigrant rights fund; community-controlled budgets in dozens of schools; a moratorium on random police searches of students; and the rejection of a two-tier health care system and increased charterization. In an analysis of the strike with UCORE and Labor Notes organizer Barbara Madeloni (2019), UTLA President Caputo-Pearl discussed "the strike not only as the last resort, but as something you do to build a social movement." (para. 24)

Organizers in this network have used the institutional and noninstitutional social actions detailed above, as well as their work in a range of social movements, to work alongside community members to challenge inequalities in their schools, unions, and society. They have done the work of a social justice union regardless of the extent to which they have won formal leadership positions in their unions. In doing so, they prefigure the vision for engaged, social justice unions that they are advancing through their work (Stark, 2019; Tarlau, 2021).

This movement links together struggles in a wide range of contexts across the United States and beyond. Organizers in the UCORE network have engaged in a number of social movements since the network formed, including but not limited to, the Occupy movement, the Opt Out movement, the Black Lives Matter at School movement, the Fight for $15 movement, the Red for Ed movement, and the Movement for Safe Schools during the COVID-19 pandemic. In the 2016 Chicago teachers strike, educators rallied and marched alongside organizers from Fight for $15 movement and the Black Lives Matter movement (Stark, 2019). Likewise, in the midst of the Red for Ed movement, the UCORE monthly national calls featured speakers from caucuses and statewide educator networks leading this work (Stark, 2023). In this way, the movement for social justice unionism can be compared to the Global Justice Movement: a networked "movement of movements" (Chihara, 2002; Mertes, 2004; Sen, 2017) that links together and propels multiple social movements.

This network realizes educational scholars' call for networks of solidarity to combat the neoliberal assault on public education. It also represents an important step toward educator unionists transitioning from taking defensive positions against neoliberalism toward offensive positions in favor of social justice-oriented reforms. Most significantly, for the purposes of this chapter, educator organizing in the UCORE network represents both an important space for connecting and supporting multiple social movements in a range of contexts, as well as a distinct movement for social justice unionism in its own right.

Conclusion

In the 10 years since the Chicago Teachers Union's landmark 2012 strike, educators in the UCORE network have continued to advance a vision for social justice unionism in the United States. They have put this vision into practice through democratic organizing within and through caucuses, grassroots networks, and teachers unions. In doing so, they have affected significant change, shifting political consciousness around issues of social justice in schools and society, and implementing more equitable policies. They have done so through a range of both institutional and noninstitutional actions, including grassroots and electoral campaigns, as well as contentious tactics, including strikes.

In this way, we can understand the work of UCORE organizers as a social movement for social justice unionism. This movement links and drives forward other social movements, including contemporary educator movements such as Black Lives Matter at School and Red for Ed, as well as broader social movements. In this way, the UCORE network can be understood as a networked "movement of movements" that sustains organizing within and across social movements that address a wide range of educational and social issues.

This movement has demonstrated the potential for educators to both defend and transform public education and other social institutions. Whether using grassroots organizing to challenge harmful policies or using the power of their union to bargain and strike for the common good, educators in the UCORE network have shown a path forward for organizers to democratically advance justice from the ground up. This path remains more vital than ever, in the face of rising fascism and, with it, white supremacy, homophobia, sexism, transphobia, ableism, income inequality, settler colonialism, and environmental degradation in the United States.

The UCORE network now includes over 40 social justice caucuses and networks committed to this work. As organizers continue to learn alongside each other in this network, they will both push back against reactionary movements and lift up and sustain movements dedicated to educational and social justice. Through this collective work, they are contributing to a movement for social justice unionism that has the potential to transform not only their unions, but also society as a whole.

References

Asselin, C. (2022). "Fighting racism through teacher union democratization: Activist educators in social justice caucuses in New York City and Philadelphia." *Critical Education, 13*(3), 44–62. http://ojs.library.ubc.ca/index.php/criticaled/article/view/186566

Au, W., & Hagopian, J. (2017). How one elementary school sparked a citywide movement to make Black students' lives matter. *Rethinking Schools, 32*(1). https://www.rethinkingschools.org/articles/how-one-elementary-school-sparked-acitywide-movement-to-make-black-students-lives-matter

Baker, R. S. (2011). Pedagogies of protest: African American teachers and the history of the civil rights movement, 1940–1963, *Teachers College Record, 113*(12), 2777–2803.

Blanc, E. (2019). *Red state revolt: The teachers' strike wave and working-class politics.* Verso Books.

Bocking, P. (2020). *Public education, neoliberalism, and teachers: New York City, Mexico City, Toronto.* University of Toronto Press.

Bradbury, A., Brenner, M., Brown, J., Slaughter, J., & Winslow, S. (2014). *How to jump-start your union: Lessons from the Chicago teachers.* Labor Notes.

Bradbury, A., Brenner, M., & Slaughter, J. (2016). *Secrets of a successful organizer.* Labor Notes.

Brenner, M. (2011, July 8). Education reform: the real deal. *Labor Notes.* https://www.labornotes.org/blogs/2011/07/education-reform-real-deal

Brogan, P. M. (2016). *Our union, our city: Teacher rebellion and urban change in Chicago and New York City* (unpublished doctoral dissertation). York University.

Chihara, M. (2002, September 24). *Naomi Klein gets global.* Alternet. http://www.alternet.org/story/14175/naomi_klein_gets_global

Dyke, E., Anderson, H., Brown, A., El Sabbagh, J., Fernandez, H., Goodwin, S., Hickey, M., Lowther, J., Price, S., Ruby, M., Self, K., Williams, D., Williams, J., & Worth, A. (2022). Beyond defeat: Understanding educators' experiences in the 2018 Oklahoma walkouts. *Critical Education, 13*(2), 77–95. https://doi.org/10.14288/ce.v13i2.186610

Dyke, E., & Muckian Bates, B. (2019). Educators striking for a better world: The significance of social movement and solidarity unionisms. *Berkeley Review of Education, 9*(1). DOI: 10.5070/B89146423

Flannery, M. E. (2022, December 6). Why do educators strike? The reasons are broadening. *NEA Today.* https://www.nea.org/advocating-for-change/new-from-nea/why-do-educators-strike-reasons-are-broadening

Givan, R. K., & Lang, A. S. (2020). *Strike for the common good: Fighting for the future of public education.* University of Michigan Press.

Hagopian, J. (2019). Jesse Hagopian talks with Gillian Russom: How Los Angeles teachers organized and what they won. *Rethinking Schools, 34*(1). https://rethinkingschools.org/articles/jesse-hagopian-talks-with-gillian-russom-how-los-angeles-teachers-organized-and-what-they-won/

Hagopian, J., & Green, J. T. (2012). Teachers unions and social justice. In J. Bale & S. Knopp (Eds.), *Education and capitalism* (pp. 141–175). Haymarket Books.

Henry, M., & Behrens, C. (2022). Columbus teachers union returning to class after approving contract with 4% annual raises. *The Columbus Dispatch.* https://www.dispatch.com/story/news/education/2022/08/28/columbus-education-association-new-deal-with-columbus-city-schools/65458868007/

Howell, C. D., & Schmitzer, C. (2022). Online and on the picket line: West Virginia teachers' use of an online community to organize. *Critical Education, 13*(2), 59–76. http://ojs.library.ubc.ca/index.php/criticaled/article/view/186613

Jaffe, S. (2019, January 23). 'This is much bigger than us, than our union, even than our city': How LA's teachers joined forces with the community and won a landmark labor contract. *The Nation*. https://www.thenation.com/article/archive/la-teachers-strike-utla-victory-agreement/

Johnson, M. (2017). Organizing for North Carolina: Social movement unionism in a Southern state. *Peabody Journal of Education, 92*(3), 127–140. https://doi.org/10.1080/0161956X.2016.1265340

Jones, D., & Hagopian, J. (Eds). (2020). *Black Lives Matter at School: An uprising for educational justice*. Haymarket Books.

Kahlenberg, R. D. (2007). *Tough liberal: Albert Shanker and the battles over schools, unions, race, and democracy*. Columbia University Press.

Kallas, J., Ritchie, K., & Friedman, E. (2022). *Labor Action Tracker. Annual Report 2022*. ILR School, Cornell University & LER School, University of Illinois. https://www.ilr.cornell.edu/faculty-and-research/labor-action-tracker-2022

Klein, N. (2007). *The Shock Doctrine: The Rise of Disaster Capitalism*. Knopf.

Kuk, H., & Tarlau, R. (2020). The confluence of popular education and social movement studies into social movement learning: A systematic literature review. *International Journal of Lifelong Education, 3*(5-6), 591–604. DOI: 10.1080/02601370.2020.1845833

Loder-Jackson, T. (2015). *Schoolhouse activists: African American educators and the long Birmingham civil rights movement*. State University of New York Press.

Madeloni, B. (2019, January 24). L.A. teachers win big and beat back privatization. *Labor Notes*. https://labornotes.org/2019/01/la-teachers-win-big-and-beat-back-privatizers

Madeloni, B. (2022, Sept 14.) *Seattle teachers end week-long strike*. Labor Notes. https://labornotes.org/2022/09/seattle-teachers-end-week-long-strike

Maton, R. (2015). Principles to practice: Philadelphia educators putting social movement unionism into action. *Workplace: A Journal for Academic Labor, 26*, 7–21.

Maton, R. (2018). From neoliberalism to structural racism: Problem framing in a teacher activist organization. *Curriculum Inquiry, 48*(3), 293–315. https://doi.org/10.1080/03626784.2018.1474711

Maton, R. (2022). Fighting on the frontlines: Intersectional organizing in educators' social justice unions during COVID-19. *Gender, Work and Organization, 30*(2), 692–709. DOI: 10.1111/gwao.12827

Maton, R., & Stark, L. (2021). Educators learning through struggle: Political education in social justice caucuses. *Journal of Educational Change, 24*, 291–315. https://doi.org/10.1007/s10833-021-09444-0

McAdam, D., and Snow, D.A. (2010). *Readings on social movements: Origins, dynamics, and outcomes.* Oxford University Press.

Mertes, T. (Ed.). (2004). *A movement of movements: Is another world really possible?* Verso.

Murphy, M. (1990). *Blackboard unions: The AFT and the NEA 1900–1980.* Cornell University Press.

Niesz, T. (2021). Activist educators and the production, circulation and impact of social movement knowledge. *Critical Education 12*(7), 5–22. http://ojs.library.ubc.ca/index.php/criticaled/article/view/186577

Owens, L. Z. (2022). (Re)Forming unions for social justice: A critical autoethnographic inquiry into racism, democracy, and teacher leadership. *Critical Education, 13*(3), 63–79. http://ojs.library.ubc.ca/index.php/criticaled/article/view/186607

Phelps, C. (2021). Why did teachers organize? Feminism and socialism in the making of New York City teacher unionism. *Modern American History, 4*(2), 131–158. doi:10.1017/mah.2021.11

Picower, B. (2013). Education should be free! Occupy the DOE!: Teacher activists involved in the Occupy Wall Street movement. *Critical Studies in Education, 54*(1), 44–56.

Riley, K. (2015). Reading for change: Social justice unionism book groups as an organizing tool. *Perspectives on Urban Education, 12*(1), 70–75.

Rousmaniere, K. (2001). White silence: A racial biography of Margaret Haley. *Equity & Excellence in Education, 34*(2), 7. https://doi.org/10.1080/1066568010340202

Schirmer, E. (2019). After Act 10: How Milwaukee teachers fought back. *Dissent, 66*(2), 48–56.

Sen, J. (2017). *Movements of movements: Part 1: What makes us move?* PM Press.

Shiller, J., & Caucus, BMORE. (2019). Winning in Baltimore: The story of how BMORE put racial equity at the center of teacher union organizing. *Berkeley Review of Education, 9*(1). https://doi.org/10.5070/B89146427

Stark, L. (2019). *We're trying to create a different world: Educator organizing in social justice caucuses* [Doctoral dissertation, University of Virginia]. LibraETD.

Stark, L. W., & Maton, R. M. (2019). School closures and the political education of US teachers. *Shuttered schools: Race, community, and school closures in American cities*, 287-324.

Stark, L. W. (2022). "Reclaiming our schools" Interviews with Black Lives Matter at School organizers Tamara Anderson and Jesse Hagopian. *Critical Education, 13*(3), 80–84. https://doi.org/10.14288/ce.v13i3.186612

Stark, L. W. (2023). Learning and knowledge-making in contemporary educator movements. *Globalisation, Societies and Education, 21*(5), 1–16. https://doi.org/10.1080/14767724.2023.2184776

Stark, L.W., Dyke, E., & Maton, R. (2022). Afterword: Reflections on contemporary educator movements. *Critical Education*, *13*(4), 50–57. http://ojs.library.ubc.ca/index.php/criticaled/article/view/186729

Stark, L.W., Tarlau, R., & Maton, R. (2024). "For once we're asking for MORE testing": Organizational infrastructure in the Safe Schools Movement during COVID-19. *Globalization, Societies and Education*. 10.1080/14767724.2023.2279049

Tarlau, R. (2021). Contentious co-governance and prefiguration: A framework for analyzing social movement–state relations in public education. *Educational Researcher*, *50*(8), 527–536. https://doi.org/10.3102/0013189X211023496

Taylor, C. (2010). *Reds at the blackboard: communism, civil rights, and the New York City Teachers Union*. Columbia University Press.

Uetricht, M. (2014). *Strike for America: Chicago teachers against austerity*. Verso.

Weiner, L. (2012). *The future of our schools: Teachers unions and social justice*. Haymarket Books.

Winslow, C. (2010). Overview: Rebellion from below, 1965–1981. In A. Brenner, R. Brenner, & C. Winslow (Eds.), *Rebel rank and file: Labor militancy and revolt from below in the long 1970s* (pp. 1–35). Verso.

Winslow, S. (2013). Chicago teachers' lesson of social justice unionism goes national. *In These Times*. https://inthesetimes.com/article/chicago-teachers-model-of-social-justice-unionism-goes-national

CHAPTER 5

The Crossfires of Hate

Shiv R. Desai

Across the nation, a slew of new bills has been introduced to reverse the progress made after years of fighting for justice, equity, diversity, and inclusion. Lawmakers in 42 states have proposed bills to restrict how K-12 teachers address racism and inequality in their classroom by primarily targeting critical race theory (CRT), a framework created by legal scholars, as well as ethnic studies (ES) coursework and other anti-racist principles (Education Week, 2021). In addition, five states have introduced bills to prohibit the teaching of the 1619 Project (Kaur, 2021), which highlighted how slavery was a foundational part of the nation's origin. Furthermore, approximately 417 anti-LGBTQ bills have been introduced in state legislatures across the United States since the start of this year alone (Choi, 2023). These bills censor the curriculum, go hand in hand with book bans that attempt to erase history and representation, and limit critical thinking and student learning. In short, these forms of legislation center ignorance and hate. The dire consequences of these laws are that they exacerbate teacher shortages, infringe on academic freedom, and create hostile learning environments where not every student feels valued.

Just prior to the COVID-19 pandemic, only a few years ago, 19 states introduced legislation supporting K-12 ES curriculum (Kwon, 2021). At its core, ES and the development of ethnic identity is instrumental in the exploration of one's history and traditions, creates a positive sense of belonging and resolution, as well as contributes to a sense of resiliency in the face of adversity due to racism and discrimination (Cross, 1991; Phinney, 2005; Umaña-Taylor et al., 2004). Furthermore, a strong ethnic identity is associated with higher self-esteem, more optimism, and fewer depressive symptoms (Phinney et al., 2007). The

ES movement is a catalyst for decolonizing and revolutionizing education for liberation. Therefore, the purpose of this chapter is to provide a brief history of educators and students working together to demand ES, which has a long, rich tradition of community-centered activism that privileges the knowledge(s), experiences, and cultures of marginalized groups (Carjuzaa et al., 2015; Grosfoguel, 2012; Salinas, 2011; Watson-Vandiver & Wiggan, 2018). I am focusing on ES because there is an extended history of activism, especially when we consider The Children's March (Birmingham), the East Los Angeles Blowouts, the Student Walkouts in Texas (Crystal City, San Antonio, Edcouch-Elsa), and the Crusade for Justice (Denver). In each of these examples, students, families, educators, and community members demanded a curriculum that reflected their lived-experiences and histories, the right to speak their native language, more teachers who reflected their communities, and centered diversity, equity, inclusion, and justice. Specifically, I am seeking to answer: What lessons do the student walkouts and the ethnic studies movement have for humanizing education?

Ethnic Studies: The Birth of a Movement

The birth of the ES movement in the United States in higher education was sparked in 1968 by the San Francisco State College's Third World Liberation Front (TWLF), a collective student group comprised of the Black Student Union (BSU), the Mexican American Student Confederation (MASC), the Philippine-American Collegiate Endeavor (PACE), Intercollegiate Chinese for Social Action (ICSA), and the Asian American Pacific Alliance (AAPA) (Hoang, 2012; Hu-DeHart, 1993; Lye, 2010; Winkler-Morey, 2010). This historic 5-month strike led by students of color had three major goals: 1) Demanded the rights of TWLF students to have access to an education that was not hindered by institutional racist policies based on testing and admissions; 2) Demanded that their educational experiences were reflective of their own identities, histories, and experiences; 3) Demanded to have the first ES program and have faculty who represented the TWLF be in charge of implementing it. These three demands highlighted the TWLF's call for self-determination, which inspired faculty, college administrators, and community members to support the establishment of an ES program. Students braved physical, emotional, and psychological violence to ensure these demands were implemented. However, this strike was inspired by national and local civil rights movements across the United States, which highlighted the struggles of marginalized groups. Out of this movement came a nationwide push that resulted in over 700 Ethnic Studies programs and departments in the United States (Hu-DeHart, 1993).

The inspiration for this mass demonstration stems from youth who were active leaders in the Civil Rights Movement. The Student Nonviolent Coordinating Committee played a critical role in helping to end segregation as well as establishing Freedom Schools (Hale, 2011). In these schools, the key principles of ES were privileged, along with students learning how to be active citizens and advocates for their community. For many students, the Freedom Schools were the first time they were exposed to and had access to education that promoted social change. In what follows, I first discuss the Children's Crusade and how it not only saved the Civil Rights Movement but also inspired all other student walkouts. Next, I highlight the importance of the East Los Angeles Blowouts and how it inspired the larger Chican@ Movement. Then I concisely describe the Texas student walkouts and the Crusade for Justice in Denver. I conclude with a recent example of the political backlash of the Tucson Unified School District's Mexican American Studies program and the overall lessons the walkouts have for our current education climate.

The Children's Crusade

Walton, Smith, and Wallace (2000) state, "A social movement may be understood as a group of persons organized in a sustained, self-conscious challenge to an existing system and its values or power relationships" (p. 110). I would argue that the roots of the ES movement has its foundation in the Civil Rights Movement. As early as 1951 in Farmville, Virginia, Barbara Johns led a strike at Moton High School to protest the inequities in education (Racine & Cook, 2005). Johns told her fellow students that if they acted in solidarity, the town jail could not hold all of them. She stated, "We knew we had to do it ourselves and that if we had asked for help before taking the first step, we would have been turned down" (Racine & Cook, 2005, p. 33). Her actions were instrumental to the *Brown v. Board of Education* landmark case. In fact, Moton High School was one of the five schools in the *Brown* case. Johns laid the groundwork on how students can utilize student walkouts to address educational inequities, racist school policies, and demand a more meaningful education that reflected students' lived experiences.

On May 2, 1963, thousands of African American elementary, middle, and high school students led one of the first student walkouts as part of the Children's Crusade by peacefully protesting the racial segregation in Birmingham, Alabama. Since so many students were arrested, some of them were incarcerated at the fairgrounds in animal pens (Hall & Lewis, 2019; Santoli et al., 2022). Their bravery continued as students showed up each day to protest their dehumanizing conditions, knowing they would be arrested, attacked by police dogs, sprayed by water hoses, and beaten by police batons. Across the country and around the world, these images were broadcasted on newspapers and evening news shows, which led to outrage from across the globe. The marches and arrests continued until May 10, 1963, when efforts by these brave children led to agreements between the U.S. Department of Justice, the Southern Christian Leadership Conference (SCLC), and local officials to desegregate stores and public facilities in downtown Birmingham and release the children (Hall & Lewis, 2019; Racine & Cook, 2005; Santoli et al., 2022).

Years of protests, lawsuits, sit-ins, and boycotts had little effect in Birmingham (Hall & Lewis, 2019; Santoli et al., 2022). In fact, it was only a few months prior that Dr. Martin Luther King Jr. had been released from Birmingham's jail where he recognized a new strategy had to be implemented to revitalize the movement (Racine & Cook, 2005). Dr. King was reluctant to use children, but members of the SCLC like James Bevel, who was a participant in the Nashville sit-in movement, initiated the idea. The Sixteenth Street Baptist Church—the site of the later brutal bombing that murdered four Black girls—was where students learned nonviolent protest tactics and planned the walkout.

At the end of the first day, when over 900 children were arrested and taken, Dr. King told anxious parents, "Don't worry about your children; they are going to be alright. Don't hold them back if they want to go to jail, for they are not only doing a job for themselves, but for all of America and for all of mankind" (Racine & Cook, 2005, p. 32). The next day, police tried to barricade the church, only to have the children find refuge in a park across from it. It was at this site these children felt the vicious wrath and sheer brutalization of "Bull" Connor, who directed local police and firemen to attack these children—some as young as six—with high-pressure fire hoses, batons, and police dogs. Again, it was these images of children being ferociously assaulted by police and violently attacked by vicious canines plastered on television and in newspapers throughout the nation and world. The Children's Crusade revived the desegregation efforts and turned the tide in the Civil Rights Movement. It was the largest of several mass protest movements in 1963 and was the precursor to the March on Washington for Jobs and Freedom. It cannot be stressed enough that these children were also suspended and/or expelled from school. Ultimately, only after the U.S. Court of Appeals for the Fifth Circuit reversed the order that the students were readmitted to school (Hall & Lewis, 2019; Racine & Cook, 2005; Santoli et al., 2022).

While the Children's Crusade was primarily organized by adults, Barbara Johns demonstrated how, in some cases, youth took the lead. The next three examples illustrate how youth and adults coordinated to create changes in education systems that disparaged and dehumanized primarily Chican@/x youth in East Los Angeles, Denver, and Texas.

Chicano/a Student Walkouts/Blowouts

Even prior to the Chican@ student walkouts/blowouts, there were several cases to end school segregation for Chican@ students. As early as *Romo v. Laird* (1925) in Tempe, Arizona, Romo filed suit against his school district on behalf of his four young children, claiming they were forced to attend a markedly low-quality segregated school (Muñoz, 2013). The court ruled in favor of Romo, but segregation still continued for the larger Mexican American community. Later, in *Salvatierra v. Independent School District* (1930) in Del Rio, Texas, the school district was sued because Mexican American students were deprived of resources given to white students (Montoya, 2001). The district judge issued a ruling that favored Salvatierra, but the state's higher courts later overturned it. Two court cases in California helped establish legal precedent for the eventual *Brown v. Board of Education* decision that ended legal segregation. In *Alvarez v. Lemon Grove* (1931), Mexicans and Mexican Americans organized to sue the school district in San Diego County, when a principal of a local elementary school prevented 75 Mexican American children from enrolling in an all-white school. This case was the first successful school desegregation court decision in the history of the United States. Lastly, in *Mendez v. Westminster* (1946) in Orange County, the parents of 8-year-old Sylvia Mendez sued the school district when she and her brothers were denied enrollment at their local school in Westminster because of their dark skin and Spanish surname (Strum, 2014). *Mendez* declared it was unconstitutional to segregate Mexican and Mexican American students into distinct schools and contributed directly to ending segregation throughout the state (Calvo-Quirós, 2014; Muñoz, 2018).

The creation of ES programs in the United States is rooted in the 1960s civil rights movements, including struggles by African Americans, Mexican Americans, Indigenous peoples, and women, among others (Wieviorka & Longerinas, 2005). For Mexican Americans, the emerging Chicano Movement, or El Movimiento, called to action cultural nationalism, political activism, and a reminder that they were stripped of their land, history, and culture (Romero & O'Leary, 2011). The Chican@/x student walkouts/blowouts were integral to the Chicano Movement and part of the larger social activism of this time (Gómez-Quiñones, 1978; Muñoz, 1989; Navarro, 1995). What is special about this type of student activism is that it entailed sociopolitical consciousness raising, social identity formation, and the adoption of Chicanismo—a more militant form of cultural nationalism (Arreola, 2004). "Through these actions, Chicano/a students demanded social justice and equal treatment in the public school system, promoted school integration, advocated recognition of Mexican culture in the public schools, and sought better educational opportunities for themselves and their Mexican-origin classmates" (Barrera, 2004, p. 94). In other words, these students carried on the Civil Rights Movement traditions that initially began with the Birmingham Children's March and continued even when historic legislation and Supreme Court decisions were passed. In each case, BIPOC youth were instrumental in helping communities gain more civil rights, assert their humanity, and create a more just society.

East Los Angeles

> The student walkouts constituted the first mass protest explicitly against racism undertaken by Mexican Americans in the history of the US, and it ignited the emergence of the Chicano Movement. The

> protests had a profound impact on the Mexican American community in LA and in other parts of the country, generating increased political awareness along with efforts to mobilize communities. (Muñoz, 2018, p. 38)

Numerous student organizations formed throughout the Southwest that assisted with the walkouts and provided trainings. The United Mexican American Students (UMAS) was the largest, and it played a significant role in organizing high school student protests in the largely segregated schools of East Los Angeles. These protests, which came to be known as "walkouts" or "blowouts," took place in the first week of March. Students held picket signs that protested racist school policies and teachers, called for freedom of speech, demanded the hiring of Mexican American teachers and administrators, and requested classes on Mexican American history and culture.

Chican@ students, with the support of Sal Castro, a Lincoln High School teacher, their parents, and other allies were fighting not only their school districts but also something larger that transcended their schools. They were fighting for an education that would humanize them, represent their communities, and no longer erase the contributions of their peoples. As Calvo-Quirós (2014) explains, "The walkouts were more than a demand for educational equality, culturally sensitive curriculums, and the elimination of racialized practices in the schools. They were also a pedagogical tool for the transformation of knowledge." (p. 158). Approximately 10,000 Chican@ students walked out of five East Los Angeles high schools—Lincoln, Roosevelt, Garfield, Wilson, and Belmont—in March 1968 (Barrera, 2004; Calvo-Quirós, 2014; Gómez-Quiñones, 1978; Muñoz, 1989; Navarro, 1995). Their demands included better educational opportunities, equal treatment, and the recognition of Mexican American cultural and academic needs. Prior to the blowouts, in the student-run newsletter *Chicano Student News: Mano a Mano,* on March 15, 1968, students wrote the article "HOW CAN THEY EXPECT TO TEACH US IF THEY DO NOT KNOW US?" (Calvo-Quirós, 2014, p. 161), where they called on school system officials to meet the following demands:

- Provide better counseling and academic assistance for Mexican-American students;

- Address the overcrowding of schools in East Los Angeles;
- Reprimand/remove educators who discriminated against Chican@ students;
- Implement curriculum reflecting ethnic Mexican culture and history;
- Promote greater community and parent involvement in school issues; and
- Hire more Chicano teachers and administrators (Rosales, 1997, p. 191).

While there were other demands, these best summarize the overall list. During this period, Mexican American students were being tracked to vocational programs, being physically disciplined for speaking Spanish, and encountering hostile school environments that pushed them out of school.

Although the East Los Angeles student walkouts did not bring about immediate reform within the local school system, school officials were pressured into at least considering the students' demands (Barrera, 2004). These boycotts emerged as the first major Chican@ student protests in U.S. public schools. As such, they impacted Chican@ students throughout the nation, particularly in schools across the Southwest. As one reporter from the *Los Angeles Times* noted, "The Birth of Brown Power" came from these East Los Angeles walkouts (Muñoz, 1989).

South Texas

A few months later, in November 1968, over 190 Chican@ students walked out of Edcouch-Elsa High School in south Texas, demanding social justice and alleging that their school system had failed to meet their educational and cultural needs. Located between the neighboring small rural towns of Edcouch and Elsa, the high school enrolled approximately 1,000 students—90% of whom were Mexican American. The 1968 Edcouch-Elsa walkout was the first major Chicano student walkout in deep south Texas (Barrera, 2004).

The students walked out for being unfairly targeted for school dress codes that had a counselor measuring skirts, shirt sleeves, and hair, as well as sideburns (Barrera, 2023). In addition, students were reprimanded for speaking

Spanish. Students were being discouraged from attending college; instead, they were told to pursue manual labor jobs, learn a trade, or join the military. Donato (1997) noted, "Mexican migrant children in the Southwest were not being served equally to whites because of indifference, because local economies depended on their labor, and because they were ethnically distinct" (p. 30). Again, students were facing similar educational barriers to the students in East Los Angeles.

Before the student walkouts beginning in October 1968, various Chican@ students, their parents, and community members began holding a series of informal meetings to address the educational issues at Edcouch-Elsa High School (Barrera, 2004). Community organizations such as the Mexican American Youth Organization (MAYO), the Political Association of Spanish-speaking Organizations (PASSO), and the Volunteers in Service to America (VISTA) were integral in these protests to help students organize and mobilize. PASSO was a conglomeration of politically active Mexican American organizations based throughout the Southwest, while VISTA served as a domestic Peace Corps–type operation (Barrera, 2004). In fact, MAYO helped organize 39 walkouts between 1968 and 1970 along with other mass confrontations to obtain civil rights, which helped students develop a strong political/militant consciousness (Navarro, 1995). Lastly, MAYO required the inclusion of parents and support from local organizations before student walkouts could occur, creating strong community engagement.

The students in South Texas had the following demands:

- Any student or teacher involved in the walkout would not face discipline;
- Students select their own candidates for student council;
- Students have the right to speak Spanish freely on school grounds;
- Blatant discrimination against Mexican American students at school cease immediately;
- New courses would be introduced as part of the curriculum to reflect the contributions of Mexican@s and Mexican American people to the state (Barrera, 2004).

The students who walked out were suspended for 3 days, and other students were expelled. The U.S. Federal District Court ultimately reversed this decision and awarded plaintiffs nominal and actual damages of $240 for school transportation expenses and tuition costs to attend classes outside the defendants' school district. In sum, these students followed the lead of the East LA students to gain educational rights and assert their humanity.

Crusade for Justice

Following the 1968 blowouts in Los Angeles, there were other high school student strikes throughout the Southwest during 1969. In Denver, the student walkouts were instrumental in the development of the Crusade for Justice and made Rudolfo "Corky" Gonzales, who coined the term Chicano, a national leader of the emerging Chicano Movement. While the protests in Los Angeles and Texas were mostly peaceful, the Denver protests witnessed violent confrontations between police, students, and members of the Crusade for Justice (Muñoz, 2018).

In 1969, after weeks of frustration from students who were being targeted and shamed by teachers if they spoke Spanish, who did not have access to Chican@ history and culture in the curriculum, and not having their concerns listened to by the administration, students from West High School in Denver staged a walkout. On March 20, 1969, a few hundred students started the walkout. One of the organizers, Emanuel Martinez, a member of the Crusade for Justice, was there with other members of the Crusade to support students who would encounter nearly 30 officers. One of the students, Nita Gonzales, "Corky" Gonzales' daughter, participated in the walkout. In total, 26 people were arrested, including 11 youth. The overwhelming force did not stop the protesters as they later marched to the Denver Police Building, City Hall, and Mayor Bill McNichols' office. The next day saw students joining in from even more city schools, representing 1,000 marchers. There was violent resistance and severe police brutality (Sanchez, 2019).

These demonstrations continued for the next 4 days and came to be known as the "blowouts." Gonzales said students presented a list of nine demands and wanted the social studies teacher fired who repeatedly insulted the students and their parents and wanted a "curriculum that represents us, that we're in that history, in that story. To have more Chicano teachers, counselors and administrators" (Sanchez, 2019). Eventually, the Superintendent agreed to change the curriculum and the teaching staff. The social studies teacher was not fired but instead transferred to another school.

Overall, these student walkouts helped kick-start what became known as El Movimiento, the Chicano Movement. A few weeks later, the Crusade for Justice held the first ever Youth Liberation Conference where nearly 1,500 young Chican@s from across the country came to Denver. A new alternative K-12 school was also born out of this movement that was led by Nita Gonzales, who remarked, "It was like a wildfire that just started to consume, travel across the states saying, 'We have a right to stand up, we have a right to live a life that we have justice and equality and it's not going to happen because someone feels sorry for us. It's going to happen when we stand up, when we say '¡Ya basta! No more. We're not doing this anymore" (Sanchez, 2019).

Unfortunately, these student walkouts would not lead to everlasting changes. The demands of these Chican@ students in the Southwest would be coddled for a few years, and, eventually, the dehumanizing conditions that led to the walkouts/blowouts would return once again. I will go into greater details in the conclusion. One thing is clear: transformative change requires constant action by the oppressed. I conclude with the last example that comes from Tucson, which has now become the harbinger of the current educational climate.

Conclusion

Tucson & Mexican American Studies

From its inception, the core demands of ES were coalitional and one of solidarity. Each underrepresented group fought against anti-imperialism (Lye, 2010), racial/ethnic equity, inclusion, justice, and educational liberation. While the Tucson Unified School District (TUSD) Mexican American Studies (MAS) program received the bulk of attention due to a targeted political backlash, TUSD actually initiated a Black Studies Department in 1980, and over the next two decades developed an ethnic studies program for the district's four largest ethnic minority groups—African Americans, Asian Americans, Mexican Americans, and Indigenous peoples (Gómez & Gabaldón, 2013). Of note, from

1867 to 1930, the majority of TUSD students were Mexican American, and in 2002, they became the majority once again. The *Fisher-Mendoza* (1976) and *Alvarez-Jasso* (1986) court cases both called for more equity for underrepresented students; however, neither of them called for a MAS program. Even before the State Superintendent of Public Instruction, Tom Horne, attacked MAS, he called for investigations to determine whether Mexican students were illegally attending public schools in U.S. border towns, complained about schools for sponsoring Spanish spelling bees, redesigned English proficiency tests in order to push English learners into regular classes more quickly even when they were not proficient, and lowered the amount of preparation teachers were required to have when serving English learners (Gómez & Gabaldón, 2013). John Huppenthal later succeeded Horne and hired a Texas-based company to audit the MAS program to see if it had violated the new anti–ethnic studies bill, SB 2281. He prematurely declared that the company found that the program had violated the bill, even though the company reported that MAS classes did not violate the law. Instead of lauding the program's success in preparing students for college, in 2012, he suspended the program (Gómez & Gabaldón, 2013).

"No other high school program has continually been vindicated by documented studies for its undeniable success in alleviating the achievement gap, graduating college-bound students, and inspiring community engaged youth" (Biggers, 2012). So, the reason for the program being shut down had nothing to do with academic achievement. Moreover, MAS was open to all students; therefore, one could not say that the program discriminated against youth from different backgrounds. However, the MAS program found new life in the Chican@ Literature, Art, and Social Studies (CLASS) program, which was created to keep the spirit of MAS alive by meeting outside of school on Sunday afternoons (Acosta, 2014). One of the guiding principles in CLASS/MAS was the "use of indigenous epistemologies that helped re-humanize the educational experience for our students; they needed to have a safe space to reflect and analyze their world, while also reestablishing their own humanity and belief in education" (Acosta, 2014, p. 4). CLASS became a space where healing and revitalization can be achieved because in the aftermath of the abolition of the MAS program, many of the teachers became marginalized, vilified, and, in some cases, fired. For students, they lost their safe space to become reconnected to ancestral knowledge, traditions, and wisdom. As Acosta (2014) notes,

"Through all the cynicism, defeatism, anguish, and rage, CLASS became an oasis of positivity, action, and personal inspiration for me to keep on pushing" (p. 7). Ultimately, students today are also in search of an oasis that privileges their true selves, their culture, and identity; moreover, they are searching for educators who will protect them from the political backlash that bans books, erases or attempts to rewrite history, and negates their humanity.

Key Lessons

Calvo-Quirós (2014) describes the Chican@ walkouts and the Chican@ Movement as a form of "epistemic resistance" to counter the amnesia that stripped away history, culture, traditions, and language from colonialism, domination, and exploitation. Calvo-Quirós explains how "erasing or limiting access to Chicana/o history, is an act of violence" (p. 156) because it divorces students from land- and place-based pedagogies and tries to erase the contributions and histories of Chican@s and Mexican@s due to forced assimilation. Therefore, the Chican@ walkouts or blowouts were an important step in regaining emancipatory knowledge, gaining new knowledge about students' communities, histories, and experiences, and advancing decolonizing practices.

It was after these protests that the existing organizations that helped high school students organize and mobilize would change their names from UMAS, MASC, and MAYO and together become the Movimiento Estudiantil Chicano de Aztlán (MEChA) (Muñoz, 2018). MEChA had three main goals: 1) To be organically connected to the Mexican American community by participating in local struggles for civil rights; 2) To establish itself as a power base on campuses to increase the presence of Mexican American youth in institutions of higher education; and 3) To play a substantive role in the creation and implementation of Chicano Studies departments and programs with curricula focusing on the Mexican American experience (Muñoz, 2018, p. 42-3).

The key lessons learned from MEChA, the student walkouts/blowouts, and Tucson is that victory for us is only short-lived. It is momentarily like an exhale. Therefore, vigilance is required at all times. The struggle never ends and must be treated like a congenital malignant. Second, solidarity cannot exist only to achieve a goal. Just as the Third World Liberation Front was a collective of different BIPOC student groups to achieve ES in higher education, solidarity must be a focal point as different groups are currently being attacked. The rights of one group can never trump the rights of the collective. Willful agitators must take the lead in order to address the wrongs suffered by one marginalized group. Third, do not ignore the powerful minority. From MAS to today's political attacks, the notion that this will pass is flawed. It never subsides but only grows stronger and more powerful until it becomes cancerous, affecting the overall system. The chief mistake of the student walkouts/blowouts was that the overall system never changed. Our community and families need leaders on the school board who do not cower to the whims of bad faith actors. Our voices need to be present at every school board meeting where we keep vocalizing that our children's needs are vital to their academic success. Our civil disobedience needs to be a serious threat that is taken sincerely by every school leader. Our children's sacredness can no longer just be tolerated, but must be firmly preserved. Finally, we cannot be afraid to challenge the premise that two wrongs do not make a right. Just as the Bible was banned in Utah (CBS Interactive, 2023), other texts can also be questioned that are part of the canon. We cannot be afraid to call out people who do not love or value our children and must bring to attention the absurdity of these laws. If LGBTQ books and curriculum are questioned, then traditional nuclear families must also be challenged. If the law states that no children should feel no discomfort with historical facts, then contest hegemony: dispute the founding fathers, Columbus Day, Thanksgiving, meritocracy, colorblindness, heterosexism, and so forth. Most of all, learn from our past and ancestors who sacrificed for so much in the walkouts/blowouts and keep fighting.

References

Acosta, C. (2014). Huitzilopochtli: The will and resiliency of Tucson youth to keep Mexican American Studies alive. *Multicultural Perspectives, 16*(1), 3–7. DOI: 10.1080/15210960.2013.867239

Arreola, P. R. (2004). Mi Raza Primero! Nationalism, identity, and insurgency in the Chicano Movement in Los Angeles, 1966-1978. *California History, 82*(2), 70–72.

Barrera, B. J. (2004). The 1968 Edcouch-Elsa high school walkout: Chicano student activism in a South Texas community. *Aztlan: Journal of Chicano Studies, 29*(2), 93–122.

Barrera, J. B. (2023). *"We want better education!": The 1960s Chicano Student Movement, school walkouts, and the quest for educational reform in South Texas*. Texas A&M University Press.

Biggers, J. (2012, November 27). With historic desegregation plan, will Tucson re-instate Mexican-American studies? *The Nation*. http://www.thenation.com/blog/171467/historic-desegregation-plan-will-tucson-reinstate-mexican-american-studies

Brown v. Board of Education of Topeka, Publ. L. No. 347 U.S. 483 (1954). https://supreme.justia.com/cases/federal/us/347/483/

Calvo-Quirós, W. A. (2014). Thank you maestro: The walkouts as praxis of "epistemic resistance." *AZTLÁN*, *39*(2), 155–165. DOI: https://doi.org/10.1525/azt.2014.39.2.155

Carjuzaa, J., Baldwin, A. E., & Munson, M. (2015). Making the dream real: Montana's Indian Education for All initiative thrives in a national climate of anti-ethnic studies. *Multicultural Perspectives*, *17*(4), 198–206.

CBS Interactive. (2023, June 5). *Utah district bans Bible in elementary and middle schools after complaint calls it "sex-ridden."* CBS News. https://www.cbsnews.com/news/bible-ban-utah-school-district-elementary-middle-complaint-sex-book/

Choi, A. (2023, April 6). *Record number of anti-LGBTQ bills have been introduced this year*. CNN. https://www.cnn.com/2023/04/06/politics/anti-lgbtq-plus-state-bill-rights-dg/index.html

Cross Jr., W. E. (1991). *Shades of black: Diversity in African-American identity*. Temple University Press.

Donato, R. (1997). *The other struggle for equal schools: Mexican Americans during the civil rights era*. SUNY Press.

Education Week. (2021, July 12). *Map: Where Critical Race Theory is under attack*. Education Week. https://www.edweek.org/policy-politics/map-where-critical-race-theory-is-under-attack/2021/06.

Gómez, C. L., & Gabaldón, S. A. (2013). A legacy of memory: the debate over ethnic studies in Arizona public schools. *AZTLÁN*, *38*(2), 163–174. https://doi.org/10.1525/azt.2013.38.2.163

Gómez-Quiñones, J. (1978). *Mexican students por la raza: The Chicano student movement in southern California, 1967-1977*. Editorial La Causa.

Grosfoguel, R. (2012). The dilemmas of ethnic studies in the United States. *Human Architecture: Journal of the Sociology of Self-Knowledge*, *10*(1), 81–89.

Hale, J. N. (2011). The Freedom Schools, the Civil Rights Movement, and refocusing the goals of American education. *Journal of Social Studies Research*, *35*(2), 259–276.

Hall, N., & Lewis, A. D. (2019). Birmingham children's crusade of 1963. In A.D. Lewis & N.A. Taylor (Eds.), *Unsung legacies of educators and events in African American education* (pp. 103–109). Springer.

Hoang, Q. (2012). Ethnic studies: The cyclical fight, conquer, and struggle. *Vermont Connection, 33*, 59–66.

Hu-DeHart, E. (1993). The history, development, and future of ethnic studies. *The Phi Delta Kappan, 75*(1), 50–54. http://www.jstor.org/stable/20405023

Kaur, H. (2021, February 11). *Bills in several states would cut funding to schools that teach the 1619 Project. But they mostly aren't going anywhere.* CNN. https://www.cnn.com/2021/02/10/us/1619-project-school-funding-cut-bills-trnd/index.html

Kwon, S. (2021). *Ethnic studies legislation: State Scan.* Region 15 Comprehensive Center. https://www.compcenternetwork.org/sites/default/files/ES%20State%20Scan%20FINAL-v1.pdf

Lye, C. (2010). US ethnic studies and Third Worldism, 40 years later. *Inter-Asia Cultural Studies, 11*(2), 188–193. DOI: 10.1080/14649371003616128

Montoya, M. E. (2001). A brief history of Chicana/o school segregation: one rationale for affirmative action. *Berkeley La Raza Law Journal, 12*(2), 159–172.

Muñoz, L. K. (2013). Romo v. Laird: Mexican American segregation and the politics of belonging in America. *Western Legal History: The Journal of the Ninth Judicial Circuit Historical Society, 26*, 97–132.

Muñoz Jr, C. (1974). The politics of protest and Chicano liberation: A case study of repression and cooptation. *Aztlán: A Journal of Chicano Studies, 5*(1-2), 119–141.

Muñoz Jr., C. (1989). *Youth, identity, power: The Chicano movement.* Verso Books.

Muñoz Jr., C. (2018). The Chicano Movement: Mexican American history and the struggle for equality. *Perspectives on Global Development & Technology, 17*(1-2), 31–52. https://doi.org/10.1163/15691497-12341465

Navarro, A. (1995). *Mexican American youth organization: Avant-garde of the Chicano movement in Texas.* University of Texas Press.

Phinney, J. S. (2005). Ethnic identity in late modern times: A response to Rattansi and Phoenix. *Identity, 5*(2), 187–194.

Phinney, J. S., Jacoby, B., & Silva, C. (2007). Positive intergroup attitudes: The role of ethnic identity. *International Journal of Behavioral Development, 31*(5), 478–490.

Racine, L., & Cook, E. (2005). The Children's Crusade and the role of youth in the African American freedom struggle. *OAH Magazine of History, 19*, 31–36. http://www.jstor.org/stable/25163740

Romero, A. J., & O'Leary, A. O. (2011). Chicana/o students respond to Arizona's anti-ethnic studies bill, SB 1108: Civic engagement, ethnic identity, and well-being. *AZTLÁN, 36*(1), 9–36.

Rosales, F. A. (1997). *Chicano! The history of the Mexican American civil rights movement.* Arte Publico Press.

Salinas, L. S. (2011). Arizona's desire to eliminate ethnic studies programs: Time to take the pill and to engage Latino students in critical education about their history. *Harvard Latino Law Review, 14*(1), 301–324.

Sanchez, H. (2019, March 23). 1969 Denver School walkout helped launch Chicano Movement. *Colorado Springs Gazette*. https://gazette.com/news/1969-denver-school-walkout-helped-launch-chicano-movement/article_042e8e70-4bfc-11e9-a52b-032ac4e13e3b.html

Santoli, S. P., Vitulli, P., & Giles, R. M. (2022). Equality in Black and white: A photographic exploration of the 1963 Birmingham Children's Crusade. *Black History Bulletin, 78*(1), 17–22. http://www.jstor.org/stable/10.5323/blachistbull.78.1.0017

Strum, P. (2014). We always tell our children they are Americans: Mendez v. Westminster and the beginning of the end of school segregation. *Journal of Supreme Court History, 39*(3), 307–328.

Umaña-Taylor, A. J., Yazedjian, A., & Bámaca-Gómez, M. (2004). Developing the ethnic identity scale using Eriksonian and social identity perspectives. *Identity: An international journal of theory and research*, 4(1), 9–38.

Walton, Jr., H., Smith, R. C., & Wallace, S. L. (2000). *American politics and the African American quest for universal freedom*. Routledge.

Watson-Vandiver, M. J., & Wiggan, G. (2018). The genius of Imhotep: An exploration of African-centered curricula and teaching in a high achieving US Urban school. *Teaching and Teacher Education, 76*, 151–164.

Wieviorka, M., & Longerinas, J. (2005). After new social movements. *Social Movement Studies, 4*(1), 1-19, DOI: 10.1080/14742830500051812

Winkler-Morey, A. (2010). The war on history: Defending ethnic studies. *The Black Scholar, 40*(4), 51–56.

Part 2:

Teacher-Activist Organizations and Social Justice Unionism

CHAPTER 6

We Refuse to Be Blamed: The Badass Teachers Association

Melissa Tomlinson

ACROSS THE NATION, perhaps even across the globe, every educator has experienced that moment of frustration about their career choice. That moment when they slam up against a system that prevents them from providing what they know deep down to their core is necessary to facilitate positive growth in their students and support them on their path towards becoming the best future self possible. Such is the nature of systemic operations that strip away individuality for the benefit of the whole. Educators are tasked with providing an efficient delivery of instruction that will maximize outputs. Unfortunately, the cost of this process relies upon overlooking outliers. If this discussion centered around a manufacturing production line, this would mean that any product deemed imperfect would be tossed, especially if such imperfections could cause potential harm. But what about when the finished product of an established system is a full-sized adult? How do educators rectify the idea that the imperfect ones should be tossed aside, or at least not given as much attention, when our work centers on children who should have unlimited opportunity to reach their fullest potential while living lives full of joy?

It is these existential questions that have kept educators awake at night, wondering how to support all the students in their class to make sure that they are achieving their fullest potential in a caring environment. But it wasn't until a shift in the overarching belief system in what the true purpose of education is became centered around the idea that schooling is the pathway to create future workers—productive members of society who would grow up to fill spots in corporations—and away from the idea that education serves the purpose of developing adults who will participate in the future betterment of society as a whole. The largest physical manifestation of this shift was the attempt to standardize education, resulting in the push for the Common Core curriculum and high-stakes standardized testing. With the passing of No Child Left Behind (NCLB) in 2002, education became a system that centered outputs instead of inputs with no regard to the outside factors that impact a child's educational success, such as class size or socioeconomic factors. In doing this, a scapegoat needed to be named when students were deemed as failing. When measurable outputs are placed upon a bell curve, as the standardized testing system is, there will always be a percentage of the data points that will lie at each end of the curve. In creating this manufactured system of rating, a never-ending culture of finger-pointing and assigning blame began, directly pointing to the educators.

Educators began to feel isolated as they fought to maintain their integrity to the profession. Most educators seem to possess this innate drive to follow the rules and to rise to meet any challenge or expectations that are placed in front of them, often at the expense of their own health and well-being. To be an educational professional means always working to improve your own understanding of education through continuous professional development and training. When the new mandates prescribed by NCLB began, school districts and educators worked hard to learn what was now to be expected from them and how they could best meet the new challenges, but no amount of training and education could negate the fact that these new mandates directly opposed what all educators know at the core of their very being, that education needs to be centered on the whole child, not the numerical grade arbitrarily assigned as a result of a standardized test. Knowing this, but still trying to do what was being asked of them, educators were starting to operate in a constant state of stress; stress that the students were also starting to feel.

Parents across the country realized the cycle that was beginning in their children's schools, a cycle of test and punish. Schools were punished for lower test scores, resulting in an increased push to teach to the test in order to raise scores, which eliminated what was deemed "extra" from educational programing, namely performing arts. The gap between educational offerings in well-funded schools and those in areas where schools were not as well funded began to grow. Recognizing their power as parents with a right to be involved in the educational process of their children, parents began to get vocal in their disagreement about NCLB and related changes to public education.

The Beginning of BATs

But what about the rights of educators? What about their responsibility to stand for what is best for their students? As educated and trained professionals in the field, shouldn't educators also have the ability to voice their opinions? To be heard and respected for their input and direction of public education? It was these questions, among others, that led to the creation of the Badass Teachers Association (BATs). BATs was formally launched on Facebook on Friday, June 14, 2013 at 4:30 p.m. and was created through the combined efforts of Dr. Mark Naison and Oklahoma parent activist, Priscilla Sanstead. Marla Kilfoyle, a teacher and parent from Long Island who became one of the driving forces behind a nationwide effort to reverse the corporate reform of public education, joined the following day. Beginning as a group that originated on Facebook as a space to share opinions and ideas about what was happening in public education, BATs later grew to become a national nonprofit network of educators, parents, and community members advocating for public education.

The original mission written by Dr. Mark Naison stated: "The Badass Teachers Association was created to give voice to every teacher who refuses to be blamed for the failure of our society to erase poverty and inequality. BAT members refuse to accept assessments, tests and evaluations created and imposed by corporate entities which have contempt for authentic teaching and learning. The BATs aim to reduce or eliminate the use of high stakes testing, increase teacher autonomy in the classroom and include teacher and family voices in legislative decision-making processes that affect students." In the beginning, the expectation for this group was to provide a space for hundreds of pro-public education individuals, eventually reaching a few thousand members, to join together in their efforts to defend public education, but the creators of this group soon realized this was not going to be a process of slow growth. Instead, educators and others who were invested in education began joining the group at an alarming rate, eager to have conversations with others that verified what they had been feeling in their isolation—a wrong turn had been taken in public education and push back was necessary. Bolstered by a blog post written on July 6th by Diane Ravitch, who was once a supporter of the Common Core and realized the harmful impact of its implementation, the Badass Teachers Association grew to 18,000 members.

To create order in some of the chaos that this growth had created, Dr. Denisha Jones created a separate space for the administrators and moderators of the Facebook group to have conversations about the different posts in the main Facebook group and make decisions about the future of BATs. This group, known as "The Cave," became the central working group for those interested in harnessing the energy of the conversations and turning it into action. The Cave acted as the leadership team of BATs and served to make decisions about member education and engagement. As members of BATs expressed interest in volunteering their time into this movement, conversations were had between those members and the current leaders to analyze strengths and needs to determine where people could fit in and contribute to the work. This was all done under the direction of the BATs General Manager, Marla Kilfoyle, who had been elected to take on this role on the third day of BATs' existence. One of these conversations led to Melissa Tomlinson joining The Cave in August.

Public education is a system that has multiple decision makers that attempt to influence and legislate over its realm. Federal mandates guide state decisions for policy and legislation that are then interpreted by local boards of education. Because of the nature of the different levels of fights that must be waged in order to stand up for students, state BAT groups were formed so that educators could connect and discuss specific issues they were facing and come together to take action within their own states. It was in the New Jersey BATs group where a conversation was started about standing up to the former bullying governor, Chris Christie, and pushing back against his narrative, stating public schools in the state were nothing more than "failure factories." At the time, Christie was running for reelection and was traveling around the state on a bus tour to show support for other candidates running on his party line. A New Jersey BAT posted in the state group about how she protested such a campaign stop in her local area by showing up with a sign asking why Governor Christie continued to portray NJ schools as failure factories when they were, in fact, one of the top three rated school systems across the nation. Members of the group commented this was an amazing idea and decided this should be done at all future stops of the campaign tour bus. Checking the schedule, Melissa Tomlinson saw the next stop was in her area in a few days, so she created her own sign to launch her statement of protest. This time, the protest act became more than just an educator standing with a sign, as Melissa's message caught the attention of Governor Christie, causing him to react in a manner that cemented his label as a bully. He cornered Melissa outside of the tour bus, pointing his finger in her face, stating: "I am tired of you people! What more do you want?" Photos of this encounter soon hit Twitter, and the altercation became national news.

BATs became a frenzy of people emboldened with the power to stand up publicly for students and for public education, armed with the understanding they were not alone in doing so, and they were supported by many others across the nation. A few weeks after this, Melissa was elected to become the Assistant General Manager of BATs and began working to bring concerted actions to harness the energy of BATs. What started as a social media space for conversations about public education soon morphed into an organizing space for action for public education.

BAT Actions

With the infrastructure that had been created within the 51 state groups (including Washington, DC), a system began where state BAT groups could assist with national actions, while the national group could assist with pulling people together to support actions that were needed at a state level. From 2014 to 2016, BATs became leaders in utilizing different online tools and social media platforms to direct people in participating in different actions to support the fight for public education. Actions took on many different forms, from completing an Action Network form letter to a legislator, or participating in a Twitter Storm to call out a bad decision made by legislators, to attending different legislative sessions to testify publicly about proposed legislation. A calendar of action items was posted monthly in the main BATs group directing members to take different actions, and a newsletter was sent out to members with different action items such as, writing to legislators, commenting on proposed changes to federal legislation, calling the U.S. Department of Education, or even creating selfies with signs that contained consistent messaging such as "Less testing, more teaching."

All of this was bolstered by the amazing work of the graphic arts items created by the BATs' "Meme Team." Using color and creativity, the memes created by the team became the most effective way to capture the attention of the average social media user in platforms that were becoming increasingly busy with different groups vying for attention. Utilizing the public-facing Badass Teachers Association public page, memes and information sent out daily became accessible to those not in the main BATs group and worked to continue to grow membership.

Over the past decade, BATs has led numerous actions that have influenced the national narrative around public education. What was once dismissed as a tin-foil hat theory about corporations trying to dismantle public education has now become the stage for the current culture wars launched across the country, holding our youth as casualties of war. BATs has had many victories as a result of different actions and campaigns, some manifesting as an immediate win, while the results of others are still being realized. BATs' first national action that showed the possibility of collective power was the BAT Swarm to call for the resignation of Arne Duncan. The phone number to the U.S. Department of Education was posted along with a script for people to use to make calls demanding the resignation of Arne Duncan as U.S. Secretary of Education. So many people participated in this action that the phone lines were tied up for hours with calls unable to get connected. By the end of the day, people taking messages knew exactly why people were calling and what was going to be said.

Sometimes, BAT actions were designed to change the narrative around public education and teachers. With the attacks on public education, the vilification of teachers increased. A big opportunity to push back against this occurred during a snowstorm in the winter of 2014 that left 8,000 students stranded in their schools in the Southeast. Georgia BAT members began posting in the group about what they were experiencing and the different lengths they were going through to keep their students safe. Immediately, the BATs seized the opportunity to showcase these amazing educators with a social media campaign to highlight their stories. The hashtag #EvaluateThat was adopted to accentuate the fact that not all the work that educators do for students is something that can be measured and evaluated.

However, social media campaigns and online organizing can only go so far. At the heart of every movement is the relationships that are built between the people that come together, united against a common issue. As BATs grew during the first years, so did the idea of coming together to meet in person. BATs within different states held meetups, got together to lobby legislative leaders to talk about public education, and connected within different union spaces. Planning started for a national event to take place in Washington, DC. Following the lead of Save Our Schools, BATs held their first rally in front of the U.S. Department of Education on July 28, 2014. Leaders in the fight against the corporate reform of public education stepped up to the mic, joining youth performers and live musicians, who instilled a sense of camaraderie and connection amongst all who joined that day. In connection with the rally, members of BATs traveled to DC a few days earlier with appointments to meet with their respective members of the Senate and Congress, armed with talking points that urged these leaders to put an end to the testing regime and to fully fund public education. Excitement levels ran high as people were meeting in person for the first time after a year of building online friendships. The movement was bolstered by these connections and more work was planned.

Two more in-person rallies were held, once again in Washington, DC on July 8, 2016, and one in Seattle, Washington on July 23, 2017. Meanwhile in Washington, DC, more meetings were held with legislators and the Quality of Worklife (QWL) team had their meeting to discuss the results of the BAT Quality of Worklife survey. The second Washington, DC rally was staged on the steps of the Lincoln Memorial and highlighted both public education advocates and civil rights leaders, including Jonathan Kozol, Diane Ravitch, Jitu Brown, and Reverend William Barber II. After a day of speeches and live music, the Badass Teachers Association led participants on a March to the White House. The day ended with a flash mob dance that renewed everyone's energy to continue the fight. The following year, Seattle was intentionally planned as the location for an event to send BATs "Back to School" as a way to come together and have some meaningful conversations about the role of educators in the fight for racial and social justice. Although a less energetic event than the first two, this conference included a powerful restorative circle led by local tribal leaders of the Suquamish Tribe and held a deeper meaning as BATs shifted their focus to a deeper understanding of the issues of inequity that are prevalent in our society.

Coalition Work

It was during these discussions that the idea of formalizing the Badass Teachers Association into more than just a Facebook group was born. Marla Kilfoyle and Melissa Tomlinson spent hours researching different nonprofit structures to decide which format was best suited for the work that BATs did. Settling as a 501c4, the Badass Teachers Association, Inc. was created to give the organization a legitimate structure to operate. This new structure allowed grants to be offered to BAT members and other organizations to assist with real boots-on-the-ground advocacy and actions that pushed back against school closures. Establishing a voluntary donation system, BATs was able to take in those donations and use them to support community groups in marginalized areas that were battling for control of their neighborhood schools. Some of the biggest fights occurred in Chicago, where Brother Jitu Brown and the We Choose network stood strong against the closing of their neighborhood schools. The Dyett High School Hunger Strike occurred in 2015 and lasted 34 days. By focusing all of their energy towards what this amazing group of people were doing, BATs worked to elevate this battle to national news. Supporting the Coalition to Revitalize Dyett High School's efforts to take the fight to the U.S. Secretary of Education in Washington, DC, BATs continued to stand in solidarity as the Coalition fought not just for their school to remain open, but demanded it to be reopened with a curriculum focused on green technology and global leadership—a fight for the school that their youth deserved.

Some of these BAT grants were used to assist BATs in educating the community through forums about predatory corporate charter school systems that were threatening their neighborhood schools, such as in Birmingham, Alabama and Camden, New Jersey. It was the cycle of school closures sweeping across the country in a repetitive pattern: Open a charter school in the neighborhood; Use standardized test scores to portray the schools as failing the students; and Offer the shiny new program of the charter school to entice families to transfer their students and cause declining enrollment in the public school. Declining enrollment equated to a loss of per pupil funding, causing program cuts and declining test scores. Coupled with the lack of cultural competency in many schools due to a teacher workforce that was majorly white, historically marginalized parents saw charter schools as a better alternative. Public education began to look internally at its own faults and role in this vicious cycle. Demands were made for culturally responsive teaching and ethnic studies, as well as educators who better reflected the demographics of the student population. BATs sought to do their part by offering grants, specifically to future educators of color to assist with the cost of purchasing necessary textbooks for their courses.

Quality of Worklife

Having the pathways to provide assistance directly to people advocating for public education resulted in individual victories in different areas, but the narrative around public education and public educators has been one of finger-pointing and blame. The idea that educators needed to prove their worth and earn respect has always been a sore spot for educators. Because of the nature of a profession of mostly women, schools had become a space for potential bullying, harassment, and intimidation of teachers and educational support professionals. Guided by the culture created by public leaders, like Chris Christie, that it was acceptable to bully teachers, school administrators bought into that narrative and often created toxic environments. This was especially true for educators who were vocally pushing back against the changes they knew were harmful to students that were being forced down into education. To shed light on the toxic environment created within education, the BATs QWL team was created. The leaders of this team all had personal experiences with bullying administrators that united them together to work hard to expose just how toxic schools had become. The tagline, "An educator's environment is a student's learning environment" was centered as the main pushback against such toxicity. To reveal exactly how extensive and pervasive this bullying culture had become, the BATs QWL team joined with the American Federation of Teachers (AFT) in 2015 to launch a survey. The response to this survey far exceeded expectations for participation, with over 30,000 responses submitted within 10 days. The data were reviewed and analyzed in order to release a report of the team's findings. The BAT QWL survey report became the first of many efforts to expose bullying and to bolster the idea that it is not acceptable for educators to be asked to sacrifice their health, wellbeing, and family relationships for their classroom. The report from this survey was used as the basis for a meeting between the BAT

QWL team, the United States Department of Education (USDOE), and the National Institute for Occupational Safety and Health (NIOSH). Plans for how to address these issues were discussed, and the BATs hoped that some positive changes would occur. Unfortunately, the 2016 elections brought about some major staffing changes within the different federal departments, and those plans became obsolete. In 2017, a second survey was created with the assistance of the scientific research community. The results of that survey verified the findings of the first survey and revealed there had not been a lot of movement towards reducing the toxic climate within schools since the initial study was conducted.

Growing Pains

The expansion of BATs was not without some major growing pains, the largest of which was developing the understanding of the role of white supremacy in our society. While public education is still a workforce of primarily women, a marginalized group of society, it is also a field dominated by white educators, with the current ethnic majority of teachers as nearly 70% white. Yet, we work in classrooms that are increasingly diverse. The need to focus on racial equity became the one divisive issue that BATs ever faced as older members pushed back against this shift in focus. Eventually, as BATs grew in their understanding of the different factors that affect public education, the understanding of the impact of systemic and institutional racism also began to develop. An education about the school-to-prison pipeline started for the leaders and members as BATs worked to establish a racially—and socially—just organization that worked to elevate voices of color and to decrease a white savior mentality that silences those voices. These new understandings spurred BATs to rewrite their mission to reflect the broader picture of their work. The mission of BATs now states:

> We, the members of the Badass Teachers Association, reject racially and socially oppressive profit-driven education reform and through our advocacy demand:
>
> - Equitable student driven policies and systems that are also equitably funded to meet the needs of ALL students and schools,

that include highly qualified and certified educational professionals

- Elimination of high stakes standardized testing as we recognize its roots in racism, arbitrary cut scores, and value-added accountability systems used to evaluate children, educators and their schools
- Educator evaluations designed to grow professional practice, without punitive measures
- Protection of balanced, student-centered curriculum which includes, but is not limited to, Performing and Visual Arts, Physical Education, Library, World Languages, Ethnic Studies developed with/by local affinity groups, Career and Technical Education, Unstructured Play and Recess
- Developmentally sound best practices and programs which augment the experiences of students with special needs, LGBTQIA+ students, students with complex trauma, students who experience institutional racism, students marginalized for socio-economic status, immigrants and those learning the English language
- Educator-designed policies, standards, and curricula that are supported by peer-reviewed research, as well as input from experienced classroom experts that includes voices from BIPoC, LGBTQIA+, and dis/abled educator communities.
- Academic freedom for educators and students, thus ensuring the best possible learning, teaching, and working environment
- Excellent public education for all students, regardless of economic status, race, nationality, gender, religion, sexual orientation, or dis/ability
- School cultures rooted in equitable practices, including the hiring and retention of BIPoC educators, that honor the culture and history of all students and strive to heal and transform past and current oppressive systems

- Safe and equitable technology—recommended screen time and content limits ensuring safe privacy practice for students and educators
- Safe, clean, well-maintained, uncrowded professional workplace environments, free from bullying and harassment of students and educators, as well as freedom from threats of violence
- Collective bargaining rights, due process, and job protections
- Legislation that unequivocally directs accountability and transparency for charter schools, and maintains the vision of public funds for public institutions, disqualifying vouchers, rebates, and tax credits that divert those funds
- Democratically elected school boards that solicit and openly work to include the input of the entire community they serve. (www.badassteacher.org/mission)

BATs and the Unions

There has always been a bigger picture to analyze in the fight for public education, and although BATs started mainly around the idea of pushing back against standardized testing, the new mission reflects the understanding there is more that has been put into place in an attempt to dismantle public education than just high-stakes standardized testing. Coupled with the fight for public education has been the attacks on unions, especially the largest unions in our country—the National Education Association (NEA) and the AFT. Leaders of BATs have, from the beginning, understood the importance of unions in providing job protections, advocating for students, and pushing back against the privatization of a public good. The BATs' spaces provided a place for conversations about both unions to happen more frequently since they were spaces that contained both NEA and AFT members. Similarities and differences were discussed and debated. Each national union holds a scheduled convention of delegate representatives who engage in a democratic process to guide the unions about their beliefs, values, and future work. BATs formed caucuses within each of the national unions to bring BAT members together around this work. With more BAT members belonging to NEA, the NEA BAT Caucus emerged as a larger group that comes together at the annual NEA Representative Assembly (RA), creating New Business Items and proposing amendments to their Resolutions and Legislative Program.

BATs have always been unionists and strong believers in the power of the union, in addition to being advocates for transparency and communication within the union. Knowing that the power of the union lies within the rank-and-file membership, BATs also became a space where educators could learn more about how the unions work and how to navigate the different structures within the union. The different BAT state groups became an important place for this work as each state union operates differently, but the theme of "Union Power" and "I am the union" remains throughout all spaces. BAT members are mentored about how to become involved with the union. Across the country, BAT members have moved into positions of union leadership at the local, state, and national levels.

This belief in union power became especially important as the national attacks on unions grew stronger. The 2016 Supreme Court case *Rebecca Friedrichs v. CTA* was a pivotal moment for educators in understanding how dangerous the corporate entities seeking to negate unions could be. The Badass Teachers Association wrote an amicus brief that was submitted to the court. Educators across the nation were tuned in to hear the case argued in court. Marla Kilfoyle and Melissa Tomlinson traveled to Washington, DC to be there in person, sitting in the courtroom as the merits of each side were presented, then rushing to the U.S. Department of Education to testify about the proposed updates to NCLB as it was morphed into the Every Student Succeeds Act (ESSA).

The campaign against *Friedrichs* served as practice for the successful blow to union organizing that came later, the decision in the 2018 *Janus v. AFSCME* case. After a victory with the *Friedrichs* case, the leaders of BATs knew that a loss was inevitable. Consistent messaging about being #UnionStrong was interwoven in all that the BATs did. This education increased to help educators realize the need for and power of a union. In the *Janus* decision, the Supreme Court ruled that union fees in the public sector violated the First Amendment right to free speech, overturning the 1977 decision in *Abood v. Detroit Board of Education* that had previously allowed such fees. However, BATs knew that positive messaging about union strength and the power of belonging to a union would not be enough. Without automatic dues deductions, the potential loss of membership numbers became the impetus for developing a deeper understanding of what meaningful organizing should look like. Leaders in BATs looked to history for guidance on how to best strengthen the union. Attending sessions from Labor Notes and other organizations taught members how to become successful organizers within unions and also how to build and strengthen relationships with community members to build coalitions and unite around common issues.

State Organizing

It was this strengthening of understanding around organizing to build power that led to the #RedforEd wave of actions and strikes that began to sweep across the country. Members of the movement in Virginia, Oklahoma, North Carolina, and other states met each other in the BATs groups and shared organizing experiences, campaign ideas, and tools used for organizing. Although these strikes did not meet the call for a national educator walkout that different members had been demanding since the beginning, the #RedforEd strike wave was successful in showing educators across the nation that if they came together, they could demonstrate their power for tangible wins. In all of these actions, BAT members could be found at the center, sometimes by showing a very public presence, other times hiding in the background to help elevate these actions.

Organizing in states that did not participate in the #Red4Ed strike wave also began. Energized by what they were watching happen in Arizona, NJBATs started to work on educating New Jersey Education Association (NJEA) members on what it really meant to organize deeply. A caucus group of the NJEA was formed, going through a few iterations until becoming NJ21United. It was this group of educators that first pushed NJEA to understand the need to state "Black Lives Matter at School." The COVID-19 pandemic in 2020 again brought the need for mobilizing as educators in New Jersey quickly realized the potential loss of life that would occur if schools were fully opened too quickly and NJ21United took the lead in the #OnlyWhenItsSafe campaign. This building and strengthening at the local and state level was instrumental as the nation began a time of upheaval and turmoil. BATs faced the 2016 election results with an understanding that the only way to come back from an election that placed a fascist as the leader of our country was to turn energy towards local movements. BATs had already been encouraging educators to consider running in public elections to center public education as a leading issue in education platforms.

Either running themselves or working closely with different candidates, BATs dove into election work. Creating lists of educators and specifically BATs members that were running for different positions, BATs worked to highlight their candidacy and hold them up as role models for other members to learn from. Current members of Congress, Gloria Johnson and Jamaal Bowman are BAT members who joined in the early days.

Organizing for Justice and Safe Schools

As the country began to reel from the different attacks on human rights that were being launched, specifically against immigrants, asylum seekers, and people of color, BATs shifted its focus even more towards organizing on a local level by encouraging members to stand up for Deferred Action for Childhood Arrivals (DACA), join the Black Lives Matter at School campaigns, and stand against xenophobia and for LGBTQIA+ rights. BAT members helped organize and showed up at protests and marches around the country. BATs joined protests in Austin, Texas against child deportation.

The Parkland school shooting in 2018 was another explosion point for the BAT movement. The previous tragedies of Columbine (1999) and Sandy Hook (2012) had been woven into the background fabric of BAT leaders, and every new school shooting brought about fresh pain and tears for the victims. Parkland was personal for us as we sat online with one of our long-time BAT members, a parent of a student at the high school, who shared real-time updates as the tragedy unfolded. BATs was not going to let this shooting get brushed aside like so many others. A call was sent out to both national unions to join with leaders in gun control organizations to make real movement towards safety in our schools. With an understanding of the impact of a police presence and militarized security systems in schools, BATs worked to guide the narrative to a more just understanding of safety, joining the idea that #CounselorsNotCops were needed in our schools to address the root causes of gun violence in schools and communities. The development of this understanding later led to the natural inclusion of BAT members in protests against police violence after the murder of George Floyd. From Seattle to New York City, BATs marched with historically marginalized communities to take a stand.

The theme of safe schools continued with the onset of the COVID-19 pandemic. As the world shut down around them, educators became the backbone of their respective communities, keeping a sense of normalcy with the shift to virtual learning, volunteering at food drives and in mutual aid networks around the country. The BAT spaces and connections became instrumental in providing lifelines for people that needed assistance with how to teach students through a screen, supporting new and experienced educators, as well as helping to fight back feelings of isolation. Even before the end of the 2020 school year, the forward-thinking BAT leaders recognized the need to be prepared for September. BAT leaders and other members became quasi-experts in air quality and other safety protections. The background work to launch the #OnlyWhenItsSafe campaign with the newly formed national educator advocacy network, National Educators United (NEU).

Due to the lack of national leadership in managing the pandemic, states were left to make their own decisions about restrictions and procedures during COVID-19. It was quickly realized that members in different states would have to organize to address what decisions were being made in their own states. Fortunately, BATs was already adept at how to organize in virtual spaces, and educators across the country came together to share safety information and campaign ideas as quick tutorials were given about different online advocacy tools. Plans for how to build air purifiers out of box fans and information about what type of ventilation was needed to effectively mitigate COVID-19 particles became widespread knowledge in the education community. Over the summer, educators met (masked) to demonstrate at different state capitols and push back against a full reopening of schools for the September 2020 school year. Organizers in New Jersey were successful at holding a day of protest at each county school superintendent's office that was followed the next day with a mock funeral march in the state capital of Trenton outside of one of the governor's daily live pandemic broadcasts. Physical safety was not the only item of safety that was advocated for. BATs soon realized the mental and emotional toll that COVID-19 was having on the youth of our nation and began an early call to have more counselors and mental health professionals ready in our schools as they reopened. Renewing the call for more counselors in our schools as a measure of safety, BATs were proactive in furthering the conversation around mental health. BAT members were directed to pay attention towards the allocation of

Elementary and Secondary School Emergency Relief (ESSER) Funds for their states and to advocate for what would help push systemic change within our schools. We knew our schools should not be allowed to merely return to the way they were before the pandemic. We knew the result of this global trauma would have a large impact upon the youth that we would now be responsible for educating.

Conclusion

Unfortunately, the system of public education is a large ship that takes a long time to steer in a different direction. Also, we are still seeing the impact of the 2016 elections manifesting as culture wars as the pendulum swings and the pushback against advances in the fight for racial justice strengthens. We now face direct attacks on a lot of the progress that was gained in human and civil rights. The battlegrounds of these fights have landed in school board meetings and the classroom. The same groups that have financed the movement to build charter schools and support voucher programs that siphon public funds are also financing the groups that are denying the rights of the LGBTQIA+ population to healthcare and safety. They deny the fact that Black history is American history and accuse educators of indoctrination and pedophilia. The Christian Nationalist movement has joined with ALEC in their attempts to dismantle the public education system and widen the opportunity gap. Emboldened by a brazen national voice, these groups seek to deny anyone of any access to resources that they have a human right to, food, safety, etc. In New Jersey, one such group has even come out against a legislative proposal to provide free lunch to all students because they think that this food will be used to poison children!

It's clear that there is still a long fight for public education that will be waged many, many years into the future. As our world moves at a faster pace every day, the landscape of challenges that educators face is always shifting. Future battles can only be imagined as new technologies such as artificial intelligence (AI) are created and become mainstream. Holding on to the national Facebook group space has allowed BATs to see future trends and help shape conversations around what they see to prepare others to advocate for, or fight back, as necessary. A greater understanding of the need to elevate the voice of those most impacted and not be the loudest voice in the room has faded BATs into the background, pushing others into the spotlight. Chances are, when there is a conversation about fighting for public education, a BAT is somewhere in the background, laying the groundwork for everyone to help defend one of the greatest common goods of our nation, the cornerstone of our democracy—our public education system.

Editor's Note: You can follow The Badass Teachers Association on Facebook, X, and Instagram. Their website is https://www.badassteacher.org/

CHAPTER 7

The Movement and the Mayor[1]

Jesse Sharkey

NOT LONG AFTER Brandon Johnson won Chicago's 2023 mayoral election, he came by the Kenwood-Oakland Community Organization's annual convention. Several hundred seniors, students, educators, and other members of the South Side community organization were gathered at King College Prep High School to attend workshops, discuss next steps, and maintain their connection with a vital part of the network of community activists, trade unionists, anti-racist organizers, and others who constitute—and identify as—the Chicago Movement. The buzz of victory still hung in the air. Conversations with people you hadn't seen in a while started with hugs or big smiles and a shake of the head. Our movement elected the mayor of Chicago. Can you believe it?

In his speech, Brandon made three points. First, he restated his commitment to the movement's demands, including housing and education, which echo the community organization's program. Second, he stressed the importance of Black and Latino unity—a timely and important intervention given the opposition to settling asylum seekers among some in Chicago's Black community. And the third point, less explicit and more visceral, was to let the movement claim him for a minute. To tell the crowd with a wink and a relaxed grin, *I know the TV cameras are on, but we all know I came out of this movement. I was a public school teacher and an organizer for the Chicago Teachers Union.* The folks he joined on a hunger strike in 2015 to save Dyett High School were sitting in the front row, and the organizers who had taken over school board meetings with him were standing just off to the side.

He told us not to let the rich and powerful divide us. He joked about how many terms Black people have for "cousin." He was speaking to his people. *Our movement elected the mayor of Chicago, y'all. Can you believe it?*

The moment he was done speaking and turned to leave the stage I was immediately reminded of the pressures on him—a police department security detail, an advance team, logistics, photographers, press liaisons, a crowd of media with cameras and microphones. It was a complete scrum, and it follows him virtually everywhere he goes in public. The end of his life as he had known it.

I first met Brandon in 2011 when he interviewed for an organizer job at the Chicago Teachers Union. I was the vice president, and he was a teacher at an elementary and middle school in the Cabrini-Green projects. CTU president, Karen Lewis and our team of rank-and-file teachers in the Caucus of Rank-and-File Educators (CORE) had just taken over the biggest local union in the city with the aim to turn the union into the kind of inspiring, socially aware, fighting organization that could transform the city's schools while building an educational justice movement. For that, we needed organizers, a job title that hadn't previously existed at the CTU. Brandon was a perfect fit: politically engaged, earnest and open to people, and motivated to fight injustice.

A pastor's kid from a family of 12 who, as he is fond of retelling, shared a single bathroom, Brandon possesses an easy good nature that can slip into the kind of facile I-can-be-anything-to-everyone style of a skilled politician. But his is not the story of a silver-tongued, charismatic young man who charts a meteoric rise up the political ladder—after all, Brandon chose a team that did not appear to be winning in 2011. In fact, we were getting the snot kicked out of us. The mayor at the time, Rahm Emanuel, came to Chicago with the clout of a DC insider (he had been President Barack Obama's White House chief of staff) and an aggressive plan to attack the teachers union and remake the schools in a corporate model. While Brandon was filling out his employment paperwork at the CTU, Mayor-Elect Emanuel was in the state capitol supporting legislation designed to strip away our collective bargaining rights and bar our ability to strike. Brandon's trajectory from the front lines of the CTU's struggles to the mayor's office mirrors the CTU's transformation from a relatively isolated and conservative union that politicians used as a punching bag to a social justice union, bolstered by a burgeoning movement that was not afraid to demonstrate or strike and could help set an agenda for the entire city.

How would Brandon withstand the pressures of office? What does it mean for our movement to have one of our own in office? How will we win our demands for housing, education, and reforming the racist injustice system? How will we build our movement to take advantage of the new horizons opening with Brandon as mayor?

The organizers at that South Side event weren't putting forward any easy or pat answers to those questions. Yet everyone, almost to a person, held to the political wisdom of an organizing tradition in Chicago that sees our most important power as flowing from our own ranks, not from high office. Few, if any, in Chicago's activist community expect the city to meet all the demands a decade of popular campaigns had generated—the price tag for our public school program alone reaches into the billions of dollars, to say nothing of our demands around housing, jobs, restorative justice, and more. Other movement ideas—like diverting funding from the police to community services—contain political risks that could undo the mayor's governing coalition. To the people at the Kenwood-Oakland Community Organization convention, Brandon's election reflected the importance of our grassroots work—a sign of our popular influence and successful organizing more than a naïve belief that electing a mayor overcomes all the financial and political obstacles to structural change.

I think the benefits of having elected an organizer as mayor fall along three lines, none of which has to do with Brandon simply delivering our political wish list to us like manna from heaven. First, the election raised expectations among working-class Chicagoans and people of color. Beyond the campaign promises alone (though those do provide a benchmark), a mayor who tells us, *This is a rich city—there's no reason it can't provide for everybody,* helps us break out of a cynical and demoralized view that this economically and racially segregated city will never change. Second, with Brandon in office, space opens up for us to win people to our ideas. As the policy proposals about housing, policing, mental health, and more from Brandon's transition report are debated and introduced as legislation, we will have an opportunity to train our activists on a new variety of political issues. Finally, all of this produces organizing opportunities and the ability to grow our unions, neighborhood organizations, and movements. If we run campaigns that produce compelling narratives, develop the thinking and ideas of our activists, and keep up the pressure through direct actions, then we can view the Johnson administration as a boon for our side.

Too often in our history we've seen reform-oriented politicians veer off course, make compromises with power, and then use their own credibility within the movement to tamp down dissent rather than encourage the activism that made their rise possible. We've also seen social movements lose their way and devolve into electoral vehicles that demobilize as soon as the campaigns end. These twin dangers can ultimately produce defeatism and a backlash we've seen captured by the right. But Brandon isn't just a politician who latched on to a social movement. He taught public school, organized co-workers, and led a militant union that was at the center of Chicago's social movements. The activists and rank-and-file members of those movements have been part of a drama whose first, second, and third acts involved movement building, strikes, and mass protests.

* * *

If you look at the forces that are arrayed against Brandon—first during the campaign and carrying on now in the same unrelenting vein—one criticism stands out above all the others: his roots in the CTU. His election was described as Chicago choosing "one of CTU's own," describing him as "a former Chicago Public Schools teacher and paid CTU organizer" by ABC7, one of Chicago's most highly rated TV news channels. Over and over again his opponent Paul Vallas, a former CEO of the Chicago Public Schools (CPS), attacked Brandon as a leader in the CTU, trying to argue that Brandon could not serve all Chicagoans because he was affiliated with the union, as if being funded by a handful of equities traders was somehow better than Brandon's support from thousands of working-class union members. Voters didn't buy it, but the attack has resurfaced as a way to criticize Johnson's decisions on issues ranging from personnel decisions to his handling of public pensions.

Chicago's most powerful businessmen and guardians of corporate interests from the Civic Committee of the Commercial Club of Chicago to the editorial board of the Chicago Tribune understand from more than a decade of bitter conflict that the CTU is an implacable foe and at the center of Brandon's victory in the mayor's race. The city's most important fighting union has been a key anchor not just in the 2023 mayoral election but for political movements in Chicago generally.

Yet, the vitality of the Chicago Movement springs from the organizing, cross-movement lesson learning, and solidarity that is at the heart of what's going on here, not from the CTU alone. Successive movements have left a rich legacy for radical politics, from the groundbreaking work against police torture to the campaign against Walmart and low-wage big-box retailers. After CORE's upset victory in the 2010 union election, the insurgent-led CTU made its relationship to other unions, community organizations, and activist groups central to its plans. One of our first acts was launching a coalition called the Grassroots Education Movement (GEM). In early 2012 we put out a report, "The Schools Chicago's Students Deserve," that not only detailed improvements the schools needed from wraparound services to arts education, but also detailed the ways poverty hurt children, along with a series of revenue-producing ideas to have the wealthy pay for them. This approach came to be called "Bargaining for the Common Good," and it helped ensure that we had common cause with other activists in the city.

CTU and other organizers found ourselves in overlapping struggles, collaborating and influenced by one another on many occasions. From the beginning of our time in office, when the Occupy movement and the Wisconsin State Capitol occupation inspired us, to the actions of teenage climate activists who helped us develop thinking about green schools, movements influenced both city politics and the thinking inside the CTU. One particularly important example occurred in late 2015 when it came out that the Chicago police had shot 17-year-old Laquan McDonald in the back and then covered it up for over a year. The Black Youth Project 100 and other young Black activists led the citywide response in a series of marches and confrontations with power that changed the way CTU members thought about the police, producing a campaign to cancel the annual $33 million police contract with the public schools.

But the bosses' focus on the CTU reflects the reality that the union provides a historical legitimacy and organizational weight that distinguishes it from other organizations and movements. That legitimacy derives in part from the CTU's role as a key voice for Chicago's Black residents, stemming from the long-standing importance of public education for Black Chicagoans, the ugly legacy of segregated schools in the city, and the important role that Black teachers played in civil rights organizing. One of them was Mamie Till-Mobley, mother of Emmett Till, who taught in the Chicago public schools for 23 years. Black teachers also played an important role in combating racist schooling, as in the 1963 boycott against segregated schools. The CTU is also among the largest and most important institutions that has had a number of Black leaders—a relative rarity in Chicago, where Black people make up more than 25% of the population—starting with Jacqueline B. Vaughn, who led the union through several strikes in the 1980s before dying in office of cancer in 1994. Vaughn's picture hung in Karen Lewis's conference room, and Karen often invoked her legacy and drew inspiration from her blunt style, including when she openly challenged Emanuel's plans to close 50 schools in 2013 by saying that "88% of students impacted by CPS school actions are African American. And this is by design," and accusing him of being the "murder mayor." The campaign she led against the closings became a rallying point for many community and social justice activists who were concerned about Chicago's stark racial and economic inequality. The current CTU president, Stacy Davis Gates, is a Chicago public school parent, former mayor Lori Lightfoot's most effective public critic, and the chief architect of our political insurgency.

The CTU's most unusual characteristic—and a source of our organizational power—has been our unwillingness to reach political accommodation with the city's power structure. The 2012 strike reminded the labor movement at large about class politics and the power of labor militancy, but what happened after the strike proved just as significant. The CTU never adopted the kind of risk-averse, organizationally-timid behavior that characterizes many unions today. Karen Lewis and the rest of the CTU leadership were not incorporated into the ruling democratic polity, nor did the union switch from industrial militancy to a lobbying strategy. Instead, we went on to wage many more strikes and campaigns, ranging from the campaign against school closings and organizing against corporate tax giveaways to a long-term strategy to remove mayoral control of the schools and participation in protests and marches against police brutality.

The CTU has been able to bring money and mass organization with citywide structure to bear in a way that has anchored Chicago's social movements since CORE's election turned the union's focus to organizing for the common good. Our roughly 27,000 members are required by statute to live in the city and are based in every neighborhood; by political necessity, we have learned how to maintain relationships with our parents (as many of us are ourselves) and communities. Chicago's more than 500 neighborhood public schools are a source of social services, including free meals (Chicago public schools served more than 21 million meals during the first six months of the pandemic, reported the *Chicago Tribune*) and are the most stable public institution in many neighborhoods. Of course they are also workplaces, and every unionized school has an elected delegate (equivalent to a shop steward in other unions) who not only conducts meetings and represents the concerns of teachers and staff to management but also maintains relationships with parents and community groups at open houses, through the local school council, and in targeted campaigns. For example, if the Chicago Public Schools' central office cuts a school's budget (a common occurrence), teachers and CTU organizers reach out to parents and local community organizations so they can plan pickets, conduct press conferences, and petition in opposition to the cuts. Public schools are a nexus between Chicago's largest local union and the city's deep history of community organizing.

Many mainstream commentators tend to ignore the social justice focus that CORE brought to the CTU and the resulting transformation of the union's relationships with parents and the community, and instead focus solely on the fact that the CTU and other unions contributed millions of dollars to Brandon's campaign. Often the same commentators thought that Vallas's huge fundraising advantage and prominent endorsements would ensure his path to office. For one candidate, money is delegitimizing; for the other, it boosts his electability. Our legitimacy, especially in the eyes of Black Chicago, our mass organization that has made us a presence in every neighborhood, and our combative stance against the political status quo means that we were a critical component of the political foment in Chicago over the past ten-plus years that led to Brandon Johnson's election.

* * *

CORE came to lead the CTU thanks to a combination of good strategy, good people, and good luck. We started the caucus as a network of activists inside the union who were dismayed at the destruction of our public schools under the banner of market-driven education reform. One of our first projects was to study Naomi Klein's *The Shock Doctrine* as a way to understand how the city's financial and political elites were using a looming fiscal crisis to attack public education. An outside observer who happened to walk by the public library in Chicago's Pilsen neighborhood would have seen Karen Lewis and the rest of the future CTU leadership with marked-up copies of the book and a pile of highlighters. But we always intended to be much more than a study group. From the beginning, we were focused on organizing co-workers and fighting for leadership of the union. Karen served as the union delegate at Lane Tech, the city's largest high school. I also was the union delegate at a large high school, as was CORE co-founder Jackson Potter, who took a leave to organize the group. Our early campaigns targeted issues of key concern to CTU members: fighting school closings, filing discrimination lawsuits after layoffs at majority Black schools, picketing principals who had committed egregious contract violations, and generally demonstrating the way the union *should* be led.

CORE benefited from a deep pool of talented members who brought valuable experience. The daughter of two Black Chicago public school teachers, Karen Lewis had taken a circuitous route to teaching high school chemistry (first came a sociology and music degree from Dartmouth, medical school, film school, and a stint as a stand-up comic), but she brought the lived experience of Black Chicago's fights against racist school policies, including the 1963 school boycott and the fight against the mobile Willis Wagon classrooms, and the 1968 strike to win permanent status for Black teachers. I came out of a radical labor organizer tradition—after college, I graduated from the AFL-CIO's Organizing Institute, worked as an organizer for SEIU 1199 New England, and spent years involved in socialist politics in Chicago.

None of this might have mattered were it not for twin crises confronting the union's leadership, a group called the United Progressive Caucus that had fought a series of militant strikes in the 1970s and 1980s but had become a complacent and entrenched bureaucracy. The first was an internal split caused by exorbitant staff salaries and overly generous perks bankrupting the union treasury. The second and more important issue revolved around the old guard's inability to block market-driven school reforms that were massively ramping up standardized testing, closing so-called low-performing schools and laying off veteran teachers, privatizing services, and increasing the number of nonunion charter schools. The Chicago Public Schools CEO was threatening mass layoffs and increased class sizes unless the legislature adopted deep pension cuts. Yet, all that union staff offered to angry members at schools that had been targeted for closure was advice about polishing their résumés. Old-guard leadership dismissed charters as an educational fad that would soon go away.

On the eve of the 2010 union election, CORE called for a mass march against the threatened layoffs. We printed thousands of beautiful full-color posters attacking the rationale for layoffs and pointing to corporate tax breaks as a source for needed revenue and distributed them in all the schools. Thousands of members turned out. While union leadership marched at the front of the event, it nonetheless was clear to most members which group had the ideas and organization to meet the coming attacks. CORE won the election and took office July 1, 2010.

Over the years that CORE has led the CTU, the union has had three presidents (I served from 2018 to 2022), conducted three strikes at CPS, waged nearly a dozen strikes in the charter sector, and survived a litany of legislative and political attacks ranging from the 2011 attempt to ban teachers strikes to Lightfoot's offensive against our COVID-19 safety protocols. These experiences produced a set of organizational conclusions that remain relevant to our challenges today. Our bitter political conflicts with Chicago's leading Democratic politicians led us to understand that we needed to form our own independent working-class-based political organization, the United Working Families. The work required to maintain our unity under unrelenting austerity imparted key lessons about democratic practices and developing internal leadership so that rank-and-file members could become union leaders and union leaders, in turn, could run for citywide office. Bargaining for common good demands taught us how to run polarizing campaigns that made audacious demands on the rich and powerful while building mass support.

* * *

When CORE first came to power, decades of social protections for teachers and students were being demolished at a fever pace. First came an attempt to dramatically increase the hours and intensity of work with no corresponding increase in pay. Emanuel and neoliberal education reformers, such as Democrats for Education Reform and Stand for Children, combined this attack on working conditions with an offensive against tenure and tried to impose punitive, test-based evaluation systems. These were the main issues that drove the 2012 strike.

But this attack on teachers quickly broadened. Chicago's financial elites in the Civic Committee of the Commercial Club of Chicago, the Civic Federation, and similar groups saw that decades of underfunding had finally caught up with the public schools, leaving Chicago Public Schools with an estimated billion-dollar-a-year structural deficit that they believed could be solved only by radical cuts. This meant determined attacks against teacher pensions and, most dramatically, Emanuel's mass closing of 50 public schools in 2013.

It's difficult to overstate the impact of the mass school closures on Chicago politics. With the exception of natural disasters such as hurricanes, it remains the largest mass school closure in the modern history of the U.S. The city administration and the mayor-appointed Board of Education released a list of 129 schools and conducted hearings to decide which of them would be closed.

Tens of thousands of people participated, arriving in buses full of students, parents, teachers, and administrators who went on to plead their case in front of private consultants brought in from out of town to sell the process. People gave searing, emotional testimony and demanded explanations. In response to that pressure, Emanuel's administration kept shifting the rationale because it couldn't tell people the truth: schools were being targeted to save money while real estate developers and corporate cronies got huge tax breaks. In the end, the board rubber-stamped 50 closings, surprising no one but hardening our resolve to ensure that Emanuel paid a political price.

CORE had come into office with an expansive view of educational justice and the belief that we needed a broad-based movement to win. The 2012 strike and especially the 2013 school closings fight forced us to conclude that we had to be serious about politics to truly affect what happens with teachers, students, and schools. The mayor's office loomed large not only because it set city policy and appointed the education board but also because the mayor exerted a tremendous amount of power over elected officials from city aldermen to statewide officials.

The people attacking our schools in the realm of public policy were Democrats—from Emanuel to a host of state and local politicians. Illinois Senate president John Cullerton worked for years to cut public pensions, and Governor Pat Quinn campaigned with an ad promising to stop "Squeezy the Pension Python." State senator Iris Martinez staffed her campaign with former board members from the charter school network her policies benefited, and state legislator Christian Mitchell joined the attack on pensions and supported expanding charter schools—both with major financial backing from neoliberal Democrats. The city council was no better.

In the summer of 2014, Karen began signaling that she would challenge Emanuel in the February 2015 municipal election and called on teachers and other movement activists to run for office themselves. Her events were well attended, and she led in early polls. At the time, I thought this attempt was premature—we didn't yet have the networks or organizational capacity to pull off a successful mayoral run, and doing so would distract our union from its other functions.

Brandon Johnson and Stacy Davis Gates, then the union's political director, were key to the union articulating a way forward. They argued that serious political engagement was necessary to achieve our goals, and they proposed a plan to address the hostility of local politicians to our interests by building a new political organization: the United Working Families party.

The UWF was the result of the CTU and allies deciding to build a political apparatus that could deliver transformative change. We wanted a political party that could formulate a platform with clear ideas for change, develop activists, train candidates, and ultimately provide a structure that could push new, pro-working-class policies through the system. We also wanted all the benefits of campaigning: the lists of supporters, fund-raising work, and reputation building. If we were going to do the hard work of challenging Emanuel and his supporters electorally, we wanted the ability to set the political agenda.

In October 2014, Karen's bid for mayor was cut short by her brain cancer diagnosis. The union was left with few options but to endorse Jesus "Chuy" Garcia, a reliable progressive but hardly the kind of combative, campaigning figure we needed to win. Without Karen, we lacked a clear path to elected office, and the political forces arrayed against us continued to intensify. The election of Bruce Rauner, a Federalist Society–friendly Republican, as governor that November signaled the start of an acute crisis. Yet Stacy's vision for building the UWF proved prescient. Too often unions are left with little to nothing to show for this kind of dramatic turn and counterturn of fortune besides a pile of flyers for a defeated candidate sitting in your junk mail. But in this case we were able to launch the UWF, which quickly began to cohere a layer of working-class activists, largely women of color, into an important political force.

Brandon Johnson gave an instructive interview about the UWF in 2014, fresh off the battle over school closures. He explained, "We just don't know who our allies are anymore. We don't know who our champions are when it comes to the issues that resonate with our members, particularly at the classroom level. So you might have Democrats that say, 'Look, I'm for public schools, I'm in favor of public education. I want to see small class sizes.' But there are no policy initiatives or legislation that speaks to that desire."

The worry was not just that Rauner would block critical funds from the schools and threaten us with bankruptcy—which he did do—but also that our own membership would become so demoralized by the severe budget cuts and worsening conditions in the schools that they would be unwilling to invest in a long-term political project that required a high degree of both unity and confidence in our ability to create change. The CTU navigated this difficult period of unrelenting austerity by mobilizing our members and simultaneously involving them in debate about strategy. This deeply democratic internal method included widespread substantive discussions, contested votes, continual political education, and political risk-taking, all of which ultimately allowed us to maintain our struggle and set the stage for later contractual advances and political wins.

The Chicago Board of Education had "solved" a series of financial shortfalls beginning in 2010 with increasingly desperate short-term gimmicks. By 2015, the cash-starved Chicago Public Schools was worried about making payroll and cutting costs in every conceivable part of its operation. In early 2016, Chicago Public Schools CEO Forrest Claypool sent a letter to the union threatening a unilateral 7% pay cut. When the union responded by notifying the district that such a cut would provoke a strike, the district further threatened mass layoffs and later, implemented unpaid furlough days. Despite some bitter internal conflict, the CTU was able to maintain unity and deepen the political involvement of our membership while facing these challenges and a near breakdown in our bargaining relationship with our employer.

Teachers and other school staff were incensed by the furloughs, not least because the board canceled days which had been scheduled for teacher planning without reducing the actual planning requirements; instead of seeing both their workload and their pay shrink slightly, teachers had to perform unpaid work. At the same time, classroom conditions deteriorated rapidly as the district virtually stopped filling vacancies. Students who were diagnosed with special needs could not get the legally mandated help, and the workload for the remaining special education teachers skyrocketed. School after school reported dysfunctional, dangerous conditions due to short staffing.

Members demanded a response from their union. But there was no short-term solution to the financial crisis undergirding the crisis in the schools. We found ourselves in a situation where most of the typical tools of unionism—grievances, public campaigns, even workplace actions—simply would not induce the employer to hire more staff or spend money they didn't have.

The debate about how to respond to the financial crisis felt chaotic, wide-open, sometimes desperate, and often uncomfortable. Some members demanded we hire more lawyers to fight the furloughs and understaffing. Others suggested that we stop writing recommendations and meeting with parents, withholding the unpaid work we typically perform after school. Some members insisted that powerful moral arguments could produce solutions, while others were angry at the union, arguing that if it couldn't protect teachers against furloughs, it should stop collecting union dues to make up the shortfall. That would have bankrupted the union at precisely the time teachers needed it most.

Rather than try to quash this debate or channel it into a legislative campaign, our union remained committed to our democratic internal method and organized discussions about what we should do. We made our response to the fiscal crisis the subject of intense school-level meetings and discussions in the union's elected bodies, including the House of Delegates (the union's largest deliberative body) and the Executive Board. We then held special citywide leader trainings, attended by hundreds of members, to take input and develop our approach. We also produced and disseminated a steady stream of high-quality analysis about the nature of the fiscal crisis, including detailed research about the role played by outsourcing and privatization, tax giveaways, and other handouts to the super-wealthy.

These discussions led to an anti-austerity campaign created with rank-and-file leaders that included a plan to "work to rule"—a concerted effort by members to perform only contractually required work and boycott unpaid duties. The plan was adopted in a vote before the House of Delegates. Working to rule proved to be difficult for teachers; many disliked withholding the extra work that makes our connections to students and parents more productive and meaningful. Other elements of the campaign were more successful: wearing union colors on Friday, distributing buttons and literature, and demonstrating against the staffing cuts. We continued to enforce hard-fought rules in the workplace, filing complaints about class size and special education workloads that emphasized the importance of our contract. The fact that the board's financial crisis meant that no relief was forthcoming did not stop us.

All the internal debate, as frustrating and discordant as it was at times, meant that our membership stayed engaged and developed a shared political perspective in the face of deep adversity. We also kept our union from devolving into a talk shop where we debated ideas but failed to involve our members in workplace actions and solidarity. Members did not just receive communications but were actively participating in face-to-face conversations, debates, votes, and actions. Those interactions led to an understanding that the frustrations we faced required a strategic response and increased people's connection to the union during a challenging time.

In order to address the financial problems, we needed long-term, structural changes to the way schools were funded. It was necessary for us to acknowledge the limitations of what we could achieve at that exact moment without letting the bosses off the hook. We also believed in putting forward a positive vision of what fully funded schools and generous public accommodations would mean for our community. So the CTU made direct demands of corporate and financial targets that allowed us to campaign for our vision and conduct broad, effective public outreach.

The first was a campaign against local banks and the Board of Education that made capital a target. Using research by the Action Center on Race and the Economy, we dug into Chicago Public Schools' rapidly increasing involvement in high-risk financial instruments and found that while local government coffers may have been dry, the wealthy corporations and financial institutions involved in those transactions were doing quite well. We argued that the board was "broke on purpose," pointing to the financial decisions that benefited the education privatizers and financiers who were then running the schools at the expense of the school system overall. One example we highlighted was a series of high-risk interest rate hedges (so-called toxic swaps) that contributed to the board owing at least $617 million to Wall Street. We demanded that the banks that had negotiated these instruments return the money to the schools, and we asked the board to sign on to this demand.

We hoped that by exposing the inner mechanisms of municipal financing, we could break the illusion that government is separate and unconnected from the financial institutions that dominate our society. We asked why Bank of America and other investment banks should make hundreds of millions in profits off the public schools at the same time that students go without basic services like counseling or special education. The point of the campaign was not to fix Chicago Public Schools' finances in the short term. We knew Bank of America was unlikely to return any profits it had made on the interest-rate market. The campaign was political—to make it clear to our members, and anyone else who was paying attention, that bosses were cutting services for the poor to protect investment bankers' windfall profits.

CTU members—joined by other union members, housing and disability rights activists, and representatives from community-based organizations such as Grassroots Collaborative, Action Now, and the Brighton Park Neighborhood Council—staged sit-ins in bank lobbies, picketed corporate offices, and spoke out in the media. When the public could see angry members making demands of bankers, it was hard to miss the larger point even if they didn't know how interest-rate swaps worked: these guys got rich while we got screwed.

The 2016 fiscal crisis did not just affect the schools, of course. A wide swath of social service providers, state universities, health care facilities, and other essential institutions were in financial freefall. We decided to organize a citywide general strike to demand that the city close corporate tax loopholes, tax the financial exchanges, end real estate development subsidies, and use the funds to invest in social services.

We struck on April 1, 2016. The coalition that took part in this mass protest included housing rights and immigrant rights organizations, other unions (though only the CTU had all of its members actually walk off the job), Black youth organizations, anti-racist and abolitionist forces, and many more. Nearly 30,000 people demonstrated in Chicago that day. The strike dominated the news, and the forces united in this coalition showed the deadlocked politicians in Springfield that more revenue was needed to fund social services—the only way forward out of the impasse we were facing.

The "Broke on Purpose" campaign, the Justice for Laquan McDonald campaign, and the 2016 general strike emphasized aspirational political goals and sharp critiques of what was wrong with the city. These were not "safe" campaigns; not all CTU members supported them. They were broadly political and targeted specific corporations and institutions, such as Bank of America and real estate developers like Ivanhoé Cambridge. Similarly, when the news of Laquan McDonald's murder at the hands of the Chicago police broke in late 2015, the CTU put itself firmly on the side of the movements, endorsing the emergency marches, passing resolutions, and engaging in local activism against the police presence in our schools. In all these cases, we took a strongly oppositional stance not just toward the Board of Education, but toward larger and more powerful forces in the city. This strategy allowed us to escape the defensive and limited prospects of making demands on a financially starved bureaucracy. Instead, we went on the offensive against some of the most powerful political and financial brokers of Chicago.

* * *

For those of us who campaigned hard for Brandon's election, the buzz of victory has faded into the demands of our work. Some who went into his administration are feeling the pressure of working under sky-high expectations and conditions they did not create. Meanwhile, progress on jobs, housing, policing, and the kind of reform that Brandon promised moves slowly. Others among us continue to build grassroots organizations and resist the urge to read every news story about the new administration as a sign of the ultimate success or failure of our project. The kind of dedication we expect from Chicago's activist community is present throughout the city: volunteers overwhelming migrant centers with offers of help for the immigrants bussed from Texas, neighborhood volunteers and CTU activists organizing youth summer programs, and hundreds coming out to join the UWF and stay involved. But we don't yet have the set of unifying demands and campaigns that we need to push for our priorities and make them a reality.

This is the kind of transition that can disorient activists. We have gone from the dynamic of opposition to the dynamic of a campaign and now to the dynamic of working with our comrade in office, all within a few short months. We will make it through this transition by talking about it—writing about it, discussing it, and maintaining our critical connections to one another. We didn't elect Brandon so that we could sit back, watch the news, and feel smart about our critique—but we also didn't agree to keep our mouths shut when immigrant families get kicked out of a shelter and are forced to sleep in a tent after arriving seven minutes past curfew. We need to do more than simply hold Brandon accountable for living up to his campaign promises; we need our movement and organizational strategies to live up to our own standards.

The work we have been doing over the past decade helps prepare us for the next set of challenges. We built the UWF to be an independent, working-class political organization in order for our forces to be able to influence government directly. Now we need to build it even bigger and use it. We learned that we can develop new layers of leadership and increase rank-and-file activism by leaning into our democratic practices and participation. Now we need to recruit new activists and involve them in the decision-making of our unions, neighborhood groups, and coalitions. And we learned how to make audacious demands on corporate titans and political power brokers. Now we must build campaigns that allow us to march, demonstrate, and call for housing, jobs, green environmental policy, and an end to the carceral state. Our movement is powerful—let's use it to make a better city.

Editor's Note: You can follow Chicago Teachers Union on Facebook, Instagram, and X. Their website is https://www.ctulocal1.org/

References Consulted:

Camarillo, E., & Miller, V. (2023, August 14). Migrant families kicked out of Rogers Park motel for missing curfew are sleeping in tents. *Chicago Sun-Times.* https://chicago.suntimes.com/2023/8/14/23832262/migrant-families-kicked-out-of-rogers-park-motel-for-missing-curfew-are-sleeping-in-tents

Chicago for the People. (2023). *Building bridges and growing the soul of Chicago: A blueprint for creating a more just and vibrant city for all.* https://www.chicago.gov/city/en/depts/mayor/supp_info/transition-report.html

Chicago Teachers Union. (n.d.). *CTU history.* https://www.ctulocal1.org/about/history/

Chicago Teachers Union. (2012). *The schools Chicago's students deserve: Research-based proposals to strengthen elementary and secondary education in the Chicago public schools.* https://www.ctulocal1.org/wp-content/uploads/2019/01/SCSD_Report-2012-02-16.pdf

Chicago Torture Justice Center. (n.d.). *Communities healing from police violence.* https://www.chicagotorturejustice.org/

Farmer, S. (2021, May 5). *Financialization created Chicago public schools' fiscal crisis.* Jacobin. https://jacobin.com/2021/05/chicago-public-schools-cps-fiscal-crisis

Grassroots Education Movement. (n.d.). *GEM member organizations.* GEM Alliance. https://gemchicago.org/gem-member-organizations/

Johnson, C.A. (2020, September 8). Six months into the pandemic, CPS has served more than 21 million free meals and won't let up anytime soon. *The Chicago Tribune.* https://www.chicagotribune.com/2020/09/08/six-months-into-the-pandemic-cps-has-served-more-than-21-million-free-meals-and-wont-let-up-anytime-soon/

Luce, S. (2006, October 3). *Movement for higher pay expanding nationally: Chicago living wage activists take on 'Big Box' retailers.* Labor Notes. https://labornotes.org/2006/10/movement-higher-pay-expanding-nationally-chicago-living-wage-activists-take-%E2%80%98big-box%E2%80%99

National Center for Civil and Human Rights. (n.d.). *Mamie Till: More than a mother.* https://www.civilandhumanrights.org/mamie-till/

Parrish, M., & Ikoro, C. (n.d.). *Chicago public schools and segregation: A historical view of how education decisions have perpetuated segregation*. WTTW. https://interactive.wttw.com/firsthand/segregation/chicago-public-schools-and-segregation

Quinn, G. (Director). (2017). *'63 Boycott* [Film]. Kartequin Films.

Endnotes

1 This chapter was previously published in the Summer 2023 edition of *Hammer & Hope: A Magazine of Black Politics and Culture*. It is republished here with permission.

CHAPTER 8

So We Stand: Minneapolis Federation of Teachers

Greta Callahan, Marcia Howard, and Brianne Kramer

MINNESOTA HAS A rich history of unionism and organizing. The first union began in Rochester in 1861 as the Minnesota State Teachers Association, becoming part of the larger National Education Association later (Crockett & Thorman, 2019). Similar to other teachers unions at this time, the union existed to improve working conditions and pay and impart more professionalism to the field. In April 1970, Minneapolis teachers illegally struck for 14 days, demanding better working conditions, salaries, and benefits (Crockett & Thorman, 2019). The Minnesota Public Employees Labor Relations Act (PELRA) was passed in 1971, giving public employees the right to collectively bargain. An amendment to the Act in 1973 created a limited right to strike (Crockett & Thorman, 2019). The district would not strike again for 50 years. On March 8, 2022, Minneapolis teachers took to the picket line again with a list of demands for the district, particularly focusing on retaining educators of color and providing hourly educational support professionals (ESPs) a living wage (Fortin, 2022). After 14 days on strike, the collective bargaining team struck a tentative agreement, ending the strike. The new contract guaranteed ESPs a more than $4/hour raise, increased hours and days for ESPs, cemented seniority-based layoff protection for teachers of color, increased mental health supports for students, provided teachers the largest raise in over two decades, and created contract-enforced class cap sizes (Bloomquist & Keefer, 2022; Shockman & Krueger, 2022). The following is a conversation between the book editor and two members of the MFT leadership team, Greta Callahan and Marcia Howard, about the union's more recent history and work.

Greta: Over 50 years ago, our union went on an illegal strike. Because of that, PELRA exists here in Minnesota, Public Employee Labor Relations Act. So basically, that strike changed our entire state forever. Since then, a lot has happened. When I got involved with MFT, we were a pop machine union. Put a quarter in and get something out. We still had great contracts and had the best insurance in the state for a single person because of a strong union, but we could barely even mobilize at that time. I also just want to say all the leaders still led us to where we are now, right? It's not like one person came in and changed that. Each person was essential, but then someone named Michelle Wiese ran for president, won, and really did everything she could do in her time to try to bring us to more of an organizing model of a union where people were flexing their muscles more. I would say we could then mobilize much better than we could in the past. I don't know if we were super-organized, but we were mobilized. Then, I was elected May 15th, 2020. So not a lot going on then (sarcasm). The conditions were prime for us to go where we had to go.

Marcia: I would agree with you. I've been in our district and our union since 1998. So, from the 20th Century to the 21st Century, and I saw us under leadership—you put it perfectly—that it was put a quarter in and you get something out. It was about service that you buy and pay for with your union dues, and that was the extent of many people and many of the members' involvement with the union. We would have an end of the year party, and that was great. However, I did see a sea change, and for obvious reasons, because I am currently occupying George Floyd Square. I'm in the middle of a social justice movement. I saw a thread begin to weave its way through our membership and our union, somewhere around 2014–2015, when people in our membership started to be willing to and able to stand with our students and our communities on the streets for Jamar Clark or marching for kids in cages. Then all of a sudden you saw members of our boards being in zip ties, arrested by the police. They started protesting with the knowledge that they may get arrested, so this idea of an activist union and activist membership came to the forefront and under fire, under criticism, from people on the right. "What are you all doing?" What helped was that we could always say: "we're standing for our students." "We're standing for our families."

In May 2020, we had a new union president, and that union president was Greta. As I was out on 38th and Chicago standing for justice as an African

American, as a resident five houses from where George Floyd was lynched, as the teacher of the girl that filmed the death of George Floyd, low and behold who's walking into the square? My union president. That, along with the membership that followed, I honestly believe paved a way for our union members to honestly get the chutzpah to start standing up for ourselves, for our colleagues, for our kids in our communities. I say the George Floyd protest was sort of proving ground and a training ground for what came afterwards, without diminishing the groundwork that our union put in from 2020 to 2022. In order to get us where we were, there was so much organization strategy and mobilization in those 2 years that I think it took even the powers that be by surprise. They didn't know we had it in us, but we had it in us. We had really great leadership and the ability to get so many of our members involved in that. As I've said before, well, they've had practice. They were on Lake Street. They were on University. They were at George Floyd Square. I mean, deep involvement in this movement for Black lives. Then, when we were able to frame our demands as a union in the language of equity and parity and the language of justice. Even with this idea of we're fighting for ourselves. You know, a lot of people would say: "What about the children?" Greta said it exactly. They were going to task us with, "why aren't you thinking of the kids?" Well, we are. Greta said that from the top of a truck in negative five degree weather. She was on the truck. She's like, they're gonna say, "What about the children?" So you respond with, "Exactly!", and we just went with that. It was remarkable.

Greta stated when she took over as union president in May 2020, conditions were created that led them to no other choice than taking the actions they did. Both women explain what was happening in the district that led up to their historic strike and demands for justice.

Greta: Well, we had just been in COVID-19 lockdown and overnight changed the way we were teaching. You know, 2 weeks, not even a week and a half later, George Floyd was publicly lynched in our city. Like Marcia said, it was her student who filmed it for the world to see. Also, in May 2020, our school board voted on a wildly unpopular and harmful district redesign. They did this while no one could attend this meeting because it was online. The redesign displaced about 10,000 students into different schools, a majority were students of color. In addition, this displaced hundreds and hundreds of teachers in our district, and what it did was really pile on to the shit show that was No

Child Left Behind and Race to the Top, where we were fresh starting staff, fresh starting admin, and creating schools where everyone was new and nobody knew what they were doing. Historical memory was gone. We knew what this was—one more way to churn and burn, to dismantle communities, to destroy public schools. I mean, things like that just harms public education in general, but this was done by our district, and through gaslighting people in the name of equity when it only made our schools more segregated. It was so harmful, and everyone was mad, not just our students who had to change schools and our teachers, but our families were furious and many spoke with their feet and got the F out of our district. Others did ride it out. In that short term and throughout the next couple of years, it just progressively seemed to get worse. We were doing so much more with so much less. We had a superintendent who hated women, hated unions, and school board members who were both incompetent and in bed with corporate ed reform groups. We always say the best organizer is the boss. September 2021, internally like Marcia said, we were doing 1,000s of one-on-ones. We were working so hard because we were like, maybe we can get our members on strike by 2025. We hadn't seen over a 2% raise in over 20 years and our education support professionals [ESPs] were making poverty wages and treated like garbage. So we really didn't have a choice.

Marcia: I think, when that was being laid out to our members about really even reaching into their memory for those who had been in the district as long as I had been. At that point, I'd been in for like 24 years. When I came to Minneapolis Public Schools, we were one of the number one educational systems in the United States. We were lauded and applauded for that. But I was there every single in-service, as teachers would go and start the beginning of the school year and be told that we are in fact, the worst. We have the worst outcomes for African Americans somehow, and I'm paraphrasing, it's as if we woke up and decided we were going to make kids of color's lives miserable. They flipped it so that instead of us being the best educational system neck-and-neck with Iowa, we could go anywhere and our license would transfer. They started telling us we're the worst. We're the worst. We're the worst every year. It was as if it was a deliberate attack on our psyche, and it was demoralizing. You saw more and more teachers just say, "Well, there's nothing I can do at this point. They are telling us that we're horrible." This is what we started talking to our members about. Me specifically, as a rank-and-file member, I'd say from the truck—"they have preyed upon white guilt way too long. In a racialized and feminized profession of white women, they have decided the way to undermine public education is to make white women feel so guilty that they run for the hills or they accept anything," including back in the day we used to make more money than all of the surrounding districts. One time I was in an in-service, and I mentioned how much I made with someone who was in the same amount of years in education as me. She turned to me and said, "Well, you're in Minneapolis. You get combat pay." Though I took a little umbrage at that, I didn't care. I made 15% more than she did. Then in 20 years, that flipped. I could make $15,000 more if I were to just go across the river. They have sold out the company store from under us. The only thing that we could do with our members was say, "You have to take a stand. It ends now. We have to take back our district and save our profession." Framing it as nothing less, nothing short of saving our union and saving public education. It resonated when you had a sea of heads nodding because it resonated with their own experience. Those of us who had been in since the 90s, we were like, "You are right. You are absolutely right." Then we came with receipts, and Greta is a powerhouse with that. Yeah, it was a perfect storm. Providence, if you will.

Despite often having the same goals, each local teachers union will focus on issues that impact their members and the students and communities they serve. This often makes union members a target of unsupportive admin and community members. The rise in conservative and neoliberal groups working to erode public education has also hyper-fixated on undermining teachers unions. Greta and Marcia spoke about what sets the Minneapolis Federation of Teachers apart from other active teachers unions.

Greta: We really are a bunch of lefty socialist motherfuckers over here in Minneapolis.

Marcia: We are some badass motherfuckers. We some bad bitches. That's why.

Greta: Yes, we are some baddies over here, and I don't know how it got to be. I do know the more we are on the ground floor, the more we are with children, the more we are seeing what is happening to public education, because we are under such threats here in Minneapolis, the more we've become this way. Whether it's billionaires, corporations, whether it's charter schools. They were trying to introduce vouchers into our state. All of that has made us this way. We don't have a choice. We are teaching real children in a super-segregated city with tons of poverty. That reality, I think, has naturally made our union into the way it is. I will also say unapologetically, Marcia and I and our board who were elected, we have helped collectively bring the people to be like, "No, you shouldn't feel shame feeling this way or supporting these things. Don't let somebody scare you by calling you a socialist or communist or leftist. The labels are irrelevant. You care about human beings and you believe that public education is meant to serve all of our students. We should not have the haves and the have nots, so hold your head up high."

Marcia: That part. Not only do we have people who are motivated by these ideologies, these ideals, we have a deep bench of people who think that way and they were duly elected, which means our membership said yes, these are the people that we want to represent us. So do we have tree hugging eco justice folks? Yup. Do we have badass leftists militants? Yup. Do we have people with deep, deep institutional historical knowledge? Yup. Also, the fact that we are still high school and elementary and middle school teachers that are with our students and their families day in and day out, and we still have the trust of the families. This isn't a radical so left that we have fallen off the edge of the earth. Right? We know the city that we live in because we're in this city as well. So for those of us who have been in the trenches, we just remind folks we know how to fight. This is a fight. Get ready to fight. You got to. If you stay ready, you ain't gotta get ready. That type of language doesn't scare our members, and it doesn't even scare our families. If anyone looks at footage or goes back and looks at our strike, almost every strike line was full of our students and our families as well. They were supplied by our families. This is what Minneapolis got up to when we went on strike. Mind you, we had just been protesting for years, right? It wasn't just George Floyd. It was George Floyd, and then it was Winston Smith, and then it was Dante Wright. We have an edifice for protest that still exists. George Floyd Square is a living, breathing memorial and place of resistance that field trips come to. So everyone has a vested interest in shaping our city and our neighborhoods in the way in which we want it to be. All of that collided with this energy behind our strike. People initially said, "Oh, this is going to be 3 days. It's going to be 5 days." How long were we out there, though? We were out there for 14 days. There always seemed to be this nascent threat of "the people are going to turn against you." When in fact, people turned against the district because they were on fuck shit, and the longer we stayed out, the more obvious it was.

Greta and Marcia went on to discuss the way in which MFT is organized and how they make decisions amongst their membership.

Greta: In our membership, we have two chapters. We have the Education Support Professionals [ESP] Chapter, which is mostly unlicensed hourly workers, and we have the Teacher Chapter, which consists of two licensed contracts, and that is the Birth to 12 contract and the Adult Education contract. In our Teacher Chapter contracts, we have nurses, social workers, occupational therapists, psychologists, you name it. If they're licensed, with the exception of principals, they're probably in our unit. Our leadership structure is proportional to each chapter's membership numbers. Then each chapter has a president, first vice president, second vice president, secretary, and then we have a joint treasurer. Our at-large members of each chapter correlate to the number of members each chapter has. We have all of those positions elected by the broader membership. Our joint board meets monthly and makes decisions about money and items we support. A lot of that can also happen at member meetings. Members can put out a resolution saying we're going to support something in the broader community, so there are always two ways to pass resolutions or initiatives.

Based on what the MFT leaders had shared, it sounded like their mission/vision of their union had changed over time, particularly as the focus on social justice became prominent. The current mission states: "The mission of Minneapolis Federation of Teachers, Education Support Professionals, Related-Service Professionals and Retirees is to promote, strengthen and improve public schools. This is done through shared decision making of those who are closest to the students. We exist to protect and promote the well-being of our members. We build with our families, students, community, district, and other labor unions a movement that fights for the resources needed to advance these principles. We accomplish this mission through sustainable organizing, collective action, collective bargaining, high quality professional practice and political activism" (Minneapolis Federation of Teachers and Educational Support Professionals).

Greta: That's funny you should ask because we didn't have one. We wrote one under our former president and recently our board updated it. We need to have the strongest public schools possible. It goes hand-in-hand with racial justice, social justice, environmental justice—strong public schools are the answer to many of the problems that we are seeing in society.

Marcia: We also tie that in with economic parity with our members. We will not have strong public schools in Minneapolis if anyone can jump ship and instantly earn more money, or if they're not attempting to attract and retain teachers of color in order to teach commensurate students, right? That is something that I'm constantly harping on, actually. Don't be shy. Talk about pay me, pay us, so I don't dismiss. I grew up in poverty. I was the kid with the free lunch, and that was back when we would have the lunch cards that were coded as to whether or not you had free lunch or reduced lunch. Because of that, the fact that almost all of our ESPs and their children qualify for food assistance. There are teachers who are educators that I work beside in the ESP chapter who literally make less than the student that they are charged with sitting beside in my classroom. He goes to Target and makes more money than she made sitting beside him, and she's college educated. I am a strong proponent of receipts. Being able to bring up those anecdotes and have the person in the audience saying, "Yep," and everyone, again, that resonance of this applies to me, this applies to my colleague. So making sure that is in our head as we are going into any type of vote, as we're going into any type of meeting with our members, which we meet in our chapter once a month. It's important that they understand that the union is them. They are the union. That as long as we have people power, we're bound together with this vision and this mission. If we keep going in the way in which we started, especially in 2021–2022 with all that strong organizing, I think we'll get closer and closer to being a vanguard against the undermining of public education and our union in Minnesota because we see what happens when you don't stand your ground. We see what happens. We've seen it in Louisiana. We've seen it in Wisconsin. We're seeing it in Florida. We need to be careful, and by being careful, we can be dangerous. Who we affect are the powers that be who really want to use Minnesota, and Minneapolis in particular. If they can break us, then we're the beta test for other cities in other states, and not on our watch. Not with MFT. So we stand.

Greta and Marcia went on to share what the current focus of MFT was, which was especially important coming on the heels of their strike and the other work happening within the union.

Greta: Everyone is quitting, as you probably know, like everywhere else. I was just with a few of our teachers at the school I taught at and they were like, "we've been up here throwing buckets of water off of this leaky ship together, and we just stood up and looked around, and nobody's there anymore. Why would we keep doing this to a sinking ship? I mean, this is why we went on strike. If we can have a strong contract, if we can retain educators, we will have strong schools. We will have the schools our students deserve." So we are already back in the next contract fight, and with that we have been working our asses off getting everything we deserve at the legislative level, and have accomplished more than we have in many of our lifetimes. So the district is about to see more money than they ever have, well, since 1991 or something. Yet, like every other district on Earth after a strike, they're like, "Oh, we have to close schools now." So a huge focus is on our community, whether that's our community coalition, our families, making sure that we are united moving into this contract campaign because we could be on the streets again in a year. Of course, we want to avoid that at all costs. Like Marcia said, we just always have to be ready. We believe if we do not win the things that our kids and staff and families deserve, the Minneapolis Public Schools will not exist.

Part of this current focus surrounds maintaining George Floyd Square, which Marcia and other community members are occupying until the city meets the demands. While the world watched from their tv screens or followed on social media, community members came together to demonstrate and demand justice.

Marcia: I was sitting here on this porch, May 25th. It was Memorial Day in 2020. I used my porch as an ad hoc classroom during COVID-19, and we were in a lockdown for COVID-19. The hullabaloo from the corner . . . it's about 263 steps from where I'm standing right now. I heard it from here. It was only later that I realized that Darnella had filmed the murder of someone at our corner store. Initially, all I did was step outside my front door and hand out hand sanitizer and masks to people who were walking by because they were heading there to protest, but eventually I would go out to see what was up. Frankly, my husband and I wound up on this porch for days and days on end as the city went into an uprising. All the unrest invited people from all points unknown. There's a lot of argument about whether, or to what extent outside agitators were here, but they were here because I sneaked down to the park at the end of my block and saw these out-of-town plates or where people who would take their plates off. I would see the scores of young white boys on bikes was the rallying cry. That's a normal occurrence; you know, someone's going to the creek, but these were people who were here for ruckus.

I'm a former Marine. I'm retired. I would be on my porch at the ready and galvanized my neighbors to prepare to basically defend our block from ne'er-do-wells.

This was not the protesters because we were, in fact, part of the protests. After the initial uprising, many of us stayed in the square to protest. They kept asking us to go and clear the area. We put up barricades, and then they said, "Why won't you leave? What do you stand for?" We said, "For justice." They made a mistake by asking, "What does justice look like?" So we went up and down the streets, in and out of houses. We asked our students, everybody who's lived under the yoke of the third precinct. "What do you want? What do you need to thrive?" Now that we're in the catbird seat, they're asking us, "What do we want? What would make us leave?" Those answers became the 24 Demands.

When we presented the 24 Demands to the city, to the county, to the state, to the then-President Trump, something interesting happened. They answered them. We wound up going into negotiations. So just like in a union, you bargain. Me and two other of my co-laborers went to City Hall and started bargaining for the 24 Demands. We've been in negotiations for the last 3 years. Watching us collectively as just the hoi polloi, just citizens, stand our ground, refuse to move under pain of death. Actually, if you're at all familiar with George Floyd Square as an autonomous zone, police were not coming in. If things would get rowdy or the powers that be sent agents in—and you don't have to believe me, go to truthout.org. or just read the DOJ report—there had been attempted incursions and undermining for years, and yet we stood our ground. That took organization. That took strategy. That took leadership. Now, I say, and I will repeat here, I don't run nothing but my mouth, but I do run my mouth. So it took me being out there 24 hours a day, sleeping out there, maybe coming here to use the bathroom. It's been 3 years. It's one of the longest political occupations in American history. Some of that was afforded by the fact that I didn't go back to school. I took a leave of absence that I was able to do because obviously, under a lot of stress, took a leave, and then AFT and MFT supported that leave. Then, I was able to organize community members, and that is paying off even now.

The connections that we are forging with community who feel an affinity for not only the fight, but the fact that we constantly say it's all connected: the fight for Black lives, the fight for Indigenous lives, the fact that our colleagues, our friends, our family were appalled by kids being in cages. It is all connected. Our health concerns, whether it is the Roof Depot and the threatened demolition of that, or the HERC incinerator, or a metal foundry that's polluting the air and making it so that many of our Indigenous students have the heart or the ribbon beside their name, and it almost always indicates that they have some respiratory infection. It's all connected. So getting people to be in that mindset is something I can either holler from a bullhorn or say at the top of a truck, or just in a chapter meeting on Zoom. So nothing's an intellectual leap or even an ideological leap now that it's all connected. I keep a body cam on when I'm outside. I have a sort of popular social media presence, where I'm showing them exactly what's happening. Now, we'll continue that because people have gotten so despondent when they realize just how much is stacked against us as educators, how much is stacked up against us in this particular district that I believe the antidote to despondency, the antidote to despair is information, where you realize, "Oh, yeah, it feels like they got you on the ropes, but did you know this and this and this?" I'm committed going into the next year of doing a better job of letting them know because where there's knowledge, there's power, and where there's people, there's power. Then you combine both of that. I'm going to want the powers that be to be shaking in their boots, not enough to get a federal indictment, but I want them to be shaking in their boots because what you're going to have is an informed membership and informed neighborhoods, informed communities, where they honestly are able to speak truth to power and have receipts to back it up, because they're really doing a number on our district.

As big of a win as we felt that we have, we have a long road to hoe. We have a long road to hoe. There are some people trying to throw salt and salt the earth. They don't care about our district, about our families, or about our members. They don't care. They don't. The call is coming from inside the house. But if you're gonna come at them, you gotta come ready to lop heads, metaphorically. Because if we miss, then it's going to be the downfall of public education in Minnesota. And if Minnesota falls, I swear to you, this is the birthplace of public education and the birthplace of charter schools. If Minnesota falls, then the entire United States is going to fall right along with it. We cannot let public education in Minnesota fall. It's not a small feat that I'm asking of our membership, but I'm going to demand that this is what they do if they give a fuck because our babies depend on it and an informed, educated, critically analytical citizenry depends on that. Some people think that I speak in hyperbole, and I'm like, "No, you don't understand. That is what is at risk." We don't want our best and brightest teachers to say, "You know what, I'm smart enough to fucking go. I'm smart enough to cut and run right now." That is what they have tried to engender. I'm not going to lie and say that it's not working. That is what we have to fight against, but I'm ready to fight.

Marcia: One thing that I do want to bring up is the fact that people are now looking at Minneapolis, specifically as a galvanizing spark for labor, period. For how much solidarity we're showing between labor unions in this state, the fact that we are in close communication, that we are in solidarity, that even young and nascent unions are looking toward MFT and they are finding support. I mean, when you look at the people who turn to MFT to be on their strike lines, to our social media apparatus, to sort of support and show solidarity. That's not a small thing. To the point where I go and I speak across the country about our union and about labor. People keep saying once is an incident, twice is a coincidence, and then three times is starting a trend. What's going on in Minnesota? They keep saying what's going on, right? Because they don't know how we got here, but I know what it looks like and lives like to be able to literally pick my phone up and call multiple union leaders and know that at the snap of the fingers, they're gonna show up. They're gonna show up. Be mindful, when we declared a strike, there were multiple [unions] who were all going to strike at the same time. We weren't playing.

Greta: So we worked closely with the ESPs, the adult educators, and we had been doing so much work with the other unions like SPFE (who was slated to go out on strike the same day as us and settled the night before), as well as those in MPS so that they were on the same timeline as us, including our bus drivers, clerical staff, and food service workers. One of them, SEIU, took a strike vote during our strike! Because the district was terrified that another one of their units was about to join us, they got the biggest raise they'd ever seen and were able to settle without hitting the streets. They were picking us off. Like Marcia said, we have so many wins from the strike that are not in our contract and that is one of them. Starbucks, Trader Joe's, everyone has called us up asking, "How did you do it? Will you support us?" I also think because it was in thick of COVID-19 they didn't think their members could get there, and they weren't there even though conditions were so bad for everyone. We helped lead the way, and we showed the world what solidarity looks like. We teachers were on the streets saying, "We are out here for hourly workers. We are on strike for our ESP colleagues. We are on strike for Black lives." That was essential. I think what Marcia and I, and people who are in agreement, also want [is] to educate other unions on, don't dumb down seniority. If that is the way you're trying to retain educators of color, that actually isn't the answer. What we were fighting for was a collective package, and what we won was one teeny-tiny piece. It was something very brave that we did to try to help retain educators of color—but spoiler alert—that alone does not retain educators of color.

The media focused on one particular piece of the contract negotiations, which focused on reduction in force (RIF) and retaining educators of color. Right-wing media took hold of this one part of the contract, spinning this into a ridiculous "reverse-racism" argument, while other media outlets did not cover all the other contractual wins MFT gained in this historic strike. The primary goal of this contract was to retain educators of color and pay ESPs a living wage.

Greta: I'd say first of all, everything we were doing or fighting for was going to retain educators of color if we won it. Our number one demand on the streets was a living wage for hourly workers who were mostly Black women. That alone was going to retain educators of color because educators does not mean someone with a license. We did have a comprehensive package that we have proposed around doing specific things to retain educators of color. Again, this is because the majority of our students are students of color. The majority of our teachers are white. Even before my time, we had been putting language out there around going out of seniority order if there are layoffs. Essentially, if the person who's lowest in the seniority number is a person of color, you'd skip them and go to the next person if there are layoffs. That had been presented in the past and didn't pass. The district was a little scared of that. This last round we not only proposed that, but had a comprehensive package around an anti-biased, anti-racist committee support council with 10 mentors of color, specifically for educators of color. There was so much to it. It was written by and for people of color. We made sure that all of our contract language went to an equity-focused team, which was people who are not on our team but were rank-and-file educators of color to look through our language and find what's missing. We actually did that with all of our proposals.

The district very much only focused on the seniority part. If they were rooted in having more educators of color, they would not have done that. They would have agreed to our proposal in a heartbeat, and they didn't. In fact, they ended up using that to stall until the very end. They wouldn't talk to us about pay. They wouldn't talk to us about class size or caseload during the strike; essentially trying to get us to just get rid of seniority in so many ways. That was an interesting part of our strike because it did gain some legs through false communication or communication with false information. At the end of the day, we, of course, stood our ground in what we believed in, but all of our demands were rooted in that.

What we ended up winning overall was a living wage for education support professionals. The highest raise teachers have seen in over 20 years. We got class size caps in the contract. We got more mental health supports for our students. We gained this language around seniority to go out-of-order if there are layoffs and excessing to retain educators in underrepresented groups. Eventually, Alpha News, which is a crazy right-wing news source here, got wind of that last part and then Fox News picked it up. So Marcia and I had to be on *Good Morning America* because the extremists are like, “Oh, they’re firing white people before people of color.” So it also is a good opportunity to do more education around what seniority even is. A lot of unions around the country will be like, “Wow, that was so brave. That was so cool.” We’re like, “Yes, AND that is not the answer. So don’t get gaslit into thinking that’s all you should focus on.” Because the truth is, we’re still not paying people like they are in St. Paul across the river. We’re still hemorrhaging educators of color when you have huge class sizes, when you have horrible working conditions, when your students are not supported.

Excessing and layoffs are a symptom of a disorganized, dysfunctional district who doesn’t plan properly or retain their students from year to year. If it was up to us, excessing and layoffs would never happen so that our students’ educational experience would be safe and stable. But it does happen, so we need an objective plan in place for when they excess or layoff teachers, so that it is fair and the least amount of harm is caused. So, like every other district, we have contract language in place that we both agreed to use WHEN the district chooses to destabilize our schools and students’ education by excessing or laying off educators. Without that language, without using seniority order, which is the fairest and most objective process, racist principals could get rid of people of color, ageist principals could get rid of those with more experience, cheap principals could get rid of the most expensive, etc. It is because of seniority that our students have a more stable education.

Marcia: We still have to educate folks. The second someone talks about school closures or layoffs, that ain’t got nothing to do with us. That has to do with the district. To be honest, the district is still on fuck shit. This is about money that they have access to, that they’re not utilizing properly because they want to create a false sense of crisis. There is a crisis in you're not paying people a wage that's commensurate with the districts around them to the point where it's almost as if you lay out bread crumbs and wonder why ants are at your picnic. You stop paying people the wage that it's expected in the Twin Cities and then wonder why an educator of color would jump to another district, especially when you've changed the ethnic dynamics of the school that they may have been in. I'll give you an example. I'm at Roosevelt High School in South Minneapolis. My school used to be 70% Black. I'm looking at the incoming freshmen, and because they did the CDD (comprehensive district design—the redesign) . . . I teach to transgress. I became a Black teacher in a Black neighborhood at a Black school for a reason. If I were to chase my students now, they not only chased Black educators out, they've been chasing Black students out of the district as well. So yes, we have a task ahead of us. I'm going to have to really, really get into conversation with folks who feel as if you use a metaphor, a sinking ship. Is this a sinking ship or is this something viable?

In 2020, before we ever went on strike, multiple newspapers said that the proposed CDD that was just being bandied about had already been sussed out and predicted to have a massive exodus of students from Minneapolis Public Schools. So sure enough, when during all the hullabaloo our students start exiting even over North Minneapolis, just going further north into northern suburbs. "Oh, wow. They must be upset about the strike." No, they weren't. This happened the exact way it was planned. When we speak of, are you trying to say that the district is making deliberate actions along with the school board, mind you, deliberate actions in order to get people to leave? Well, yeah, they call that churn. I am a colonized person, descended from enslaved people. What we know if we look at history is when someone wants to colonize, they go into the land, and they cause turmoil, and you cause people to leave as refugees. Then you announce and pronounce there's nothing to see here. Nothing is worthy. This is all primitive. This is all just land. Then, all of a sudden, you realize that there is wealth there in the form of whatever resources that were there all along. You bring in people to take it over when there's blood in the street by land, and the blood was created by this turn that was instigated by the district itself, and the high money developers, and so called philanthropic organizations, that have invested for long-term goals of using our buildings to take public money to fund charter schools that discriminate, with no regard for ADA, with no regard for adding desegregation. So they're going to have for-profit, CEO-controlled, private education, and they're going to say, "Well, it's the failures of public school." No, it's the undermining. That's the way capitalism works.

Greta: And they're gonna do that on public dollars.

Marcia: Because the first thing you know . . . I've owned four restaurants. You never spend your own money. Right? You don't spend your own money. We're calling it out. There are people who are mad. They're mad at Greta for calling it out. Mad at me for calling it out, but we'll continue to do that.

It is important to note that these contractual wins were voted on by 75% of union membership, which was a majority of white women. Greta and Marcia were asked how they were able to mobilize this high percentage of members.

Greta: The same way I get 25 kindergarteners and Marcia gets 200 high school students to believe that reading is the coolest thing on earth. When we surveyed our members, shocker, their number one priority was *not* to retain educators of color. It was *not* for ESPs to earn a living wage. But the leadership we had and have was unlike anything we had before. Our leadership did then and does now reflect our students. People knew conditions were bad. They knew that they had to get out on strike. We never said you don't deserve a raise, but we knew exactly what we were doing with communication. I really believe that we did not F up in how we were communicating what we were fighting for to the public and to our members.

We still have those people who are like, "I didn't get a raise." Bye, be angry, but this is the direction our union is going in, and if you don't like it, you can step up and try to do something about it. That was just the initial part of it. Marcia was running George Floyd Square and was not elected in our union at that time. I always say we are such a good team. We're just as paranoid as the other person is about everything happening, but also we complement each other so well. When I was in the darkest pits of hell negotiating, she led our union on the streets. I led behind closed doors and she led the streets. She helped me as doubt crept in, as fear and uncertainty crept in because that was the boss's full-time job. Marcia kept our members grounded every single day and every single member will say that now. They'll say, "if Marcia wasn't out there on the truck, talking me down from the ledge every single day, I would have jumped ship and people didn't." We had 95% of our members on the line on day 14. That is unheard of. Without her, it wouldn't have happened.

Marcia: The thing that helped me out was number one, we had practice at being at George Floyd Square and Minneapolis had practice. I'm going to be honest, looking at me when we have dances in high school, you have a chaperone, and a lot of people because I have a huge social media presence and they trust me in an autonomous zone with gunshots and agents of chaos all around. They trust me to bring them information that's accurate. When I was on the truck, when we were on the strike line, the fact that I would literally leave GFS every morning and show up to strike lines and constantly reiterate this: our bargaining team, we have to support them behind those closed doors. They are the fist; we are the glove. We have to strike together. We cannot be separated. We have to trust that our elected leader was going to do what we sent her in there to do; that our bargaining team was going to do what they do as fear and doubt and uncertainty crept in personally with people. How are we going to get paid? How much is this going to affect us? Is this going to affect our pension? Then I was constantly being the person to say this is why we're out here. This is what you're going to do. I'll admit this here, and at some point, I'll write about this: racial dynamics actually have a deleterious effect, right? If you fall into stereotypes, if you play into racial stereotypes or dynamics, you can't do that long term. However, short term, the heuristics, the rule of thumb of knowledgeable sage, Black woman that they trust . . . Plus, I'm going to be straight with you. I'm a teacher, 24 years here in the same school, mind you. This isn't just pie in the sky that we're talking about. These are real things. When we give anecdotes, she [Greta] and I can talk about our real colleagues, our real coworkers, our real friends, our real students, our real families. So when I'm looking people in the face and I'm looking at them, and I say, "I make $84,000 a year," I'll be damned if I'm going to talk to somebody making $15 an hour and give up on them. Because I can count on one hand the amount of times I've taught with more than one Black teacher at Roosevelt, but I can tell you on two hands every day that I'm with ESPs of color. If we're going to stand here, and it's 12 degrees, and you're telling me that we can kvetch about what we're getting paid when we know that our colleagues are getting this . . . Being able to hold them to the fact that we are. What they gonna do? Look to the left, look to the right, and tell these sisters they don't deserve the money? Is that what they gonna do? No, they won't. So it took a little bit of reminding them constantly. That if the least of us ain't getting it, the most of us ain't getting it. We had to use that as the barometer for success—that amount of solidarity between chapters.

Frankly, it's a class issue. Always has been, right? Getting them to see that's what we have to do. If we're not fighting for them, then how am I going to trust you if you fight for me as a Black person? This is where we got them. Those same white teachers were on the street. I don't care if all they did was put a sign on their door, "Black Lives Matter," as if it was the blood of the lamb to keep the protests from going over to their property. They can always think about, "Okay, where was I during George Floyd? What have I been in this protest?" A lot of people were in that sort of, "I have to walk that talk," so we benefited from that. I don't think just during the strike. I think our students have benefited from that because a lot of people have done a lot of soul searching about where they stand and how is that practice within their classroom? So praxis, practice, what does it look like as a teacher in a predominantly student of color district? It made it . . . I won't say easier, but what it did do was make it more harmonious to work in concert with the people. I mean, Greta and the whole bargaining team, they worked overnight. Every hour that the Lord sent them, they were working, and by the end they were so obviously punch drunk from the down and dirty tactics that were happening that people will ever know just how bad it got. Because, again, the powers that be were trying to do something more than just negotiate a contract. I can look and look at her and say what they did was not historic. It was *heroic* that they survived that with their skin intact. Because I can't. Girl, I'd have been in jail. It was so dirty. So when they came out and we had our TA—our tentative agreement—I actually did a social media post. I said, by all means, you can vote yes on this or no on this, but understand, those are our fighters. You can rub their shoulders and say, "Go back in there." Do you want our fighters to go back in there another round? Do you trust that they're going to be victorious? If we think we've gotten what we can get this round, understand 2 years, we're going to be right back out here. Maybe not in a strike, but in negotiations.

I had so many people inbox me and say, "I didn't know what to do until I saw that post" because they were conflicted. Then thank God for whatever reason, everybody was sick towards those last days, and not just COVID-19. I don't know if it was stress or whatever, but I wound up being there during the reading of our strike vote and managed to get the exact moment—not the strike vote, but the agreement. At the moment when we all agreed to accept the TA, people were in tears and hugging each other and joyful. I've had other people come to me and say, "I didn't know which way to feel until I saw that." I think that speaks to how powerful collective action is about that sort of feedback, making sure that we are open with our emotions about things and understand that there is such a thing as communal emotion. By seeing us joyful in our War Room at the local union, got people saying, "Okay, this is good." The day we walked back into school . . . the tears because that's where we wanted to be, but we weren't going to just accept anything. Right? We wanted some wins, and we got some. But that's just the beginning, and that's all we keep saying. It's just the beginning.

Greta: I mean, people who went in to get a raise were spewing snippets of Marcia's speeches, saying "I am here for my colleagues. I am here for them." It was just beautiful and eventually effortless. That's leadership.

In addition to some of the contractual wins, the union also saw several other things happen to benefit union members.

Greta: We got rid of our superintendent. We got rid of a horrible school board member, and the head of HR, who resigned in the middle of our strike. They couldn't even make it the 3 weeks. We've flipped our entire school board since then, and we are in the search for a better superintendent. Those are things that are not on paper but were essential and were some of our goals behind the scenes. Here's who we want to get rid of in this process, and I'm sure they had the same for us, but we are still here.

The conversation closed with their ideas for what MFT would focus on next.

Marcia: I believe for our organization's next steps is that we walk with more member knowledge. I have really, really thought about what is good in action, inoculation for what we call lovingly "fuck shit." That can be psychological, and our morale—how do we guard against that? I think member knowledge and education is going to be key. We'll get more buy-in to action because we cannot have 80 people doing the work for 4,000. It needs to be a deep enough bench where no one gets burnt out. No one wants to be looked at as a guru. Nobody wants to look like we're talking from down on high. Our members should be coming in and out of our local, like this they house, right, because it's theirs. This idea of I don't run nothing but my mouth. Greta don't run nothing but her mouth. This is our union, and then they take charge for our collective good because we have our communities and our kids and our colleagues in mind. That's going to be the next steps for me.

Greta: We are at the threat of losing our public schools, which is the best thing government has ever done, besides mail. Public schools serve every child.

So, it is only up to us, and our union is the only thing standing in the way of us becoming a city of charters and a state of vouchers. So it's like Marcia said, it is every 2 years we are negotiating again. We learned so much from the strike, and we're not messing around. We have such a beautiful community coalition right now. We are working hand-in-hand with our families, with our students, and with each other, and those at the top of our district don't know what the fuck they're doing anymore because they've all jumped off and are looking for other jobs and have gone somewhere else. At New Teacher Orientation, we have new educators telling us, "It's because of your strike and strong union that I left my district. I want to work for MPS because of MFT." I promise you that's not happening at the management level.

We are it. We are our only hope. Our kids deserve that. Our city deserves that. We truly, truly in our heart of hearts believe that. This is the answer to a thriving, beautiful city. I always think of Derek Chauvin, who murdered George Floyd. We need our roots to be healthy and to get everything we need along the way in order to be the best, healthiest tree, which in turn makes the best, healthiest forest. Who were his teachers? How strong were his schools? How much nurturing and critical thinking happened in his formative years? It starts at birth. We are a piece of that and by having strong public schools, we can create wonderful people who know every kind of person and care about others and have the time to learn those lessons because right now, that's being stripped from us in the classroom. I can't tell you how many times I had a principal come in and ask, "Why are your kids painting? Where are they playing? What learning target does that fulfill?" But we know as educators that stuff is essential. Our kids need the arts. They need to be nurtured. They need to play with kids who are not the same as them. They need to gain critical thinking skills. They need an educational system drenched in humanity!

We cannot keep doing this. Our kids are not robots. We are not going to answer to the 1% anymore. We are not going to let them grow up and work at Kraft and never question why a few people hold all the wealth, others hold the guns, and the rest of us are struggling. No, it is up to us. So everything we do, every move we make—is about our kids. Our public schools. *That* is our North Star.

Editor's Note: You can follow Minneapolis Federation of Teachers on Facebook and X. Their website is https://www.mft59.org/.

References

Bloomquist, M., & Keefer, W. (2022, March 8). *What to know about the Minneapolis teachers union strike.* MplsStPaul. https://mspmag.com/arts-and-culture/minneapolis-teachers-union-strike/

Crockett, K., & Thorman, C. (2019). *The history of Minnesota's teachers' unions: From 1861 until today.* Educated Teachers. https://www.educatedteachersmn.com/app/uploads/2019/04/TeachersUnionHistoryPaper-3.2019.pdf

Fortin, J. (2022, March 25). Minneapolis teachers reach a deal to end their strike. *The New York Times.* https://www.nytimes.com/2022/03/25/us/minneapolis-teachers-strike.html

Shockman, E., & Krueger, A. (2022, March 25). *Deal reached to end Minneapolis teachers strike; classes expected to restart Tuesday.* MPR News. https://www.mprnews.org/story/2022/03/25/tentative-agreement-reached-to-end-minneapolis-educators-strike

CHAPTER 9

Black Lives Matter at School and the Ongoing Pursuit of Educational Justice for Black Lives

Denisha Jones

> *"What, to the American slave, is your Fourth of July?*
> *I answer: a day that reveals to him, more than all other days in the year, the gross injustice and cruelty to which he is the constant victim."*
>
> —FREDERICK DOUGLAS, 1852

> *"What, to the Black child, is your institution of public schooling?*
> *I answer: an institution that reveals to them, more than all the other institutions, the gross injustice and cruelty to which they are the constant victim."*
>
> —DENISHA JONES, 2023

IN ONE OF his most famous speeches, Frederick Douglass shames America for celebrating freedom and liberty, commemorating the signing of the Declaration of Independence while continuing to uphold the legal chattel enslavement of Black people. He questions why he is being asked to celebrate the supposed independence of a nation and the greatness of the men who declared the men of this nation to be equal, but did not include him and did not bestow this independence to all. Before delivering those infamous lines shared above, Douglass clarifies that given the irony of a nation celebrating freedom and equality while maintaining enslavement, the time has come to denounce this country for its ongoing crimes against humanity. He exposes the many contradictions in celebrating liberty, denouncing tyranny, offering prayers, and giving thanks as nothing more than a vain sham full of mockery and hypocrisy. Despite his intense admonishment of this American farce, he ends his speech with a renewed commitment to hope that this empire, like others before it, will fall, knowledge will spread, and people worldwide will hear each other's calls for freedom.

When asked to write a chapter about the work of education justice activists, advocates, and agitators working within the current neoliberal assault on education, I felt it was time to denounce America's institution of public schooling. Before I could properly tell the story of how a grassroots uprising for educational justice for Black lives took root, I felt it was necessary also to point out the irony and many contradictions embedded in America's supposed "Great Equalizer" (Johnson, 2006). As a public school survivor, teacher educator, and education justice activist, I often question how I am expected to remain invested in this farce we call democratic public schooling and prepare others to participate in this institution. Though the work of education activists keeps me somewhat hopeful that we will one day achieve education justice for all, it does not make the painful realization that the institution of schooling is a weapon of education colonization (Spring, 2016) any easier to accept. Thus, in the spirit of Douglass, I will first expose how the institution of schooling in America has been a tool to erase Black humanity before I offer the national Black Lives Matter at School movement as an example of contemporary Black fugitive pedagogy (Givens, 2021). However, first I must share how I have come to differentiate education from schooling and why that is an important distinction for understanding the ongoing pursuit of educational justice for Black lives.

Education for Liberation vs. Schooling for the Status Quo

In rewording Douglass' quote, I specifically used the institution of public schooling instead of education because I remain committed to believing in education as the practice of freedom (Freire, 2005; hooks, 1994). Nonetheless, I acknowledge that the institution of public schooling, often used interchangeably with public education, is the master's tool to maintain the status quo. To reconcile the lesson from Audre Lorde (1984) on how the master's tools will never destroy the master's house and the declarations from hooks and Freire that education must be the practice of freedom, I distinguish between schooling to uphold systems of oppression and education for liberation. The American public schooling system was designed to educate its children, but as an institution, it does not pursue freedom through education for all. In fact, it has been routinely used to deny educational freedom to Black, Indigenous, and People of Color (BIPOC) since this country was founded.

Though many of the scholars whose work I will share do not always make this distinction, I will make critiques against schooling while offering education, specifically liberatory education, as the goal of education activist work. Shujaa (1993) provides a helpful explanation of how education and schooling differ when he shares his view "that schooling is a process *intended* to perpetuate and maintain the society's existing power relations and the institutional structures that support those arrangements" (p. 330) and "education, in contrast to schooling, is the process of transmitting from one generation to the next knowledge of the values, aesthetics, spiritual beliefs, and all things that give a particular cultural orientation its uniqueness" (p. 330-1). He argues that though there is significant overlap in the processes of education and schooling, "the failure to take into account differing cultural orientations and unequal power relations among groups that share membership in a society" (p. 329) keeps those overlapping processes from achieving the same goal.

Shujaa (1993) offers a conceptual model to explore how schooling maintains existing unequal power distribution and argues that for Black people to achieve the goals of schooling, they must have an education intentionally aligned with a cultural orientation guided by Black history and identity. Public schooling in the United States does not include a cultural orientation that uplifts Black humanity; thus, it cannot ensure that Black children experience the democratic ideals of schooling. Education for liberation and the practice of freedom acknowledges the relationship between schooling and oppression and seeks to unshackle our agency to disrupt the cycle of socialization (Harro, 2002). Thus, I offer this chapter as a response to work that Shujaa (1993) noted needs to be done:

> The critical task confronting us is broadening our understanding of the role that the strategic differentiation of education and schooling can play in the success of African-American resistance to political and cultural domination and in guiding the development

> of a new world order in which egalitarian relationships between cultures and replace exploitative hierarchies. (p. 349)

Schooling as a Tool to Erase Black Humanity

Scholars have documented the many ways that education has been used to deny equal rights to Black people since they arrived in chains in 1619 (Boutte & Bryan, 2019; Busey & Dowie-Chin, 2021; Dumas & ross, 2016; King, 2014; Ladson-Billings, 2003; Mayorga & Picower, 2018; Spring, 2016). For most people who understand this history, it was easy to believe that racist ideas led to racist practices, but historian Ibram Kendi (2016) contends that it was the opposite, and racist ideas were used to justify racist practices, mainly the chattel enslavement of Africans. Slavery was not a new practice in other parts of the world, but the chattel enslavement of a race of people was new and thus warranted new ideas to justify building a Christian nation with slave labor.

Spring (2016) documented how the need to justify stealing the land from the Indigenous led English settlers to justify their beliefs in cultural superiority through "the growth of white racism and cultural chauvinism" (p. 4). As the spread of white supremacy became tethered to the birth of a nation, deculturization became the tool, and schools became the vehicle to maintain dominance over those deemed inferior. Spring (2016) defined deculturalization as "a conscious attempt to replace one culture and language with another that is considered 'superior'" (p. 1) and one of several "educational methods of colonization" used by English colonizers. He notes that Indigenous, Black, and Latinx groups "primarily experienced cultural genocide, deculturalization and denial of education" while "immigrant groups have mostly experienced assimilation and hybridity" (p. 5). I contend that the process of deculturization combined with anti-Blackness has resulted in numerous attempts to erase Black humanity through public schooling. Furthermore, the current neoliberal populist attacks on teaching history, which have led to a resurgence in book bans and legislation prohibiting teaching critical race theory (CRT), is the newest method of schooling colonization.

Dumas and ross (2016) define anti-Blackness as more than racism targeted towards Black people, but "refers to a broader antagonistic relationship between blackness and (the possibility of) humanity" (p. 429). Black people remained trapped in an identity that limited them to property, and any attempts to engage as full citizens were met with recurring types of anti-Black violence. Boutte and Bryan (2019) identified five types of "anti-Black violence in schools: (1) physical, (2) symbolic, (3) linguistic, (4) curricular and pedagogical, and (5) systemic" (p. 5). To underscore how American schooling has historically and currently engages in education colonization, I will provide examples of how physical, symbolic, and curricular and pedagogical anti-Black violence was enacted in the past and are alive and well today.

Table 9.1.

Types of Anti-Black Violence in Schools

Types of Anti-Black Violence in Schools (Boutte & Bryan, 2019)	**Definition**	**Historical Examples**	**Contemporary Examples**
Physical	Physical assault, abuse, and brutality	Denial of education	Disproportionate use of suspension and expulsion Educator and school police brutality
Symbolic	"A metaphorical representation of violence that stems from, 'racial abuse, pain, and suffering against the spirit and humanity of Black people'" (Boutte & Bryan, 2019, p. 6)	Freedom vs. Equality Separate but (un) equal	Spirit-murdering (Love, 2019 and Williams, 1987) Protecting the comfort of white children over the accurate teaching of race and racism
Curricular and Pedagogical	Overuse of Eurocentric curriculum and instilling narratives of racial inferiority about Black people through deficit-based pedagogy, practices, and curriculum.	Teaching anti-Black and pro-white narratives in the curriculum Centering invisibilizing and marginalizing knowledge (King, 2004)	Banning divisive concepts Revised history standards

Denial of Education and Spirit-Murdering

The dehumanization of freed and enslaved Black people began with the denial of education, then shifted to deculturalization. I argue that denial of education is an example of physical anti-Black violence perpetuated by schooling, as it constituted an assault on the Black body and mind to remain shackled, ignorant, and inferior. Enslavers feared the ability of education to liberate the minds of the enslaved; thus, they instituted laws to make it illegal to teach an enslaved person to read and denied them access to education (Spring, 2016). Physical anti-Black violence in schools today is frequently documented with video recordings of violent assaults by school resource officers and educators (Dumas & ross, 2016; Love, 2019; Mapping Racial Trauma in Schools, n.d.). However, I would add the well-documented disproportional use of suspension and expulsion that often begins in preschool (Jones & Levin, 2016) as contemporary examples of physical anti-Black violence in schools. Denying and limiting Black children's right to access educational opportunities is an act of dehumanization planted long ago and continues to fester within the institution of schooling.

Symbolic anti-Black violence in schools can best be understood as spirit-murdering (Love, 2019; Williams, 1987), or how racism murders the spirit of Black people. When it was no longer possible to deny Black people their education, the institution of schooling attempted to kill their spirit to strip them of their humanity further. Spring (2016) noted even when northern states called for abolition, and the population of freed Blacks grew, freedom did not lead to equality. Though some acknowledged the contradictions of purporting to be a country for freedom while actively enslaving a growing segment of the population, America quickly found ways to offer freedom to Blacks and deny them equality and their humanity. Thus, the doctrine of separate but (un)equal was hatched, and schooling became a prime vehicle to spread education segregation. As the abolition of slavery spread through the North, inferior and under-funded schools for Black children allowed for deculturalization to take root. Black children were taught to internalize lessons of inferiority and accept white dominance as the natural order.

The culture wars in education erupted after the uprising for racial justice in the summer of 2020 led to a spate of legislation banning the teaching of race, racism, sex, and heterosexism in K-12 schools across the country (Jones, 2024). Though many of the laws were packaged under the anti-CRT hysteria promoted by conservatives, one aspect they have in common is that they privilege protecting the comfort of white students by banning any discussions or training on race and sex that would cause them to feel guilt or any type of psychological distress (Pendharker, 2021). With this type of vague language, the bills have the intended chilling effect, leaving many teachers unsure if they can move forward with essential lessons on discrimination and inequality for fear that a student could be upset and then can face punishment, including personal fines and loss of district funding (Florido, 2021; Pendharker, 2021). Passing laws that protect white students' feelings over teaching the truth about racism is a contemporary form of spirit-murder and dehumanization of Black children.

Teaching Black Inferiority Then and Now

Historian, father of Black history, and founder of Negro History Week, now known as Black History Month, Carter G. Woodson (1933) documented early forms of curricular and pedagogical anti-Black violence in his book, *The Mis-Education of the Negro.*

> The so-called modern education, with all its defects, however, does others so much more good than it does the Negro, because it has been worked out in conformity to the needs of those who have enslaved and oppressed weaker peoples . . . The problem of holding the Negro down, therefore, is easily solved. When you control a man's thinking, you do not have to worry about his actions. You do not have to tell him not to stand here or go yonder. He will find his "proper place" and will stay in it. You do not need to send him to the back door. He will go without being told. In fact, if there is no back door, he will cut one for his special benefit. His education makes it necessary." (p. 4)

Woodson describes how various aspects of the curriculum were designed to teach disdain for Black people by omitting them from the study of literature or history, or teaching Black people as diseased criminals in medicine and law. Thus, education for free Blacks was inherently tied to fostering Black inferiority through the curriculum and instruction.

Givens (2021) documented how Black teachers and parents had no control over the curriculum, as the local school board and educational administrators, all of who were white, enforced a scripted curriculum that reinforced deculturalization. Though many Black educators resisted the anti-Black curriculum and engaged in what Givens (2021) calls fugitive pedagogy, the school system remained hostile to the education of Black people. A curriculum that failed to prepare Black people with the needed skills to find work and demeaned their culture by regulating them to segregated, inferior schooling is a curriculum that inflicts violence. Unfortunately, the end of school segregation did not include an end to anti-Black curriculum and instruction. Instead, the all-Black schools that found ways to build up Black children despite the official curriculum were closed, their beloved teachers were fired, and Black children were turned over to white teachers who continued the practice of deculturalization.

Deculturalization results from the types of knowledge taught in schools. In her study on the evolution of African American culture-centered knowledge and curriculum transformation, J. E. King (2004) delineated four categories based on the interests they serve. Marginalizing and invisibilizing knowledge were linked to an indivisible interest, emphasizing sameness and hegemony, and expanding and deciphering knowledge connected to communities of interest, autonomy, and difference. As the American institution of schooling progressed from denying education to Black people to deculturalization, marginalizing and invisibilizing knowledge became the norm. One example of marginalizing knowledge is the selective inclusion of Black people in the curriculum to reinforce white dominance. Invisibilizing knowledge "simply obliterates the historical presence, unique experience, contributions, and perspectives of diverse people in the development of the United States and Western civilization" (King, 2004, p.362).

In his overview of Black teachers who authored history textbooks, L. J. King (2014) offered examples of how social studies education included marginalizing and invisibilizing knowledge. One social studies curriculum included messages on the need to train Black people in Western civilization to overcome their inherent deficits and gain the skills needed to be civilized while simultaneously fostering narratives on the impossibility of Black humanity. "Early social studies textbooks promoted and sustained a specific construction of Blackness, which was part of an apparatus of racial oppression that denied personhood, thus creating an ontological truth that non-Whites were abnormal, childlike, and innately inferior to Whites" (King, 2014, p. 4). The social studies curriculum enacted deculturalization by denying Black humanity and agency and linking citizenship with whiteness.

After *Brown vs. Board of Education* outlawed segregation in 1954, marginalizing and invisibilizing cultural knowledge remained entrenched in the curriculum. However, it became more subtle as various groups began demanding cultural pluralism in schools. A resurgence of anti-Black curricular and pedagogical violence is being perpetuated through the laws banning CRT and other approaches to teaching diverse perspectives in schools. Although President Biden rescinded the previous administration's executive order that launched the current attack, state legislatures nationwide continue the fight. As of April 2023, 18 states passed laws that ban teaching CRT, while 17 states have tried or are trying to enact similar legislation (World Population Review, 2023). Many of these new bans also target discussions about gender identity and teaching about sexism and LGBTQ history under the label of "divisive concepts." Stitzlein (2022) noted how these "laws label certain understandings of or beliefs about race, gender, and sexuality, as too divisive or inappropriate for classroom curriculum and instruction, or even for the professional development of teachers" (p. 597). Naming essential topics such as white supremacy, intersectionality, patriarchy, education justice, racial prejudice, and even social and emotional learning as divisive ensures the school curriculum will continue to center marginalizing and invisibilizing knowledge.

Another example of anti-Black curricular and pedagogical violence in schools today is the revising of social studies standards. In July 2023, after instituting the Don't Say Gay law, Stop W.O.K.E. (Wrongs to our Kids and Employees) Act, and asking Advancement Placement (AP) to revise its new African American History course, Florida was once again in the spotlight of the culture wars, after releasing their revised history standards. Many took issue with a benchmark clarification that called for instruction on the skills enslaved people developed and could use to their benefit, prompting outrage on various social media platforms. Harriot (2023) reviewed all the standards and found several instances of whitewashing Black history, including instruction on how Black people owned slaves and only one mention of racism and no mention of white supremacy. Florida is leading the movement created to silence the work of racial justice in education by rewriting standards and labeling important topics as divisive.

This movement, like others before it, reminds us that the institution of schooling was never designed for Black children and will continue to conspire against the realization of their full humanity. We must create our own Black educational fugitive spaces to achieve education justice. The rest of this chapter explores one such space, the national Black Lives Matter at School movement, as contemporary fugitive pedagogy for Black lives. Though this work primarily happens in schools, our work transcends the institution of schooling and instead fosters education as the practice of freedom.

Black Lives Matter at School as Contemporary Black Fugitive Pedagogy

Black Lives Matter at School (BLMAS) is a national movement organized locally by educators, activists, and youth. In 2016, educators at an elementary school in Seattle hosted the first teach-in for Black Lives, which led to a citywide one-day teach-in later in the semester (Au & Hagopian, 2020). In January 2017, educators in Philly instituted the first BLMAS Week of Action (WOA) using a Global Black Lives Matter organization statement to develop a curriculum centered on 13 guiding principles (GPs). In the summer of 2017, a group of organizers began meeting regularly and formed the national BLMAS steering committee and local BLMAS organizing groups to launch the first national BLMAS WOA in the spring of 2018. In 2020, we instituted the Year of Purpose to ground our 13 GPs throughout the academic year. Today, our national steering committee continues to support local groups in planning for the WOA and Year of Purpose by curating our free curriculum materials and resources.[1]

My research on BLMAS has examined the pedagogy of BLMAS (Jones, 2020) and how teachers use the 13 GPs to foster Black cultural citizenship education (Jones, 2022; Jones & Mathews, 2023; Mathews & Jones, 2022). The rest of this chapter will explore BLMAS and the 13 GPs in relation to Givens's (2021) Black fugitive pedagogy. "Fugitivity—and fugitive pedagogy in particular—is the metanarrative of black educational history. It is a social and rhetorical frame by which we might interpret black Americans' pursuit to enact humanizing and affirming practices of teaching and learning" (Givens, 2021, p. 11). Though Givens and others have provided us with a historical analysis of the ongoing struggle for Black education, we must also look to contemporary movements for education justice that are creating "new scripts of knowledge" (2021, p. 126). Some might argue that the fugitive educational practices of our ancestors are no longer needed in our current post-*Brown* school integration era. But in the 18 states that have made it illegal to teach Black Lives Matter, I argue that the work of BLMAS constitutes a contemporary Black fugitive pedagogy that provides contemporary Black cultural knowledge that reclaims Black humanity, teaches Black ways of being and knowing, and centers Black joy.

Table 9.2.

Black Lives Matter at School (BLMAS) 13 Guiding Principles (13 GPs) as Black Fugitive Pedagogy

13 GPs	New Scripts of Knowledge	Fugitive Pedagogy Race Vindicationism (Givens, 2021)
Black Families, Black Villages, Unapologetically Black, Black Women	Reclaiming Black Humanity	Rejecting the Master Narrative and Resistance
Collective Value, Restorative Justice, Globalism, Diversity	Teaching Black Cultural Knowledge and Ways of Being	Self-Determination and Diasporic Citations
Empathy, Loving Engagement, Queer-Affirming, Transgender-Affirming, Intergenerational	Centering Black Joy	Resilience and Black Rationality

Reclaiming Black Humanity: Resistance and Rejection of Master Narratives

Similar to how textbooks authored by Black teachers rejected master narratives and documented the ongoing work of Black resistance (Givens, 2021), four of the BLMAS 13 GPs reclaim Black humanity: Black Families, Black Villages, Unapologetically Black, and Black Women.

Table 9.3.
13 GPs Reclaiming Black Humanity

Black Families	We are committed to making our spaces family-friendly and enable parents to fully participate with their children. We are committed to dismantling the patriarchal practice that requires mothers to work "double shifts" that require them to mother in private even as they participate in justice work.
Black Villages	We are committed to disrupting the Western-prescribed nuclear family structure requirement by supporting each other as extended families and "villages" that collectively care for one another, and especially "our" children, to the degree that mothers, parents, and children are comfortable.
Unapologetically Black	We are unapologetically Black in our positioning. In affirming that Black Lives Matter, we need not qualify our position. To love and desire freedom and justice for ourselves is a necessary prerequisite for wanting the same for others.
Black Women	We are committed to building Black women affirming space free from sexism, misogyny, and male-centeredness.

The naming of Blackness in these four principles serves as a space to center our humanity within a pedagogy that must bear our names and reject deficit narratives that equate Black history with suffering, pain, failure, and personal choices (Kirkland, 2021; Mathews & Jones, 2022). Given the negative portrayal of Black families and communities within pop culture and the absence of their positive depiction in K-12 curriculums, these four GPs allow students to understand how we honor ourselves and our families. Additionally, they name our continued resistance against patriarchy, nuclear family structures, sexism, and misogyny as part of the work to make Black Lives Matter.

Teaching Black Cultural Knowledge and Ways of Being as Self-Determination Through the Diaspora

To transform the curriculum, we must move away from marginalizing and invisibilizing cultural knowledge and instead utilize expanding and deciphering knowledge. Through expanding knowledge, we can extend our understanding of Black life by including various narratives and perspectives. With deciphering knowledge, we can support the development of our cognitive autonomy to delegitimatize anti-Black frameworks (King, 2004). Thus, as a contemporary Black fugitive pedagogy, BLMAS offers four GPs that instill Black cultural knowledge and ways of beings: Collective Value, Restorative Justice, Globalism, and Diversity.

Table 9.4.
13 GPs Teaching Black Cultural Knowledge and Black Ways of Being

Collective Value	We are guided by the fact all Black lives matter, regardless of actual or perceived sexual identity, gender identity, gender expression, economic status, ability, disability, religious beliefs or disbeliefs, immigration status, or location.
Restorative Justice	We are committed to collectively, lovingly, and courageously working vigorously for freedom and justice for Black people and, by extension, all people. As we forge our path, we intentionally build and nurture a beloved community that is bonded together through a beautiful struggle that is restorative, not depleting.
Globalism	We see ourselves as part of the global Black family and we are aware of the different ways we are impacted or privileged as Black folk who exist in different parts of the world.
Diversity	We are committed to acknowledging, respecting, and celebrating difference(s) and commonalities.

Our commitments to supporting all Black lives with restorative practices across the globe align with the self-determination and diasporic inclusion embedded in fugitive pedagogy (Givens, 2021).

Centering Black Joy: Resilience and Blackness as Rational

The history of denying education and deculturalization ensured the normalization of Black suffering (Dumas, 2014) and the exclusion of Black joy from our classrooms. Love (2019) differentiates Black joy from joy because it embraces Blackness within its complete humanity and celebrates Black identity as beautiful. Duncan, Hall, and Dunn (2023) offer this definition, "Black joy, then, is consciousness, embodied knowledge, and a fugitive space that refuses Black oppression and suffering both individually and collectively" (p. 3). The remaining five BLMAS GPs center Black joy: Empathy, Loving Engagement, Queer Affirming, Transgender Affirming, and Intergenerational.

Table 9.5.
13 GPs Centering Black Joy

Empathy	We are committed to practicing empathy; we engage comrades with the intent to learn about and connect with their contexts.
Loving Engagement	We are committed to embodying and practicing justice, liberation, and peace in our engagements with one another.
Queer Affirming	We are committed to fostering a queer-affirming network. When we gather, we do so with the intention of freeing ourselves from the tight grip of hetero-normative thinking or, rather, the belief that all in the world are heterosexual unless s/he or they disclose otherwise.
Transgender Affirming	We are committed to embracing and making space for transgender siblings to participate and lead. We are committed to being self-reflexive and doing the work required to dismantle cis-gender privilege and uplift Black transgender folk, especially Black transgender women, who continue to be disproportionately impacted by trans-antagonistic violence.
Intergenerational	We are committed to fostering an intergenerational and communal network free from ageism. We believe that all people, regardless of age, show up with capacity to lead and learn.

These principles embody our commitment to engaging with each other and building joyful homeplaces for ourselves and others (Love, 2019). They also align with narrative constructions of resilience and the ability of Black people to be rational, documented in Black fugitive textbooks (Givens, 2021).

My research with a group of teachers who taught the 13 GPs over 4 years documented how BLMAS engages with education as the practice of freedom. Early childhood teachers used diverse books to support young children as they grappled with big ideas, recognized and collaborated on how to deal with injustice in the present, and situated themselves as change agents (Jones, 2022). Other teachers engaged in critical race pedagogies while teaching the 13 GPs that allowed their students to unlearn and relearn Black history, recognize and challenge systems of oppression, and engage as active contributors in the work for Black liberation (Mathews & Jones, 2022). All the teachers fostered critical civic empathy when they taught the principles of empathy, loving engagement, and restorative justice as relational civic practices (Jones & Mathews, 2023). Though we only studied a small group of teachers, we believe that additional research on BLMAS will showcase the unlimited possibilities for reclaiming Black humanity in education. The BLMAS movement invites teachers to abandon the dehumanizing work of schooling and embrace liberatory education for Black lives.

Conclusion: Collecting on the Education Debt Owed to Black Children

In addition to developing curriculum materials to teach the 13 GPs, BLMAS is guided by four demands: (1) End "zero tolerance discipline" and implement restorative justice; (2) Hire more Black teachers; (3) Mandate Black history and ethnic studies in K-12 curriculum; and (4) Fund counselors, not cops (Jones & Hagopian, 2020). As we engage in the ongoing struggle for educational justice, these demands serve as points of organizing around the changes we must secure if Black lives are to matter in our schools. Whether we use the education debt framework (Ladson-Billings, 2006) or the demand for education reparations (Love, 2023), we must be unequivocal in our insistence that Black children are owed a debt that must be paid. The debt formed when schooling was used as a weapon to deny Black humanity and continued to accrue as we engaged in ongoing fights for freedom through education. The harmful nature of school reforms and attacks against teaching truth precludes us from accepting any claims that the debt has been paid.

Our four demands provide an immediate payment towards the debt by centering truth. Implementing restorative justice and banning all zero-tolerance and punitive discipline measures will pay down the debt owed from the school-to-prison nexus. Hiring more Black teachers will pay down the debt incurred when, instead of equalizing funding for Black schools, integration was used to fire Black teachers and force Black children into the classrooms of a hostile white teaching force. Mandating Black history and ethnic studies in every birth-16 institution of learning will pay down the debt from centuries of overfeeding society, a bland false narrative of Eurocentric superiority. Funding counselors and getting cops out of our schools pays down the debt of racial trauma and toxic racist stress waged on the minds and bodies of Black people, further victimized by the dehumanization of American schooling.

Schooling is the master's tool and cannot destroy the white supremacist, capitalist, hetero-patriarchal roots of the master's house. Black Lives Matter at School is a movement grounded in teaching truth. Truth exposes the many facets that keep the master's house operating. Teaching truth supports learners' ability to recognize and name the systems of oppression that operate to keep them from living their life as fully human citizens. Instead of succumbing to the poison that is internalized racial inferiority, truth seeks to transport our minds and hearts to a space free from blame and self-doubt, where our greatness shines unencumbered by whiteness. Through principles grounded in contemporary Black cultural knowledge and universal demands that center Black joy and reinforce our commitment to teaching and honoring Black humanity, Black Lives Matter at School is the people's tool we desperately need.

Editor's Note: You can follow Black Lives Matter at School on Facebook and Instagram. Their website is https://www.blacklivesmatteratschool.com/

References

Au, W., & Hagopian, J. (2020). How one elementary school sparked a movement to make Black students' lives matter. In D. Jones & J. Hagopian (Eds.), *Black Lives Matter at School: An uprising for educational justice* (pp. 33–45). Haymarket Books.

Boutte, G., & Bryan, N. (2019). When will Black children be well? Interrupting anti-Black violence in early childhood classrooms and schools. *Contemporary Issues in Early Childhood, 22*(3), 232–243. doi.org/10.1177/1463949119890598

Busey, C. L., & Dowie-Chin, T. (2021). The making of global Black anti-citizen/citizenship: Situating BlackCrit in global citizenship research and theory. *Theory & Research in Social Education, 49*(2), 153–175. https://doi/10.1080/00933104.2020.1869632

Dumas, M. (2014). 'Losing an arm': Schooling as a site of Black suffering. *Race, Ethnicity, and Education, 17*(1), 1–19. http://dx.doi.org/10.1080/13613324.2013.850412

Dumas, M. J., & ross, k. m. (2016). "Be real Black for me": Imagining BlackCrit in education. *Urban Education, 51*(4), 415–442.

Duncan, K. E., Hall, D., & Dunn, D. C. (2023). Embracing the fullness of Black humanity: Centering Black joy in social studies. *The Social Studies, 114*(5), 241–249. DOI: 10.1080/00377996.2023.2174926

Florido, A. (2021, May 28). *Teachers say laws banning critical race theory are putting a chill on their lessons.* NPR. https://www.npr.org/2021/05/28/1000537206/teachers-laws-banning-critical-race-theory-are-leading-to-self-censorship

Freire, P. (2005). *Pedagogy of the oppressed* (30th Anniversary Edition). Continuum.

Givens, J. R. (2021). *Fugitive pedagogy: Carter G. Woodson and the art of Black teaching.* Harvard University Press.

Harriot, M. (2023, July 27). *Florida's Black history standards are even worse than reported.* The Grio. https://thegrio.com/2023/07/27/floridas-black-history-standards-are-even-worse-than-reported/?fbclid=IwAR3ECca6Yu_JjPIuRKud2R42hFFfd1VnUENQVkalgIky86w_oSwcUwmizoY

Harro, B. (2002). The cycle of socialization. In M. Adams, W. Blumenfeld, R. Castaneda, H. Hackman, M. Peters, & X. Zuniga (Eds.), *Readings for diversity and social justice* (pp. 16–21). Routledge.

hooks, b. (1994). *Teaching to transgress: Education as the practice of freedom.* Routledge.

Johnson, H. B. (2006). *The American dream and the power of wealth: Choosing schools and inheriting inequality in the land of opportunity.* Routledge.

Jones, D. (2020). The Black Lives Matter at School pedagogy: Affirming Black lives, resisting neoliberal reform, and reimagining education for liberation. In D. Jones & J. Hagopian (Eds.), *Black Lives Matter at School: An uprising for educational justice* (pp. 200–207). Haymarket Books.

Jones, D. (2022). Enacting cultural citizenship education for Black liberation: A dream for social studies education. In A. E. Vickery & N. N. Rodriguez (Eds.), *Critical race theory and social studies futures: From the nightmare of racial realism to dreaming out loud* (pp. 120–129). Teachers College Press.

Jones, D. (2024). Activist research in social studies education: Renewed scholarship for a better world. In S. A. Mathews (Ed.), *(Re)Envisioning social studies education research: Current epistemological and methodological expansions, deconstructions, and creations.* IAP.

Jones, D., & Hagopian, J. (2020). *Black Lives Matter at School: An uprising for educational Justice.* Haymarket Books.

Jones, D., & Levin, D. (2016). Preschool suspensions do more harm than good. *Education Week, 35*(22), 26.

Jones, D., & Mathews, S. A. (2023). The Black Lives Matter at school guiding principles: Fostering Black cultural citizenship through critical civic empathy. In K. E. Duncan (Ed.), *Civic engagement in communities of color: Pedagogy for learning and life in a more expansive democracy* (pp. 155–170). Teachers College Press.

Kendi, I. X. (2016). *Stamped from the beginning: The definitive history of racist ideas in America.* Nation Books.

King, J. E. (2004). Culture-centered knowledge: Black studies, curriculum transformation, and social action. In. J. A. Banks & C. A. McGee Banks (Eds.), *Handbook of research on multicultural education* (pp. 349–378). Jossey-Bass.

King, L. J. (2014). When lions write history: Black history textbooks, African American educators & the alternative Black curriculum in social studies education 1890–1940. *Multicultural Education, 22*(1), 2–10.

Kirkland, D. E. (2021). A pedagogy for Black people: Why naming race matters. *Equity & Excellence in Education, 54*(1), 60–67. DOI: 10.1080/10665684.2020.1867018

Ladson-Billings, G. (2003). Lies my teacher still tells: Developing a critical perspective towards social studies. In G. Ladson-billings (Ed.), *Critical race theory perspectives on the social studies: The profession, policies, and curriculum* (pp. 1–11). Information Age.

Ladson-Billings, G. (2006). From the achievement gap to the education debt: Understanding achievement in U.S. schools. *Educational Researcher, 35*(7), 3–12. https://doi.org/10.3102/0013189X035007003

Lorde, A. (1984). The master's tools will never dismantle the master's house. *Sister Outsider: Essays and Speeches.* Crossing Press.

Love, B. L. (2019). *We want to do more than survive: Abolitionist teaching and the pursuit of educational freedom.* Beacon Press.

Love, B. L. (2023). *Punished for dreaming: How school reform harms Black children and how we heal.* Macmillan Publishers.

Mapping Racial Trauma in Schools. (n.d.). *Home* [Facebook page]. Facebook. https://www.facebook.com/mappingracialtrauma

Mathews, S. A., & Jones, D. (6 April 2022). Black lives matter at school: Using the 13 guiding principles as critical race pedagogies for Black citizenship education. *Journal of Social Studies Research,* 47(1), 15–28. https://doi.org/10.1016/j.jssr.2022.03.001

Mayorga, E., & Picower, B. (2018). Active solidarity: Centering the demands and vision of the Black Lives Matter movement in teacher education. *Urban Education,* 53(2). 212-230. https://doi.org/10.1177/0042085917747117

Pendharker, E. (2021, June 30). Four things schools won't be able to do under 'critical race theory' laws. *Education Week.* https://www.edweek.org/policy-politics/four-things-schools-wont-be-able-to-do-under-critical-race-theory-laws/2021/06

Shujaa, M. (1993). Education and schooling: You can have one without the other. *Urban Education, 27*(4), 328–351.

Spring, J. (2016). *Deculturalization and the struggle for equality: A brief history of the education of dominated cultures in the United States.* Routledge.

Stitzlein, S. (2022). Divisive concepts in classrooms: A call to inquiry. *Studies in Philosophy and Education, 41,* 595–612. https://doi.org/10.1007/s11217-022-09842-8

Williams, P. (1987). Spirit-murdering the messenger: The discourse of fingerpointing as the law's response to racism. *Miami Law Review, 42*(8), 127–157. https://repository.law.miami.edu/umlr/vol42/iss1/8

Woodson, C. G. (1933). *The Mis-Education of the Negro*. Associated Publishers.

World Population Review. (2023). Critical race theory ban status [Interactive Map]. https://worldpopulationreview.com/state-rankings/critical-race-theory-ban-states

Endnotes

1 I joined the national steering committee in 2017 and organized locally in Washington, DC and then New York. For more information on the history of the BLMAS please see our edited book *Black Lives Matter at School: An Uprising for Education Justice* published in 2020 and check out our website www.blacklivesmatteratschool.com.

CHAPTER 10

National Educators United (NEU): Collective Action Outside of Formal Union Spaces

Janette Zahia Corcelius, Rebecca Garelli, Melissa Tomlinson, Stephanie Price, Katie Ehrlich, Ivonne Rovira, and Brianne Kramer

THIS CHAPTER WAS a collaboration between National Educators United members and the book editor and was primarily developed from a group interview. The authors would like to thank the following people for their contributions to the organization that led to this chapter: Frank Adamson, Josh Austin, Darrin Hoop, Carla Okouchi, Tia Edison, Gabriela Mitchell, Kenyatta Dean Bacon, Sarah Steinhauer, and Greg Tichenor.

The #RedforEd wildcat strikes in predominantly red states in 2018 began an increased wave of organizing as educators in "right-to-work" states discovered new possibilities they could utilize in their respective states. The strikes also provided a spotlight for families and communities to better understand the importance of fighting for strong, well-funded public schools. On the heels of this groundswell movement, a new organization for educational activism was born. National Educators United began December 14, 2019 as a group of educators from Arizona, California, Indiana, Kentucky, New Jersey, Oklahoma, Oregon, Virginia, Washington, and West Virginia who came together from other activist groups and organizations to create a new space to educate and organize supporters of public education.

Once the group began, members quickly joined, soon amassing to a 6,600 member group. There is no hierarchical leadership structure. Decisions are made by consensus by those who volunteer their time to plan initiatives. They plan to hold open meetings to discuss the direction and structure of their leadership as the group continues to grow. Members of the core group who began NEU provided more context to the organization's beginning.

Rebecca Garelli: National Educators United emerged out of the #RedforEd strike wave of 2018. Many of us started having conversations, some of us in Arizona, where as you know, this is the land of all bad things in education, and really looking for ways to come together with other folks who are fighting the same fight. So we began conversations about trying to find some sort of system where we could build some sort of national coalition, knowing that the strike wave had so much momentum at the time, and knowing that it was getting a lot of coverage. Folks being more aware than they had been in thinking of consciousness, like more people were consciously aware of teachers fighting back, teachers willing to take risks, willing to speak up, willing to organize their co-workers.

A few of us in Arizona had been talking about it, and then we reached out to other folks that we knew. I've known Ivonne in the past, and Melissa in the past, and our paths have crossed just from #RedforEd organizing, and BATs obviously is a reason many of us are here and know what we know. I had done some work with Josh Austin and California Educators United, helping him build that sort of statewide solidarity system. I was working behind the scenes with just Josh Austin quite a bit, just really in camaraderie of like, how did you build your movement? How can we do this outside of California? The conditions aren't the same. Josh Austin was a huge collaborator and [an] original organizer of National Educators United (NEU). Josh then brought in Frank Adamson, a powerhouse in the research world who worked with folks at the Stanford Center for Opportunity Policy in Education (SCOPE) and organizations fighting privatization internationally, and is well versed in education research. I've known Darrin Hoop for a long time and worked with him through the #RedforEd movement getting our story out there. Darrin really wanted to form #RedforEd Solidarity Network, which still exists on Facebook, with the intention of really focusing on uplifting issues across the country and building solidarity. Darrin was someone who built solidarity with many of the strike leaders. He sent pizzas to us and really organized Go Fund Me's for different struggles. I just want to make sure that he is definitely mentioned and acknowledged for really uplifting the solidarity piece. So it was really this kind of coalition of people, and those folks knew other folks.

Then I met the Virginia folks from Virginia Educators United, like Janette and Carla, and then Washington Educators United, Katie, Darrin, and also Steph in Oklahoma. We all kind of just got together in this group, with the help of Frank's brilliance with the research behind creating a really strong set of demands, I know all of us helped create those demands collectively. Melissa has been in this world forever and knows all the things and how to speak the language and what would really resonate with people. So we really started with the crafting of the mission, the values, and the demands. So that's kind of how it started coming out of the #RedforEd movement.

We had this group behind the scenes working on stuff before our launch in December. I remember talking to people in the Chicago Teachers Union about a national movement back in June of 2019. That's kind of how it all kind of happened. I think we were riding this wave of incredible momentum and power. UCORE, the United Caucuses of Rank and File Educators, has been around for a long time, but sometimes people do not know about UCORE, and, two, what happens to people if they're not part of the union? Where's the space for them to organize? There's no labor formation or organization to plug those people in. Yes, we want all people to be in the union. However, look at where I'm at. I'm in Arizona, 60,000 teachers [are] here. We have 60,000 teachers in the classroom that are certified working in the classrooms, but only 1/3 of them belong to the union. So that means 40,000 teachers were not plugged into any kind of labor organization or formation. So we focused on organizing the unorganized. My mission and vision for helping grow NEU was not only about pro-unionism, but getting people plugged into a space who don't have a pathway. What if you're in a charter school? What if you're in a private school? I mean, there's more than just us in public education. So opening a space for those to learn to grow and to really help people learn how to organize.

Janette Zahia Corcelius: The #RedforEd movement happened in red states (with the exception of California and even Washington). The #RedforEd wildcat strikes in 2018 happened in states where the educator unions didn't have public-sector collective bargaining. It was a shining example of what's possible in places where organizing feels impossible. I hear a lot of educators in the South say, "we don't have a union," or "our union is weak," or "we don't have collective bargaining and we're not allowed to strike because it's illegal." We have to educate them on the facts. Being from Virginia, where I taught for 6 years, the state affiliate didn't want to call itself a union for a really long time—it just called itself a professional association. This comes out of the service model and business unionism that has proliferated since late 1970s, early 1980s. People just see the union as a service or they treat it as a professional organization. They didn't see it as a way or a means to organize. A lot of dues money goes towards lobbying and not new organizing or teaching members how to organize. Leaders and staff are finally realizing, "Oh, we got to organize and beef up our unions because of what's happening in Florida" because of the bill that was brought forth and pushed by Ron DeSantis that indicates, if your union has less than 60%, you'll automatically be decertified. So now, Florida educators are realizing, "I'm going to lose my public sector union and my collective bargaining rights if we don't have enough members."

That organizing push has cropped up out of dire necessity and survival instincts. Our national affiliates need to adopt an organizing model while they have co-opted social justice unionism. Until then, the reform caucus movement will continue to blossom and it is incumbent upon rank-and-file members to determine the direction of their union. We learned from Joe Burns' book, *Class Struggle Unionism*, how important bottom-up organizing and rank-and-file militancy is for our movement. And while educators are professionals, we are also workers . . . therefore working-class people. We need unions, just like everyone needs a union. I'm really thankful that my mentor, Carla, brought me into the NEU and VEU spaces because it taught me how to organize and it taught us to put the pressure on our state affiliate and our local. We also garnered so much knowledge in the UCORE space and decided to start a statewide caucus, VCORE.

Another thing that sets NEU apart from other groups is there is no hierarchy. Anyone who would like to participate in any initiatives is free to do so. This was especially true during COVID-19, when needs were high and there was consistent work to do. There were also groups built within NEU where people could participate in various ways. The other committees that NEU members can be a part of are Racial Equity, Building Statewide Groups, and Fighting Austerity. NEU also has state groups operating in Arizona, California, Florida, Indiana, Kentucky, Louisiana, New Jersey, Oklahoma, Oregon, Virginia, and Washington.

Rebecca Garelli: I think what we were really focused on is teaching people how to set up organizing spaces. We've had some success, and many of us in this NEU group have had success building statewide, whether you technically call it a caucus, or for us we don't call it a caucus because we call it a statewide movement. What we kind of learned early on is that people were hungry and looking for information and support on how do you build a movement like this? What steps did you take? What structures are in place? What kind of systems do you have? What kind of mailing lists do you have? I mean, basic logistical things, right down to you can't email people on Gmail because you can't have over 500 people. Teaching people little tiny tips on how to build big lists, and how you use lists to organize, and how you target certain lists.

Then, I think what's unique about what we did is we went full blown on how to organize in a digital space, especially during COVID-19. I think we were very open about—anybody's welcome. You don't have to belong to this group. You don't need to pay dues—we're doing this for the good of the cause. We believe in this, and we want to help you learn how to organize. How do you organize, build the logistics, the structures, targets for Twitter storms? How do you advocate online? How do you build community meetings and town halls where anybody's welcome to get information and really think about systems and networks for raising awareness? That's kind of like what our mission was at the beginning.

People don't know what they don't know, so how can we help people get the information they need to understand that we are all under severe attack? Intentional and aggressive agendas to destroy the professions that we love deeply and destroy our public school systems, which are the cornerstone of democracy and all those things. So I think for us, we're different because it isn't this entity for which you must belong, right? There's no gateway. There's no gatekeeping. You don't have to come in. It's open to all if you want to come and learn how to organize, come and join with us. This is what we're doing. We will show you some things we've learned. We're not perfect. We're not full experts. A lot of us have experience, though. So we're trying to put it to the test and teach you how you can make change, especially during COVID-19. We built organizing toolkits for people to take, make copies of, and use. So people had mimicked our actions. I think that's what makes us different.

Ivonne Rovira: I would like to speak to that generosity. I'm in Louisville, which is . . . Louisville is to Kentucky as Austin is to Texas. You know, it's a big blue. I think back to this [which] started shortly before COVID-19 went crazy, and it really changed the trajectory here. A week before school was going to open, we were going to go pedal to the metal and open. That changed it for the biggest cities in Kentucky. They helped us organize these amazing town halls where you did as Rebecca said. You didn't have to sign up. You signed up to go to the Zoom meeting. That was it, and then you brought it back to where you were. I really do think it changed. I don't think Kentucky is the only one where things were really safe, where we weren't killing kids and parents and what have you because there was one town hall after another on different aspects. There were experts coming in and saying . . . some guy who was like the air expert of the planet, talking about how fans aren't gonna help you. Stupid stuff people were saying that's not going to help you. A mask and a fan is not going to help you. It got us through a really terrible time and it was not just for pupils. It was for parents. It was for teachers. It was for the whole community because there were places where people were dying by the droves from COVID-19 that started at a school, and then just spread. I think it wasn't just us that benefited. I think there were other states where we took the ball. Thank you, Rebecca. She gave us permission to redo this just for northern Kentucky where they were organizing. We had a town hall just for them where they asked questions, and it was great. It was great. Like she said, it was like one-stop shopping. It was statements you could release, fact sheets, organizing tips, posts. It was everything you wanted. It was amazing.

Stephanie Price: What set us apart was our intentionality, from the very beginning, about building solidarity between other groups. We did the City Waste Union town hall with the sanitation workers and other solidarity efforts too. We partnered with Black Lives Matter at School to support Trans Day of Remembrance and the National Week of Action. We really worked hard to uplift others' struggles beyond just educators and education. Often, that isn't happening in the spaces we're in. We tend to get so focused on what's happening right around us and not thinking about how it's all interconnected. Something I feel stood out about our efforts is not just the incredible organizing and the toolkits, but also talking about how it's important to recognize there are other struggles going on in the world. They are all interconnected. When we lift each other up, we are stronger for it. That's something that really stands out to me.

Melissa Tomlinson: Rebecca touched upon this when she said there was no ownership over anything that we did, but it goes a little deeper. We worked really hard to not create any kind of hierarchy. Anybody that wanted to jump in and do some of this work, that had an idea, that had access to information, especially during COVID-19, our thought was, "Come on board. Let's do something." We set up working teams based upon different time periods of what was going on. I think that's a really big difference between us and bigger education caucuses. The caucuses work hard to include more voices, but there's still somewhat of a structure there. You ask us what the structure of NEU is, and to us it's a group of people that get together and talk, and that's about it. Then a second piece that kind of ties in starts with the Badass Teachers Association (BATs). BATs has been kind of in a pigeonhole of being a space for information and for conversations to happen. What NEU did was take that and from just conversations and transformed to action. The two groups worked hand-in-hand, especially because myself and Rebecca and others, we're all in both organizations. It's very easy to make that transition from what BATs does to what NEU does. Technically, it's basically one group. Most people go to both groups. It's just that one's an organizing one, and one has more of a communication and messaging function.

Katie Ehrlich: We've developed committees within NEU to research and share publicly on various topics, and we put on town halls to spread the message. We worked together technologically and took on roles in town halls to share the work. We had specialized committees run presentations and we just basically volunteered to help with anything we could. I was on the Safe Return to Schools committee, so I was one of a group of people that were doing research on COVID-19 and the risks of being in schools during a global pandemic. We put together a slide deck to present information in multiple town halls. We had all these different committees come together depending on the need of the day.

People within NEU formed a leadership group, and the people in that group varied depending on who had the time and was willing to take on that role at any given time. Those in leadership, in addition to any other volunteers, would get together prior to town halls to prepare. We would ask, "Who wants to do this? Can you help with that? Great, let's go do this." Our town halls would be live streamed on Facebook and we would share it in each of our state Educators United groups on Facebook, as well as other teacher groups like BATs. We used

Action Network to get the word out about the town halls and people signed up to attend on Zoom. Many others watched the live streams on a Facebook group they were a part of. We had so many people join the space so that we could publicize and just get out there. Each new person that attended expanded our Action Network list, and there were even more people getting information about upcoming town halls. There were so many people watching and commenting and engaging in the town halls both on Zoom and on Facebook. It was really great to see all of the engagement from educators, to parents, to nurses, to just everyone. It was awesome.

Their online focus was important, especially as school buildings nationwide closed in mid-March 2020 and instruction and student supports moved online or remote. The pandemic also drove many teachers to seek support from different organizations like NEU. The leaders were asked if they believed the COVID-19 pandemic contributed to the fast growth of their organization.

Melissa Tomlinson: I'm going to say, absolutely. It's always easier to organize when you're organizing against a common enemy or a common threat than it is to organize in times of peace. But that's not to say, it's not just as important to make sure you're organizing during peaceful times as well.

Rebecca Garelli: I agree. I think we filled a huge need. There was a very big opportunity there. We were organizing in our own states anyway, so it was great to have like-minded folks who could get together and build stuff together so that we could then turn around and flip out to our own organizing structures. I definitely think people were looking and desperate. In some cases, especially in red states where we had people losing funding due to horrific legislation being passed if they had a mask policy, like here in Arizona. I think that did fill a need. It definitely propelled our momentum because people were, I think, looking for some support, knowledge, information, tools, and resources that they could flip and say, "Okay, now I can use this. I can start conversations." We brought in some experts, industrial hygienists that Melissa brought in from New Jersey public schools to speak on air quality and give us the tools on how we choose air cleaners for the right square footage. How do we determine which air cleaners will work for the size of our classrooms? How do I build an organizing structure to address concerns? Basically, how do I help people build step-by-step processes where they can identify a need, take the next step, and identify some leaders that can help them? We built some town halls around—this is how you can do this, step one, step two, step three, and built toolkits that were accessible and usable. During some of our meetings, we would role play in breakout rooms and have people fill in these organizing tools to take back with them, so they had some support. So I just wanted to add in that organizing piece.

Like other grassroots organizations, NEU has developed a mission statement and vision. Their mission statement is: "National Educators United is a grassroots group of educators and allied stakeholders organized to achieve its vision through a variety of actions." The organization's vision indicates the group's priorities:

> We believe that every child without exception, including undocumented ones, deserves a high-quality, free, public education with wrap-around services to meet the needs of the whole child. Every educator should be treated and compensated fairly for the invaluable role they play in the communities they serve. Educators have the right to promote and defend democratic, social-justice unions and caucuses and to organize alongside grassroots networks and community organizations. This overarching vision is captured in our slogan: "Public Schools Students and Educators Deserve." (National Educators United, n.d. -a)

Melissa Tomlinson: I think it's important to note that, like Stephanie said, we were intentional in a lot of this work, and that goes for creating that vision/mission. Making sure that we looked at it with a racial justice lens. Making sure that we looked at it in terms of fighting against neoliberal corporate reform of public education. Making sure that it went beyond just public education as its own silo, also addressing some of the issues that impact public education.

Rebecca Garelli: I would add on that we were also intentional about considering and acknowledging what our unions have not been doing that we ourselves are determined to do.

Stephanie Price: That's what I was thinking about, too. Like Rebecca said, what's not happening within our unions and what needs to change? Especially for those of us in red states where racial justice is not an issue being tackled within our unions. Students who are Black and Brown and educators who are Black and Brown are constantly being oppressed and terrorized in the public school system. We sat down and discussed as a group what our values were and what was important to uplift in public education. We were very clear from the beginning that NEU stood for ending all forms of oppression.

Rebecca Garelli: It connects to what Janette brought up earlier. All of us own the NEU space. We're sick of business unionism, sick of this top-down structure, and really believe in the power of rank-and-file strategy, the power of collective action, and the power of us organizing ourselves, with ourselves, for ourselves. I think all of us, really, that's one of our strongest values is that bottom-up is the only way to go because top-down has not been working, and top-down is not going to give us the schools we deserve. It goes beyond that cliche of "you are the union." What does that mean? What does that look like on a day-to-day basis? What *does* that mean? It means you have your boots on the ground. You're willing to speak up. You're willing to work with others and do the work. What does *that* look like? Well, let's learn how to organize. Let's learn how to get people into a space with commonly and widely deeply felt issues, and then begin the process of moving forward on those issues. I think, for me, personally, and I know all of us in this space, it's what the unions are not doing and what they should be doing, and let's go do that. Let's build power the way we know power is built.

The initial goals of the organization were:

- Unite across states in unions, caucuses, and other grassroots networks as a collective group of educators to build a national movement
- Build capacity for collective action in our different states and local contexts to meet our demands
- Assist each other in learning how to more effectively organize
- Push education to the forefront of the national conversation before and after the 2020 presidential election
- Replace charter schools, education reform, standardized testing, scripted curriculum, and the corporatization of education with fully funded, democratically operated neighborhood community schools with [sic] that center racial equity and social justice
- Fight for the rights and respect of all education workers

- Create a society that highly values the education and care of all children, including undocumented ones, for the future that we all want for our families and communities (National Educators United, n.d. -a)

NEU also has crafted a set of demands that they organize around. There are three primary areas that they have identified as priorities:

Racial Equity and Social Justice (Support the Black Lives Matter at Schools demands):

- End zero tolerance, and implement restorative justice
- Mandate Black history & ethnic studies in K-12 curriculum
- Hire more Black teachers
- Fund counselors, not cops
- Require culturally sustaining teacher training and trauma-informed, healing-centered practices
- Create nurturing schools where students are safe from all forms of oppression
- End child detentions and family separation
- Fight for justice and dignity for immigrants and all people
- Provide equitable and affordable housing for all families
- Enact universal healthcare and childcare
- End child poverty and close the income inequality gap

Fully Funded Public Education Through Progressive Taxation:

- Ensure adequate class size, caseload limits, and student supports
- Mandate professional and equitable wages
- Provide a public defined-benefit pension system
- Enact progressive capital gains and income taxes
- End tax cuts, breaks, and loopholes for millionaires and corporations

Pro-Public Education and Anti-Privatization:

- Adopt a model of community schools with democratic governance
- Prohibit new charter schools
- Unionize existing charter schools and hold them accountable to our communities
- Advance democratic, social justice, class struggle unionism
- Eradicate vouchers and neo-voucher systems
- End scripted curriculum and the replacement of in-person teachers with online classes
- End high stakes accountability systems and linked teacher evaluations (National Educators United, n.d. -b)

Ivonne Rovira: I think most of our problems are created in a factory. They're cookie cutter, the same bills. That's one of the things that Rebecca was so brilliant to figure out, that we were all battling the same problems because they're all created in the same place. ALEC makes up a bill, it's one-stop shopping. Those who want to be bought and those who want to buy are in the same place. Then there's legislation to tie them together. We once had this guy. He got defeated. He had a charter bill where he forgot to replace the "your State Department of Education here." It was Bill Moffit, you don't know about universal find and replace? Clearly not. He'd gone and filled that in by hand, but the boy missed one. He just got caught. It's happening everywhere.

Rebecca Garelli: I talked to quite a lot of people in the different Educators United groups. Some have formed caucuses that are part of UCORE in addition to having a statewide Facebook group or a network or a structure of some kind. Our focus now is getting back to our roots. We're doing a book study. Bought books for everybody; shipped them out in the mail. We're focusing on reading *Secrets of a Successful Organizer* right now. When you think of the nation at one time, I did map this out, there were many statewide educator groups we connected with, but due to frequent turnover and lack of capacity, many organizers that joined NEU at its inception left to focus on local struggles. That kind of happened quite a bit where folks love the idea of building this national movement, right? Everybody's excited about a national movement. Everybody wants a national teacher strike, but really, what does that look like? Well, we need actual people who are willing to volunteer, who have the capacity, and are willing to commit for a long time. It's not going to happen overnight.

I think the momentum of the #RedforEd movement, at least from where I was sitting as someone who was being contacted quite a bit from people in many states going, "how did you guys do that?" Starting with California Educators United, I went out there and spent some time with organizers. We discussed lessons learned from the strategies and tactics of building this movement to learn how to apply to struggles in California, a place with strong bargaining rights, where LA's got UTLA (United Teachers Los Angeles) and a caucus that took over. What's there actually morphed into, and many of the California folks who run that joined NEU and various committees, and I received a really nice email from David de Leeuw, one of the CEU organizers, that described that the good thing about NEU—what we took away from it was the power of solidarity. He explained that they built this solidarity newsletter, which seems like something small, but it was taking all the actions from the Bay Area in California, synthesizing it, and showing people how they can get involved. For example, California Educators United produced a newsletter in 2019, and they led the Adopt a Striking School initiative for the UTLA and OEA (Oakland Education Association) strikes in 2019. They have camaraderie and people on the picket lines, and they embraced the power of solidarity from being involved in the NEU space. Florida wanted something that looked a little more like Arizona because our conditions are the same. I think it became nuanced. There's Kentucky, Oklahoma, Melissa's group formed into NJ21 United, which is a union caucus. So there's that structure for their conditions. So it's all variable, dependent on the conditions and who's willing to do the work. We had Indiana Educators United for a while. Then there was turnover, and then it was capacity building. It was really beautiful to see it all come to fruition and manifest itself during the #RedforEd movement.

There's still people going, "now we're thinking about it." I know it was 5 years ago, but how do you build a movement like that? How do you do that? Some people are coming into that, wanting that manifestation to happen now. Then what kind of morphed from all that is then we began working with the Demand Safe Schools group, which was led by folks with CTU and UTLA. We were in that space working together during COVID-19. We're all trying to uplift the same message and all using our networks and sharing each other's information and inviting folks. So I think it's just kind of this. It's never been done before. We have a national union, a 3 million member union, the biggest public sector union, but they're not doing what the members want. People want this to happen, but in reality, it's incredibly difficult and challenging to sustain this movement. Different conditions, and different people coming in and out that it's hard to move forward with all that spiraling going on.

Stephanie Price: I would just add to what Rebecca said that part of the challenge was a lot of what we tried to do was based on social media. Think about how hard it is to get people to act, to do something, even when you're face-to-face, but when you are on the interwebs trying to organize and get people committed to action, it's even harder. I think it certainly posed a particular challenge.

Members have participated in many different actions that solidify the group's commitment to the goals and demands that they have created.

Janette Zahia Corcelius: We've done everything as a group: organized around the #OnlyWhenItsSafe campaign, George Floyd uprising/Black Lives Matter movement, Stop Asian Hate, Teach the Truth, and more. We wrote and issued public statements and response letters together where one person (usually Darrin) would craft an initial draft and others (usually Carla and I) would edit. You would have many people's eyes on a document and since all the work we did nationally was virtual, we utilized Zoom, Google Docs, Facebook chat, and our Facebook group and page. In regards to our organizing materials, Rebecca was the Google Docs master. The way she knows how to put things in chapters and categories. I learned so much about organizing through NEU and everyone's struggles.

Organizing terrains between our states vary. Privatization, vouchers, charter schools, and the destruction of public education is a threat everywhere. In the suburbs and rural areas, it comes from the right-wing—which is an obvious enemy—but in the cities, it comes from wolves in sheep's clothing, neoliberal democrats.

Rebecca Garelli: I want to circle back to our accomplishments. As I was listening to Janette and all the beautiful words, she said that I 1,000% understand and agree with, I was reviewing all the things that we created, distributed, participated in, developed, and made available. Some of our main accomplishments were bringing in experts in the field, like the air quality industrial hygienist and building toolkits that many of us were building in our own states to build direct action. Week-long actions and combining both in-person safe actions and online actions. Teaching people step-by-step; how do you use targets and build a Twitter storm to uplift messages? How do you get out in the streets and build a motor march to raise awareness of the unsafe working conditions at schools? We built everything from graphics to messaging to here's the slide deck, take it, and go make sure you have a way to build lists at the events. That way, you can build a list in order to use that list for the next thing. How do you build momentum when you are organizing and move people through some organizing steps? A town hall is a beautiful thing because you can not only get people into a space to educate and inform them, but then you can also teach them to use the tools.

Some of that work we did, and Melissa is very good at teaching people how to use the toolkit in a real setting. So role playing, how do you identify issues and take it to the next level? How do you involve folks in organizing? How do you build a petition? Do you need us to help you build a petition? I remember building petitions for all kinds of people, like can you help us get something out? Yes, we can do that. We've got the systems. We've got Action Network. We can build things, building national petitions, and really just working our lists to try to get these things out. Then we built a cumulative list (it's on our website), called an organizing dashboard.

We made a one-stop shop collection powerhouse of every resource we use for organizing. Things from Labor Notes, things from New Jersey, from Arizona, from Washington, from California, so people could take it and go. I remember seeing our toolkits show up in Florida, show up in California, just spread and people were like, "Thank you, I have no time to build this. Thank you for helping. Can you make us a graphic that looks like your graphic, but can you put our name on it?" So we flipped things for people. They would use it and take it to a toolkit. Just really user-friendly. I remember getting a lot of messages about gratitude. For us, we really burnt ourselves out during this time. Quite frankly, we worked our tails off day-in, day-out, hours upon hours upon hours, building these toolkits. Virginia Educators United put out incredible toolkits, and NJ 21 United, and then Arizona. We were building all kinds of stuff here, just helping people. I would borrow from New Jersey and borrow from Carla and Janette, borrow, borrow, borrow and get those things. Washington was putting on town halls at the time. We were doing town halls in Kentucky and taking our sort of master slide deck for town halls and then flipping them out to other states. We were just trying to get this cycle of organizing going and saying, we're willing to do the work. Come, learn, and go because it's gonna take all of us and we need all that boots on the ground. So I feel like that was a lot of accomplishments. My favorite part of seeing that success was seeing that stuff pop up in other states across the nation.

The leaders were asked what they believed their primary accomplishment was or what action they believed had the greatest impact.

Melissa Tomlinson: I would definitely say the success of our #Only-WhenItsSafe campaign. I know for a fact that schools would have opened earlier had we not started pushing back immediately. We would have lost a lot more lives in this country than we did.

Ivonne Rovira: We were going to start school, I'm just going to make it up—on a Wednesday, like we usually do. They called a special meeting on a Thursday, so we ended up starting like three days later to get everything together to go virtual. I'm with Melissa. They would have been pedal to the metal even in the bastion of liberalism that is Louisville. That's how close they cut it. So they are clearly without everything I learned here, and the rest of us in our state . . . There are a bunch of us. A lot of people would have died.

Katie Ehrlich: That's exactly what I was just going to say. We probably would have returned to schools in-person and more people would have died, if not for what NEU did with those town halls and educating people on clean air and COVID-19. I remember having to teach people that COVID-19 doesn't care about all these things. COVID-19 will do this. Here is the science behind it. People didn't get it for the longest time. Doing all of that helped keep everyone safe, and it pushed the hand of the unions (AFT, NEA), and those in positions of power. I think we pushed them to make a safe decision for everyone.

Rebecca Garelli: I have actual tears in my eyes just thinking about this because the #OnlyWhenItsSafe campaign . . . I'm a science teacher, so organizing with science is literally what we needed. I felt most proud to be using science and organizing in tandem. Helping people understand the science of air particles was my personal favorite accomplishment. Thankfully, Melissa knew the industrial hygienist who taught us how to use the Harvard tool, which I have now taught to 1,000s of people, and we had over 20,000 views in no time at all.

At the town hall, we showed how to use the Harvard tool, and this tool taught people how to input their classroom sizes and then it would output. It was just a spreadsheet. Really complicated if you're not savvy. So we sat there, and we explained it step-by-step. How do you measure for your classroom? Then we brought in, how do you measure for radius? If I'm standing here, it's from the midpoint to out here. Draw a circle. We showed them the mathematical reasoning behind why you shouldn't have X amount of kids in the space, and then how to determine the right air cleaner for the classroom size.

This knowledge helped me push my own kids' school to have air cleaners in every single room. Because I had the knowledge, I showed up at the governing board meetings and emailed the district administrators and gave them the information on how to pick an air filter. Then we taught people how to build their own Corsi Rosenthal boxes using materials that cost $88 that were available at home improvement stores. We made a video and a toolkit with instructions for building these. I saw these DIY boxes popping up on social media in classrooms all over, and our toolkit getting shared, and I just was just so proud of the science behind the organizing because, well, I am a science teacher.

Moving forward, NEU will need to build a strong bottom-up, nationwide movement to meet our demands. This requires a mixture of old and new methods: deep organizing at school sites and other workplaces, in unions and community organizations, across multiple and diverse sectors, in coalition to take unified collective action of increasing size and intensity, combined with the rapid spreading of information through online means.

Stephanie Price: The thing that's really been on my mind lately are the continued targeted attacks against trans folx, LGBTQ+ folx, and Black and Brown folx. It's an organized movement to continue systems of oppression that have been upheld for hundreds of years. They're very smart about the way they're spinning the narratives. Something we need to start thinking about is how we build a movement to combat this. It's violence. It is violence against so many people in this country. As educators, we have a responsibility to teach all students. We have to support them, make sure they're safe, and let them know they matter. These bills being passed, books being banned, curriculum being whitewashed, and identities being attacked . . . it's all creating an unsafe environment. This has been on my mind for a while. I've been thinking about how we come back together as a group and fight for change. It's going to be incredibly important moving forward, especially because some of the rhetoric being pushed is so sneaky and insidious. Even in more progressive places like Washington, this is starting to creep up. We have parents showing up at school board meetings, pushing exclusionary and harmful policies. They don't believe in supporting our Black and Brown students, our trans students, our Queer students or educators, or anyone. How do we fight against this? Regarding accomplishments of the group, our COVID-19 organizing was necessary and important. I also want to say how incredible it's been to be part of such an awesome group of folks who've come together from across the country to do this work. The way we've respected, supported, cared for, and built each other up has been amazing. The love we have in this group of folks is an accomplishment in and of itself, especially considering some of us have never even met in person! I love you all.

Rebecca Garelli: First, I am crying by the way. You're beautiful and I heart you very much. You're right. I definitely was lost without you all, personally. One thing I really am thinking we need to talk about and organize around is, and I know it's because of where I live, is universal vouchers. I'm talking $900 million will be drained from public school funding because of universal vouchers in Arizona. It was determined during the previous year's legislative session that it would only be $30 million, and therefore, the state never budgeted for this program. So now you have homeschool moms here who have multiple children earning $7,000 per child via vouchers, therefore effectively making more money than actual certified teachers. This is literally happening as we speak. As you know, Arizona is ALEC's playground. If they can make things happen here, they will happen in other places. So for me because of where I am, part of what I believe we should do, and I've already had people in Michigan reach out because they are worried it's coming their way. They start whispers as you guys said. Florida has been asking us.

So I'm just thinking with the copycat bills and the model legislation, and Doug Ducey, who is our former Governor now becoming the head of that PAC? That's his new mission. We are in trouble. We are in serious, deep trouble with public education because they have found ways to take our money and use it for anything they want, including Charlie Kirk's nationalist school that has popped up in Arizona as a charter school. So for me, that's issue number one in getting people to realize. Most people don't know what's happening. Back to the basics.

People don't understand the power behind ALEC and the think tank power in the model legislation, copycat bills, and 35 states where these model legislations just keep being churned out. We need to tell people what is happening because you're going to watch us have no money very soon.

Editor's Note: You can follow National Educators United on Facebook, Instagram, and X. Their website is https://www.nationaleducatorsunited.org/

References

National Educators United. (n.d. -a). *About.* https://www.nationaleducatorsunited.org/about

National Educators United. (n.d. -b). *Demands.* https://www.nationaleducatorsunited.org/demands

CHAPTER 11

NYCoRE's Inquiry-to-Action Groups: Developing Political Education Toward Liberatory Futures in Education

Jennifer Queenan, Natalia Ortiz, and Pam Segura

WHILE TEACHER ACTIVISM[1] has received more attention in the press over the last several years with the Red for Ed waves of teacher strikes, teacher activism is not new. We are writing this chapter as members of the New York Collective of Radical Educators (NYCoRE), a teacher activist group founded in 2002. NYCoRE is part of the Teacher Activist Group (TAG) Network, "a national coalition of grassroots teacher organizing groups. Together, we engage in shared political education and relationship building in order to work for educational justice both nationally and in our local communities" (Teacher Activist Groups, n.d.). While the coalition is no longer meeting due to capacity, the groups in this network remain in touch. In this chapter, we will give a brief background regarding NYCoRE's history and structure and then focus on one aspect of NYCoRE's work that we are all deeply engaged in: political education through Inquiry to Action Groups (ItAGs).

When NYCoRE was founded, there were not many radical[2] groups for teachers to join in New York City if they wanted to organize with others beyond the walls of their classrooms. The United Federation of Teachers (UFT) had/has a history of racism that one can trace back to the Ocean Hill Brownsville strike (Back, 2001; Podair, 2002) and UFT leadership has consistently avoided addressing social justice issues (Asselin, 2019; Schirmer & Tarlau, 2022; Weiner, 2012), as social justice caucuses within the UFT, like the Movement of Rank and File Educators have continuously named. There were several factors that led to the founding of NYCoRE. In NYCoRE meetings, we often talk about what we are confronting as a Hydra[3] with "the internal organs of the Hydra [being] neoliberalism, structural racism, Whiteness and White supremacy, racial capitalism, and accumulation by dispossession" (Picower & Mayorga, 2015, p. 5). If we use the Hydra as a framing, then the heads of the Hydra that contributed to NYCoRE's founding include the privatization of and disinvestment in New York City public schools under neoliberal policies, racism in the UFT and a lack of organizing spaces for radical educators, and government actions post-9/11, including military recruitment of Black and Brown youth in public schools.

The first NYCoRE meeting, where the six founding members came together to discuss ideas for the group, took place in October 2002. Jessica Klonsky and Lisa Adler met beforehand while attending protests against the U.S. military's response to 9/11. Jessica and Daniel "Herm" Jerome knew one another through previous political work and Jessica reached out to Herm after she and Lisa decided they wanted to bring together teachers to push back against military recruitment in schools. Herm knew Keith Catone, Chris Maestro, and Ariana Mangual Figueroa because they were all teachers at Banana Kelly High School and brought them in. NYCoRE opened meetings to other participants in 2003 and started a public email listserv in 2004.

While NYCoRE initially came together around antiwar sentiments, the founding members never intended for NYCoRE to be a single-issue group. In the early days, NYCoRE developed points of unity through study—modeled after the Black Panthers and Young Lords—as well as a mission statement. Our mission is as follows:

> New York Collective of Radical Educators (NYCoRE) is a group of current and former public-school educators and their allies committed to fighting for social justice in our school system and society at large, by organizing and mobilizing teachers, developing curriculum, and working with community, parent, and student organizations. We are educators who believe that education is an integral part of social change and that we must work both inside and outside the classroom because the struggle for justice does not end when the school bell rings. (New York Collective of Radical Educators. n.d. -b)

The first points of unity were finalized in 2003. They were revised by NYCoRE leadership in 2014 and again in 2022. Our most recent iteration of our points of unity is below:

1. **We believe in education that centers collective liberation and self-actualization for everyone.** Currently, racism, especially anti-Black racism, neoliberalism, and racial capitalism, are driving forces in educational systems, policies, and practices. These forces perpetuate the systematic and historical oppression of BIPOC and other marginalized folx; they work in concert with all forms of oppression to perpetuate a school system that is antithetical to collective liberation. As educators, we have a responsibility to address systems of oppression and their manifestations as they impact our students, our profession, and public education as a whole.
2. **We believe that humans are complex and beautiful and cannot be evaluated by a number.** We oppose high stakes standardized testing, as well as punitive grading measures, because they are tools of corporatization, stratification, and social reproduction meant to rank students and teachers rather than recognize their humanity. We recognize the racist history of standardized testing in the eugenics movement. We support creative approaches to develop local, holistic assessments that provide more insight than one-size-fits-all exams and numerical grades. Rather than replacing tests with tests, we believe schools need to develop more democratic, student-centered systems of assessment and grading.
3. **We believe education should center healing and address the systemic causes and impacts of harm using transformative justice practices.** Punitive disciplinary measures and policing inside and outside of schools disproportionately criminalize low-income students, BIPOC students and students with disabilities, and are not an answer to crime and other social problems. Accountability approaches should work toward transformative justice and foster community accountability. Educators and schools should build restorative justice practices,[4] honor and name the Indigenous roots of this work, and develop an understanding of the systems of oppression that many of the harms in our society come from.

Note: We recognize that restorative justice intends to restore back to the conditions that were present before the harm happened and that schools are often inherently violent places, making restorative justice challenging. In other words, do we really want to restore back to a violent, oppressive environment? We also recognize that transformative justice practices often operate outside of institutions as they currently exist and so we are using restorative justice as actions that are currently being attempted in schools. However, we envision a world where educational spaces use transformative justice practices but also know that we have a long way to get there.

4. **We believe schools should be places of global solidarity and sanctuary so that people can live in their full humanity.** We oppose state violence in any form—military recruitment at school sites, policies that encourage marginalized students to enlist, the presence of police and metal detectors in schools, the idealization of war in our curriculum, the presence of ICE in our schools, and other measures that encourage increased contact with law enforcement, to name a few. These efforts are an extension of an imperialist, colonialist and racist strategy to protect and promote U.S. world dominance and oppress BIPOC and poor peoples around the country and world. As educators, we should create curricula that critically examine U.S. imperialism and colonization and fight for schools as true sanctuaries.
5. **We believe school funding policies should ensure equitable resources for all through transparency and accountability to community members.** The prevailing funding structure based upon property taxes discriminates against low-income communities and urban areas, which disproportionately affect BIPOC students. Approaches to educational "reform" that rely on private philanthropy, venture capital, and other nonpublic forms of funding, along with the ciphering of public funds to charter schools, are part of a broader trend of divestment from public education. The current system of mayoral control in many urban areas gives politicians and public education leaders unchecked power to decide how taxpayers' money is allocated in public schools. School district and individual school budgets should

be determined by all stakeholders, especially parents and students. Funding high-quality and equitable public education is a public responsibility that should be shared for the benefit of the common good.

6. **We believe schools should be affirming spaces for every human's varying gender and sexual identities.** Schools often perpetuate cisheteropatriarchy. People who identify as (or are perceived as being) women/girls, gender nonconforming, nonbinary, transgender, lesbian, gay, bisexual, queer or questioning (LGBTQAI+ and beyond) are verbally, physically, and emotionally abused in and outside of schools in addition to being excluded and othered in curriculum and by the school community. All school community members must cultivate spaces that actively affirm LGBTQAI+ youth, families and staff. This can be done through centering queer joy and play, providing gender affirming health resources, LGBTQAI+ forward curriculum, comprehensive sexual education, and access to gender neutral bathrooms, among other actions.
7. **We believe schools should be places of questioning and critical thinking.** The current factory model is not student-centered and devalues teacher expertise; stifles creativity due to standardized tests/curriculum and the elimination of the arts, health, and movement classes; polices bodies and language; generates burnout due to lack of school staff support and large class sizes; and more. We believe all students deserve school environments that nurture creativity and inquiry, foster love, and embrace their communities. Teaching and learning should enable students to see themselves as transformative agents of change.
8. **We believe schools should be part of their communities.** Top-down bureaucracy, mayoral control, and racism lead to a lack of relationships and trust between schools, families, and the communities they serve. Thus, schools are often distant and far removed from the lives of students. Schools should be loving, healing-centered spaces where all community voices are heard. There should be mutual accountability between families, community members, and school workers in addressing the needs and care of the local and NYC-wide community. Genuine school and community solidarity has the power to transform our society and create radical possibilities.

9. **We believe all students deserve an environment where they can flourish physically, intellectually, and emotionally.** Our education system promotes an ableist, Eurocentric, English-dominant, deficit-based framework in which many students cannot thrive, and their strengths and differences are ignored or penalized. This mistreatment, miseducation, and misidentification disproportionately impacts disabled students and multilingual learners, especially those with multiple marginalizations. Schools must be spaces in which all students receive holistic support, which includes academic, social, emotional, language, and health services that are true to their individual needs. All students deserve the right to live fully self-determined lives.
10. **We believe in the power of social justice unionism to transform our schools and ultimately our world.** The United Federation of Teachers was founded on anti-socialist and anti-Black racist views through red-baiting, and later, striking against the Black community in the 1968 Ocean Hill-Brownsville Strike. This history, along with the UFT's bureaucracy and lack of transparency, has disillusioned many members and pinned its members against the students and families they serve. The UFT must recognize the impact of its actions by paying reparations to the Ocean Hill-Brownsville communities and creating more democracy among its rank-and-file members and accountability within its leadership. As UFT members and educational stakeholders, we should organize to transform the UFT to be a social justice and rank and file led teachers' union, in solidarity with students and community, in order to radically improve the working and learning conditions of school staff and students.
11. **In order to combat economic, social, and political systems that actively silence Black, Indigenous, People of Color, women, and gender expansive folx, NYCoRE is committed to being an intersectional, anti-oppressive organization.** We maintain a majority of women, gender expansive, and BIPOC representation in our leadership and strive[5] to do the same in our community. (New York Collective of Radical Educators. n.d. -c)

NYCoRE membership currently consists of three levels: a core or leadership body, active members who facilitate and participate in events and projects, and a listserv of supporters. We—the authors of this chapter—are all core members of NYCoRE. Natalia began teaching and joined NYCoRE in 2006 as an active ItAG participant. She joined the core in 2009 and in 2012, Natalia left the classroom and went on to complete a PhD in Urban Education. She is currently a Clinical Assistant Professor at New York University (NYU) in the Department of Teaching and Learning. Jenna is a white, queer educator. She first got involved with NYCoRE in 2011 while student teaching. She taught English as a New Language at a public high school in Brooklyn for 7 years before leaving to begin a PhD in Urban Education at the City University of New York. Pam began attending NYCoRE monthly meetings and participating in ItAGs in 2016. Pam recently left the classroom to study General Psychology at the New School for Social Research after teaching in nonprofit and K-12 settings for nearly 10 years.

Broadly, NYCoRE's work consists of creating a political home for radical educators, providing critical professional development, and connecting educators to action, whether that be specific organizing campaigns led by other groups, attending protests and other political actions together, or supporting educators in creating change in their school buildings (Queenan et al., 2024). Historically, NYCoRE also organized around specific issues through working groups. Over time, NYCoRE has had working groups on issues such as counter-military recruitment, anti-high stakes testing, fighting against the criminalization of youth, affirming queer youth and educators, a specific space to support new teachers, an Educators of Color affinity group, an Anti-Racist White Educators affinity group, standing in solidarity with undocumented youth and families, and fighting ableism in education. However, with the onset of the pandemic, most groups stopped meeting and we are currently rethinking the role of working groups in NYCoRE's structure.

Inquiry to Action Groups

NYCoRE members began holding ItAGs in the winter of 2004, calling on the group's internal network of radical teacher activists to facilitate (Picower, 2015). This political education model was inspired by Freire's praxis, using reflection plus action and dialectical relationships, as well as engaging with West Coast educator scholars who were investigating their own questions and creating circles of dialogue with and amongst teachers, calling them critical inquiry groups. Our definition of an ItAG is as follows:

> An ItAG is an Inquiry to Action Group. It's similar to a study group, but the goal is that after the group inquires into a particular topic, they will together create action around their area of study, making it a true community of praxis. The topics and themes chosen are always consistent with NYCoRE's points of unity. (New York Collective of Radical Educators, n.d. -a)

ItAGs bring about educational justice by creating the following three conditions for social justice–minded, public-school educators (Picower, 2015): (1) a political home that provides a sense of emotional groundedness and social connections with other teachers; (2) critical professional development that counters the harm from traditional, top-down approaches of education and teacher education; and (3) leadership experiences that are centered on sharing rather than amassing power. These three conditions sustain the profoundly difficult work of social justice–minded educators. The ItAG space helps repair some of the harm that many social justice–minded educators witness and experience in their school through providing opportunities to build and strategize with other like-minded educators. In addition to a healing space, ItAGs also create the opportunities for teachers to begin their political awakening.

ItAGs create a political home for educators who already have radical, leftist politics, marginalized identities and those who are curious and looking to sharpen their political consciousness (Picower, 2015; Queenan et al., 2024). These educators are often encouraged to be apolitical in school and, when they are not, are at greater risk of being targeted and/or pushed out of schools (Burciaga & Kohli, 2018; Castaneda et al., 2006; Retta, 2021). A political home through the ItAG, in turn, allows social justice–minded educators to develop an action plan from a series of discussions and learning experiences that have a critical power analysis. These experiences lead to long-term friendships, continued engagement with NYCoRE, and solidarity between organizing groups. This is an integral part of NYCoRE's mission and vision beyond the ItAGs: loving relationships cultivate stronger bonds between people and lead to deeper movement work (Brown, 2017; Freire & Freire, 1997) and, in turn, help remedy the wounds from the conflict, abuse, and harm that is enveloped in social justice education and liberation work (Pour-Khorshid, 2016).

ItAGs led by educators are an example of critical professional development (CPD) (Kohli et al., 2015). Through CPD, teachers are positioned as active agents in their own learning and pushed to center students and families with a justice lens. ItAGs function as critical professional learning spaces because they are self-directed, there is shared power between facilitators and participants, and it is not top-down technical training. Through ItAGs, teachers have the opportunity to interrogate problematic systems within their school districts; they can feel, think, mourn, process, and challenge in ways that honor their expertise and humanity (Picower, 2015). ItAGs and teacher CPD are a subset of political education, an education accessible to educators that offers critical inquiry and an investigation of power and collective agency led by and for the educators themselves. We need political education spaces, like ItAGs, that function outside of institutions in order to help us envision liberatory education spaces for our society more broadly.

Upon nurturing emotional groundedness, social connections, and intellectual play, ItAGs provide new ways of embodying leadership. Teachers who have participated in Inquiry to Action Groups leave with emotional, intellectual, and professional skills (Picower, 2015). Throughout the ItAGs, participants practice leading critical discussions based on both text analysis and lived experience, strengthen their understanding and work in adult learning spaces, and engage in action research. This leadership is premised on shared power, transformative justice, and critical relationships.

The Action in Inquiry to Action Groups

NYCoRE ItAGs center community and political education because we believe these are necessary prerequisites for action, whether that action is a shift in personal practice or on-the-ground organizing to change material conditions. We see political education as "a particular theoretical framework for supporting and encouraging social change, but in each specific context that framework takes on a unique form appropriate for a specific group of people of a particular culture in a specific community" (Boyd, 2012). Over time, NYCoRE ItAGs have covered a variety of topics, as illustrated in Table 1. Each ItAG takes its own approach to action and learning that is specific to the topic and sociopolitical context of the moment. The emphasis in ItAGs is "on collective rather than individual learning, and the use of an action-reflection-action approach to learning commonly referred to as praxis" (Boyd, 2012), which many have learned about through reading texts like Paulo Freire's *Pedagogy of the Oppressed.*

Table 11.1.
NYCoRE ItAGs Offered by Year and Title

2023	**2022** (Remote)	**2021** (Remote)	**2020** (Pandemic Year, transitioned to remote)
Radical Visions: Educators as School Abolitionists	Radical Visions: Educators as School Abolitionists	Radical Visions: Educators as School Abolitionists	ReTIE: Reimagining Trauma-Informed Education
Musical Circles: Restore and Transform	The Transformative Power of Art	Envisioning Democracy in Schools: The Roots of Resistance for Community Control of Schools	From Sí Se Puede to Pa'lante: Ethnic Studies in New York City
Dreaming Disability Justice: Reorienting towards Inclusion	Dreaming Disability Justice: Reorienting towards Inclusion		
	Queer and Beyond: Reflecting on the Schooling of Gender Identity and Sexuality		
	From Framework to Practice: Creating the Learning Communities We Deserve		

Table 11.1. continued
NYCoRE ItAGs Offered by Year and Title

2019	2018	2017	2016
NYCoRE Creates!	Critical Ethnic Studies: Disrupting the Histories of Colonialism in STEM	AFFIRMATIONS: Honoring Self & Community Care for & with Educators of Color	STEM Education: Unpacking the Hidden Curriculum
Radical Mamas	Care-giving, Risk-taking, & Role-making: Learning from and Connecting with Mama-Activists and their Children	Care-giving, Risk-taking, & Role-making: Models of Mama-Activists Around the Globe	Not Just a Suspension Alternative: Tracing the Cultural and Philosophical Roots of Restorative Justice
Toward a Freedom School: Permission to be Radical	Youth Spectatorship in Media and Film	Clown Class: Searching for Fun in the Classroom	Time to Act: Reflecting, Unpacking, and Confronting Racism Through Theatre
This is what an Anti-Racist school would look like. How do we get there?	MADLib: Musicians Actively Designing Liberation	MADLib: Musicians Actively Designing Liberation	Storytelling to Heal Ourselves and Educate our Youth
Digital Storytelling with Teachers For Educators of Color	Liberation not Deportation!: Youth and Educators Collaborating for Undocumented Resistance in Schools	Radical Imaginations: Education Beyond Racial Capitalism	Critical Educational Leadership
		Islamophobia in Context: How to Respond as Educators and Allies	
		The Power of Art and Healing	

Table 11.1. continued
NYCoRE ItAGs Offered by Year and Title

2015	2014	2013	2011
Don't Call Me Baby: Speaking about Sexism	Mindfulness in Teaching and Action: Building a Radical Practice	No Human Being is Illegal: Transforming NYC Schools into Supportive Spaces for Undocumented Youth	Interrupting Islamophobia
Pushing Back Against Pushout: Restorative Approaches to School Discipline (Teachers Unite)	Critically Unpacking Race with Educators of Color	What does Mayoral Control got to do with it?	Queer! Fag! Tranny! Dyke! : Exploring Gender, Sexuality, and Anti-LGBT Bullying
Teaching Cuba: Another World is Possible	Beyond Scores, Ranks & Rubrics: Re-imagining Teacher Evaluation	The Criminalization of Our Youth: What is it? Why is it happening? How can radical educators challenge it?	Filling in the Gaps: Support and Action for Developing Teachers
#Beyond the Marches: Living, Teaching and Organizing through the Intersections	Migration is Beautiful: Empowering Undocumented Students to Advocate for Themselves (NYSYLC)	Listening to Marginal Voices: Exploring Queer Latino Identity	My Classroom is Anti-Racist: Theory to Practice to Action
Transforming the Curriculum: Social Justice Pedagogy Meets Mandated Curricula	Engaged Pedagogy: Building Emotionally Responsive Practices into our Classrooms	Stand Up, Fight Back! Teaching Young Children to Take a Stand	
Meet me Half-Way: #Undocumented Students and #OurSchools (NYSYLC)			

Table 11.1. continued
NYCoRE ItAGs Offered by Year and Title

2009	2008	2007	2006-2005
Social Justice in Teacher Education	Making Schools Responsive to Immigrant Youth	African Diaspora Cultural Arts Education and Social Justice in the Classroom	Transforming Mainstream Curriculum into Social Justice Teaching
Teachers as Organizers	Education for Liberation: Bringing Freire & Boal's ideas into NYC Public Schools	Radical Math	Authentic Assessment in a Test Crazed Context
Revolutionizing the Classroom: Transforming Mainstream Curriculum into Social Justice Teaching	Unveiling Islam for Greater Community Awareness	Creating Safe Community for LGBT Youth and Straight Allies	Creating Powerful Parent/Teacher Relationships for School Change
What does it mean to be a Radical Educator? A Space for Beginning Teachers to Explore and Learn	Bridging the Gap: CBO Partners working in schools for social change	Media Justice	See All That You Can See: Understanding and Teaching About the Military Industrial Complex from a Systemic Perspective
Combating the Banking Mentality: Integrating Media and Youth Culture into the Classroom			
Rethinking Discipline/ Building Community			

In order to reflect on what actions ItAGs have led to over the past 18 years, we looked through descriptions of past ItAGs, many of which can be found on NYCoRE's website, contacted previous ItAG facilitators to ask about the actions that emerged from their ItAG, and used our own memories. These memories came from ItAGs we were involved in or knew about through our roles as NYCoRE core members: Pam and Natalia through serving as ItAG co-coordinators, and Jenna through conducting oral histories and collecting other documentation from former NYCoRE core members. We then compiled a list of actions from each ItAG to analyze.

We recognize that action is an amorphous term that can be used in many ways. As educators, we believe deeply in the importance of defining and clarifying meaning. With that being said, the actions in ItAGs are "always left up to the participants and facilitators. It takes different forms depending on the topic and the people involved" (New York Collective of Radical Educators, n.d. -a). Generally, however, actions in ItAGs focus on the participants taking the learning from the ItAG and applying it—acting on it—outside of the ItAG, whether in their schools, personal lives, or more broadly in New York City and beyond. In examining the list of actions that emerged from NYCoRE ItAGs, we were able to identify four main types of actions: shifts in personal practice, the development of a public resource, engagement in a public action or presentation, and the formation of a working group. Below, we describe each in more detail.

Shifts in Personal Practice

The majority of ItAG actions focused on shifts in participants' personal practices, either in their classrooms, more broadly in their schools, or in day-to-day interactions in their lives and communities. These shifts include changes to participants' curriculum and pedagogies; adaptations in school culture and structures, such as starting an after-school club or speaking with administration about a school policy; and changes in participants' ways of being that resulted from developing radical consciousness in the ItAG community around various systems of oppression and how they manifest. Some examples[6] from past ItAGs include (New York Collective of Radical Educators. n.d. -a):

1. Radical Visions: Educators as School Abolitionists (2023)—Each participant was assigned a buddy to stay in touch with after the ItAG to continue to workshop and brainstorm ways to bring more humanizing, restorative practices to their schools and classroom practices.
2. Care-giving, Risk-taking, & Role-making: Models of Mama-Activists Around the Globe (2017)—"Each week, ItAG members will read about, engage in dialogue with, and learn from other radical mamas with the goal of developing strategies for radical mothering as educators in this historical moment."
3. Islamophobia in Context: How to Respond as Educators and Allies (2017)—"Participants will develop strategies for addressing Islamophobia in schools and/or communities." This ItAG also compiled resources to use in addressing Islamophobia in curriculum.
4. Mindfulness in Teaching and Action: Building a Radical Practice (2014)—"We will also begin to cultivate our own practices, collectively and individually, through a variety of different meditation exercises."
5. Applying Popular Education to the Classroom (2010)—"Texts will include excerpts from *Pedagogy of the Oppressed* [red edition], *Games for Actors and Non-actors,* and assorted letters and "talking chapters" by Freire and others. The goal is to bring these texts to life and make sense of them for NYC Public Schools, finding ways for people to put radical pedagogy into their daily practices, while also using theater of the oppressed tools and practices."
6. Combating the Banking Mentality: Integrating Media and Youth Culture into the Classroom (2009)—"Participants will create a vision of the kinds of classroom environments they hope to create through the integration of youth culture and will be introduced to a variety of strategies and methods. Participants will gain a better understanding of what resources and strategies they can use to create interactive classrooms that build on students' interests."
7. See All That You Can See: Understanding and Teaching About the Military Industrial Complex (MIC) from a Systemic Perspective (2006) —"During the final weeks participants will be encouraged to focus

on designing curricula, resources, and potential actions that can be used to teach a systemic understanding of the MIC in a variety of educational contexts."

Development of a Public Resource

Several ItAGs decided to produce a resource of some type, such as a curriculum guide, or list of resources for informing oneself around the ItAG topic, which were then typically shared via a pdf on NYCoRE's website or through the creation of a separate website. These resources often took time and labor beyond the 6 to 8 weeks of the ItAG and were put together by participants as well as facilitators. Some examples from past ItAGs include (New York Collective of Radical Educators, n.d. -a):

- Time to Act: Reflecting, Unpacking, and Confronting Racism Through Theatre (2016)—"This ItAG will be part of a larger research project that documents how applied theater and theater of the oppressed techniques can be used with teachers to facilitate conversations about and around Race and Racism."
- No Human Being is Illegal: Transforming NYC Schools into Supportive Spaces for Undocumented Youth (2013)—After the ItAG, a group of participants continued to meet to create a website on supporting undocumented youth in schools, which can be accessed at: https://teachdreamnyc.wordpress.com/
- African Diaspora Cultural Arts Education and Social Justice in the Classroom (2007)—Teacher participants created a curriculum guide with lesson plans tailored to their student's needs that addressed a social justice issue while learning about African diaspora cultural art. The Guide can be downloaded at: http://www.nycore.org/newsite/wp-content/uploads/Cultural_Arts_ITAG_BOOK.pdf

Engagement in a Public Action or Presentation

Several, although not many, ItAGs coordinated a public-facing event, such as a march or performance, or connected with local grassroots activism. In years where the NYCoRE conference took place, all ItAGs were invited to do a workshop at the conference to share their learnings with the broader NYCoRE community. More recently, since the start of the pandemic, NYCoRE has hosted an ItAG closing event at the end of ItAG season, in which ItAG participants share their experiences with other ItAGs. In 2023, we hosted an open meeting to close out ItAGs and invited the broader NYCoRE community to come to learn from each ItAG. Some of the public actions that ItAGs have organized include (New York Collective of Radical Educators. n.d. -a):

- Musical Circles: Restore and Transform (2023): From one of the facilitators—"We got to create a collaborative composition like a quilt, putting together everyone's verses on the topic of "I am" and we got to support and uplift one another by adding improvised background vocals and building off of each other's lines and experiences." This ItAG included both students and educators.
- Care-giving, Risk-taking, & Role-making: Learning from and Connecting with Mama-Activists and their Children (2018)—The ItAG facilitated the first ever Children's March at the NYCoRE 2018 Conference, inspired by the Children's Crusade in 1963.
- Migration is Beautiful: Empowering Undocumented Students to Advocate for Themselves, facilitated in collaboration with the New York State Youth Leadership Council (2014)—Participants learned about and participated in the NYSYLC campaign to pass the New York Dream Act.
- The Criminalization of Our Youth: What is it? Why is it happening? How can radical educators challenge it? (2013)—"The goal of this ITAG is to investigate the criminalization of our youth, find ways to challenge what has become known as the School-to-Prison Pipeline, and connect with grassroots activism."
- Public Education for the 99% (2012)—"The ItAG will collaborate with members of Occupy the Department of Education (DOE), Occupy Wall Street (OWS), and will be action oriented throughout the process."

- Interrupting Islamophobia (2011)—The ItAG culminated in the Coming Out Muslim theater performance, performed by Terna Tilley-Gyado and Wazina Zondon.
- Queer! Fag! Tranny! Dyke!: Exploring Gender, Sexuality, and Anti-LGBT Bullying (2011)—"As a closing to our ItAG, participants will plan and participate in a political action that will address a specific issue that relates to anti-LGBT bullying."
- Radical Math (2007)—"Participants will work together to create a presentation(s) for a conference on Math Education and Social Justice occurring in New York this April."

We want to pause here to note and reflect on the fact that ItAGs typically do not lead to school or city-wide organizing to change the material conditions that exist in schools. However, some of the ItAGs (as well as other work NYCoRE has done) did/does connect with groups in New York City that were/are doing on-the-ground organizing and campaign work.

Formation of a Working Group

Several ItAGs determined the need to continue meeting to support shifts in personal practice, sharing resources, and connecting to organizing and advocacy campaigns in New York City. To do so, these ItAGs became working groups in NYCoRE and continued to meet at NYCoRE open meetings as well as separately. These working groups include (New York Collective of Radical Educators. n.d. -a):

- Dreaming Disability Justice: Reorienting towards Inclusion (2023)—While this group did not become an official NYCoRE working group, as working groups are not currently functioning in NYCoRE, the group decided to stay in touch via a discord group to continue to share resources and discuss practice.
- No Human Being is Illegal: Transforming NYC Schools into Supportive Spaces for Undocumented Youth (2013)—After creating the website mentioned above, this ItAG continued to meet as the Teach Dream working group. Teach Dream officially joined the New York State Youth Leadership Council as their educator team in 2020.

- My Classroom is Anti-Racist: Theory to Practice to Action (2011)—This ItAG led to the formation of the Anti-Racist White Educators Group, a White affinity space/working group in NYCoRE.
- Creating Safe Community for LGBT Youth and Straight Allies (2007)—This ItAG became the NYQueer working group, which "focuse[d] on gender and sexuality as they relate to school communities" (NYQueer, n.d.).

Reflections and Conclusion

For 17 years, NYCoRE and its educator members, through ItAGs, have been organizing political education that is by us, for us, and outside of the top-down professional development bureaucracy. ItAGs have led to shifts in personal teaching practice and pedagogy, the creation and sharing of public resources that further the conscientização of teachers (Freire, 1970), public actions, the making of public art and sharing of knowledge in conference spaces via workshops, and lastly, the continuing of praxis via a working group model. It is our belief that ItAGs set the stage to further educational changes in our classroom and beyond, providing the political education necessary to further NYCoRE's ultimate goal, which is "to have liberatory educational practices/pedagogy, classrooms, and public schools for our students, families, teachers, and communities as a microcosm/model/example for society at large/the society we'd like to create." ItAGs create spaces to practice the liberatory educational pedagogies and practices we wish for in all educational spaces in the future. More broadly, we believe that developing political consciousness through engaging in political education is a necessary part of revolutionary, liberatory work. Beyond developing a deeper critical analysis, ItAGs activate educators to contribute in some way to the change needed in schools as we work toward liberatory educational spaces.

Over the years, NYCoRE has been asked by other organizing teacher activist groups, and individual educators trying to bring together teachers at the local level, how to create Inquiry to Action Groups. The Education for Liberation Network featured a NYCoRE ItAG How To as part of their EdLib Lab, which, while no longer publicly available, was up on the website for over 10 years. In addition, we have had calls and meetings to discuss our ItAG model with educators across the country, have been invited to present and lead workshops on

ItAGs at the Institute for Teachers of Color Conference as well as the Abolitionist Teaching Network, and were featured in *The Assembly*, a journal for public scholarship on education. Our ItAG model has supported the creation of new teacher inquiry spaces, and is part of a larger network of teacher inquiry groups across the country, creating professional learning praxis circles outside of the top-down professional development structure. Some of these groups include People's Ed Movement Teacher Inquiry Groups in the Bay and Los Angeles, California; Teachers 4 Social Justice Study Groups in San Francisco, California; Teachers for Social Justice in Chicago; and more.

While ItAGs are only one piece of our work, we chose to write about them here because we see a particular need for ItAGs, and other teacher inquiry groups like them, in the sociopolitical moment we are currently in. Across the United States, educators and students are experiencing continued budget cuts and the gutting of public education (Picower & Mayorga, 2015; Zimmerman, 2023). They are being told to go back to "normal" when we know the normal prior to the pandemic was harmful (Love, 2020; Villavicencio, 2022). In addition, the proliferation of government policies that critique and limit the discussion of racial oppression and queerness (amongst other critical theories) continues to silence and marginalize liberatory classrooms (Belsha, 2022; Waxman, 2022). It is no surprise to us, given these conditions, that so many teachers are leaving the profession (Barnum, 2023). Educators need spaces to learn and grow that are also healing, which we believe ItAGs provide. With this context in mind, we close with some questions we are in continual reflection around regarding our Inquiry to Action Groups:

1. What do educators most need in the current moment? How can ItAGs meet these needs? What political education do educators always need, regardless of the current socio-political context?
2. How can ItAGs be both responsive to the current moment while also understanding that the fight is ongoing?
3. How are ItAGs, if at all, working to help change the material conditions in schools?
4. What is our responsibility, as a group grounded in New York City, to national and international educational justice movements?

5. Particularly with the ongoing pandemic in mind, how do we continue to hold ItAGs while meeting the multiple needs of our participants: in person, hybrid, virtual, etc?

Editor's Note: You can follow New York Collective of Radical Educators on Facebook, Instagram, and X. Their website is http://www.nycore.org/

References

Asselin, C. (2019). *See value in the tension and see opportunity there: Teacher union democratization in two social justice caucuses in New York City and Philadelphia* [Doctoral Dissertation, City University of New York]. CUNY Academic Works.

Back, A. (2001). Blacks, Jews and the struggle to integrate Brooklyn's Junior High School 258: A Cold War story. *Journal of American Ethnic History 20*(2), 38–69. https://doi.org/10.2307/27502676

Barnum, M. (2023, March 6). 'I just found myself struggling to keep up': Number of teachers quitting hits new high. *USA TODAY*. https://www.usatoday.com/story/news/education/2023/03/06/more-teachers-quitting-than-usual-driven-stress-politics-data-shows/11390639002/

Belsha, K. (2022, April 12). *Schools grapple with new restrictions on teaching gender and sexuality.* Chalkbeat. https://www.chalkbeat.org/2022/4/12/23022356/teaching-restrictions-gender-identity-sexual-orientation-lgbtq-issues-health-education

Boyd, D. (2012). *Under the radar: Popular education in North America.* COMM-ORG Papers. https://comm-org.wisc.edu/papers2012/boyd.htm#about

Brown, A. (2017). *Emergent strategy.* AK Press.

Burciaga, R., & Kohli, R. (2018). Disrupting whitestream measures of quality teaching: The community cultural wealth of teachers of color. *Multicultural Perspectives, 20*(1), 5–12, DOI: 10.1080/15210960.2017.1400915

Castaneda, C., Kambutu, J., & Rios, F. (2006). Speaking their truths. *The Rural Educator, 27*(3). https://doi.org/10.35608/ruraled.v27i3.490

Freire, P. (1970). *Pedagogy of the oppressed.* Herder and Herder.

Freire, P., & Freire, A. M. A. (1997). *Pedagogy of the heart.* Continuum.

Kohli, R., Picower, B., Martinez, A., & Ortiz, N. (2015). Critical professional development: Centering the social justice needs of teachers. *International Journal of Critical Pedagogy, 6*(2), 7–24. https://doi.org/10.1080/19415257.2020.1814387

Love, B. L. (2020, December 3). Teachers, we cannot go back to the way things were (Opinion). *Education Week.* https://www.edweek.org/leadership/opinion-teachers-we-cannot-go-back-to-the-way-things-were/2020/04

New York Collective of Radical Educators. (n.d. -a). Inquiry to Action Groups (ItAGs). http://www.nycore.org/projects-2/itags/

New York Collective of Radical Educators. (n.d. -b). Mission. http://www.nycore.org/nycore-info/mission/

New York Collective of Radical Educators. (n.d. -c). Points of Unity. http://www.nycore.org/nycore-info/points-of-unity/

NYQueer. (n.d.). *About NYQueer.* New York Collective of Radical Educators. http://www.nycore.org/projects-2/nyqueer/

Picower, B. (2015). Nothing about us without us: Teacher-driven critical professional development. *Radical Pedagogy, 12*(1).

Picower, B., & Mayorga, E. (2015). Introduction. In B. Picower & E. Mayorga (Eds.), *What's race got to do with it?: How current school reform policy maintains racial and economic inequality, Volume 2* (pp. 1–20). Peter Lang.

Podair, J. E. (2002) *The strike that changed New York: Blacks, whites, and the Ocean Hill-Brownsville crisis*. Yale University Press.

Pour-Khorshid, F. (2016). HELLA: Collective *testimonio* that speak to the healing, empowerment, love, liberation, and action embodied by social justice educators of color. *Association of Mexican American Educators Journal, 10*(2), 16–32.

Queenan, J., Ortiz, N., Segura, P., Frascella, R., Troiano, A., & Velazquez, E. (2024). Learning from our history: The role of the New York Collective of Radical Educators in movements for educational justice. *Radical Teacher, 128.* https://doi.org/10.5195/rt.2024.1010

Retta, M. (2021, January 21). Teachers say they've faced scrutiny, discipline for progressive views. *Teen Vogue*. https://www.teenvogue.com/story/teachers-backlash-progressive-views

Schirmer, E., & Tarlau, R. (2022). "Never let a good crisis go to waste": Labor organizing during COVID-19. *Journal of Labor and Society (2022)*, 1–34. https://doi.org/10.1163/24714607-bja10069

Teacher Activist Groups. (n.d.). *Teacher Activist Groups.* The National Network of Teacher Activist Groups. https://teacheractivists.org/

Villavicencio, A. (2022, November 2). *Why schools' going back to 'normal' won't work for students of color.* The Conversation. https://theconversation.com/why-schools-going-back-to-normal-wont-work-for-students-of-color-192228

Waxman, O. B. (2022, June 30). Anti-'critical race theory' laws are working: Teachers are thinking twice about how they talk about race. *Time*. https://time.com/6192708/critical-race-theory-teachers-racism/

Weiner, L. (2012, January 15). Teacher unionism reborn. *New Politics*. https://newpol.org/issue_post/teacher-unionism-reborn/

Zimmerman, A. (2023). *NYC education department faced with another round of budget cuts.* Chalkbeat New York. https://ny.chalkbeat.org/2023/4/4/23670470/nyc-school-education-budget-cuts-eric-adams-david-b

Endnotes

1 We use activism here, rather than organizing, in order to be consistent with previous documentation and naming of NYCoRE's work as well as the broader Teacher Activist Group network. However, we believe that some of the work NYCoRE does can also be defined as organizing.
2 We use radical in order to acknowledge the explicit decision made by NYCoRE founding members to use the word radical in NYCoRE's name. To them (and us), being radical involves a commitment to system-level change and is embodied in the tagline in our mission statement: "the struggle for justice does not end when the school bell rings."
3 "Those who are familiar with Greek mythology know that the Hydra was an immortal multi-headed creature. Any attempt to slay the Hydra was a struggle in futility and hopelessness, because if one head were removed, the Hydra would grow back two more in its place . . . . NYCoRE made the connection that each of these Hydra heads was analogous to one of the market-based reforms unfolding in our city . . . . NYCoRE observed that when one project was being addressed, other projects were lined up to continue moving a privatization agenda forward. The group realized that focusing on one head meant that our attention was often drawn away from the larger forces, or Hydra body, driving reform—namely, the form of capitalism that some describe as neoliberalism" (Picower & Mayorga, 2015, p. 5) and more broadly, racial capitalism.
4 By restorative justice practices, we are referring to three tiers of practices typically referenced in conversations about restorative justice. Tier 1 includes community and relationship building, Tier 2 involves community and relationship repair and conflict resolution, and Tier 3 incorporates a reintegration process after a removal or other kind of absence from the community.
5 We know the majority of educators are white women. Striving to do this has not always meant that our spaces have majority BIPOC representation.
6 The explanations in quotes come directly from the ItAG descriptions on NYCoRE's website (New York Collective of Radical Educators. n.d. -a). Those not in quotes come from the authors' memories or conversations with the ItAG facilitators.

CHAPTER 12

Privatization Doesn't Stop at Borders: The Trinational Coalition in Defense of Public Education

Rosemary Lee and Brianne Kramer

VALUABLE INPUT TO the chapter was also contributed by Maria de la Luz Arriaga, (UNAM, Mexico), Larry Kuehn, (BCTF, Canada) and Domenic Bellissimo (OTSSF/FEESO, Canada), founding members of the Trinational Coalition.

The Trinational Coalition in Defense of Public Education has had many participants over our 30-year history. Some are now deceased, some are long-term participants, and some have joined us in the last years. Nonetheless, as an organization, we have maintained our unwavering defense of public education and solidarity within and across our borders. We have extended our work to those in other countries as well. In telling our story, we have included the voices of some of the founders of the Coalition and the most recent participants. We hope that readers, who believe that through reclaiming public education we can build a future world for and with our kids for all of humanity and life on the planet, will join us across North America.

What? Education is a Commodity Now?!

In the late 1980s, trade unions and organizations in the United States, Mexico, and Canada began meeting over concerns about the North American Free Trade Act (NAFTA) that was being negotiated. NAFTA would create a free trade of our three countries by eliminating tariffs on goods, jobs, and services exported and imported across our borders. A number of academic activists, who were already fighting against cuts to public education funding, became alarmed when they found out that NAFTA would turn education into a commodity to be bought and sold on the world market! The activists held a conference in January 1993 entitled, "The Future of Public Education in North America," that was sponsored by Evergreen College's Labor Education Center in Olympia, Washington with funding from union organizations from all three countries. Their goal was to establish a North American Public Schools Commission to defend public education against NAFTA's plans to privatize public education. Dan Leahy, past Chair of Evergreen's Labor Education Center and former Trinational Spokesperson, provided a brief history and description of the organizational structure of the Trinational Coalition: "More than 200 union delegates attended this first conference. Forty delegates came from Mexico, representing all levels of the education system. We also had delegates from Canada, the Caribbean, and Latin America. At this moment, we adopted a trinational plan and the *Olympia Declaration*, which advocates education as a social right." (Leahy, 2010, p. 2)

Formation of the Coalition

In October 1994, in Zacatecas, Mexico, the Labor Center organized a follow-up conference with the intention of forming a North American Public Schools Commission that would be independent, funded by union organizations that would implement ideas in the "Olympia Declaration." This second conference was attended by the Canadian Teachers' Federation, the Ontario Secondary School Teachers' Federation (OSSTF) based in Toronto, and the British Columbia Teachers' Federation (BCTF) based in Vancouver, the National Education Association (NEA), and union leaders from Mexican universities and secondary schools. Instead of a commission, the delegates agreed to establish a Trinational Coalition to coordinate unions' actions and support public schools across North America. The organizational principles established were free, nonformal participation of organizations, no formal membership required, and organizations would be involved in financing/organizing projects or conferences. At this time, the coalition was coordinated by Dan Leahy, a professor at Evergreen State College, Larry Kuehn, the research director at BCTF, and Maria de la Luz Arriaga, a professor at the National Autonomous University of Mexico.

The Role of Unions

In February, 1995, a conference was held in Mexico City and we set up a Mexican section of our coalition, with local and regional associations belonging to the National Union of Education Workers (SNTE) in Mexico City, Michoacan, and Oaxaca, and university unions in Zacatecas, Queretaro, Chapingo, and Mexico City. Although the national sections' project has never come to pass in Canada and the United States, the Mexican section has been operational since its inception in 1995. Besides organizing and participating in several Coalition projects, the Mexican section has also published the *Coalition* magazine, a forum for articles critical of neoliberal policies in education. The Canadian Teachers' Federation (CTF) has played a key role from the start by promoting the coalition in provincial organizations and by coordinating solidarity actions. Several provincial organizations have also been very active in the coalition: BCTF, OSSTF, the Manitoba Teachers' Society, the Fédération nationale des enseignantes et des enseignants du Québec (FNEEQ-CSN), and the Confédération des syndicats du Québec (CSQ). The Canadian Association of University Teachers (CAUT) joined the coalition and hosted the sixth conference in Toronto in May 2003. Despite their involvement in the first conference, NEA declined to participate and AFT has never gotten involved in the organization.

The Accomplishments of the Coalition

Coalition conferences have been held in Mexico, Canada, and the United States. Below is a list of each conference the Trinational Coalition has held:

1993—"The Future of Public Education in North America," Olympia, Washington
1995—Morelia, Mexico
1997—Vancouver, Canada
1998—Queretaro, Mexico
2000—Zacatecas, Mexico
2003—Toronto, Canada
2006—Oaxaca, Mexico
2008—"Public Education is not for Sale," Los Angeles, California

2010—"Building Public and Democratic Education in North America," Montreal, Canada
2012—"Putting the Public Back in Education: Alternatives for the Future," Mexico City, Mexico
2014—"20 Years Building Alternatives to Neoliberal Politics in Education," Chicago, Illinois
2016—"Reversing Austerity and the Privatization of the Right to Education: Building Alternatives to the Neoliberal Agenda in Public Education," Vancouver, Canada
2018–"Internationalism, the Axis of the Fight to Defend Public Education as a Social Right," Orizaba, Mexico
2021–"Through the Pandemic: Education for Transformation," Online via Zoom
2022–"Rebuilding Community Through Public Education," Oaxaca, Mexico

The conferences have featured guided tours of local schools and are multilingual, utilizing numerous translators. With support from the other Trinational sections, Rosemary organized a mini-conference in 2009 in Santa Fe, New Mexico with Indigenous teachers from British Columbia, Guatemala, Chiapas, and New Mexico. While the attack on public education continues, its forms and intensity changes as the crisis of global capitalism intensifies. In each conference, we select keynote speakers to address the theme of the conference. Our workshops discuss related topics that are of particular concern. A panelist from each country gives a short presentation on the topic as experienced in their country, then most of the workshop is spent in discussion. On the final day of the conference, the rapporteurs present summaries and proposals from all of the sessions. Participants then draw up a final "Declaration," immediate actions on urgent issues, and a plan of future work.

Some of the topics discussed in workshops have included:

- manufactured austerity to justify cuts to funding education
- the use of high-stakes standardized testing, with particular note of the detrimental effect of the PISA examinations and the monopoly of companies like Pearson at the global level
- charter schools, vouchers, and federal policies

- new methods of privatization
- the use of digital technology to replace teachers that is often unavailable to students
- advanced attacks on labor rights at all levels of education
- violent and sometimes deadly attacks on teachers and students
- the increasing precariousness of professors
- the across-the-board inability for education workers, families, and students to afford housing and to live in their communities

For example, our last conference in 2022 had the following workshops: Building Organizational Links with the Community/Collective Work Based on a Community Philosophy; Pedagogical Work Experiences that Link School and Life; Resistance to the Incursion of Transitional Technology Companies into Public Education; Organizations and Social Movements Reconstruct the Community/Collective Forms of Organization; The Community as the Ideal for Social Life; and Resistance from the Social Fabric.

In the name of fighting for an education for the future, we have held workshops that championed the fight for an education that serves our poorest and most discriminated students and communities; these have encompassed social justice unionism, negotiating for the common good, community-based schools, Indigenous traditions, collective education in lieu of competitiveness, strategies and experiences for countering the censure of "woke" education in our educational institutions, and what broad-based education that prepares students as creative, critical thinkers should be. We employ interpreters and equipment to provide simultaneous translation throughout the conference.

The Trinational's deep commitment to education and social justice is also reflected in solidarity projects between conferences too. A number of us have given workshops and spoken at union conventions, public forums, and protests, supported strikes and mass actions, and written letters to government officials and union leaders in each other's and our own countries. We have learned to use social media for posting information, holding Zoom conferences and live streaming events. When the 43 students at the school for rural teachers in Ayotzinapa, Mexico disappeared, the Trinational participated in the marches and protests in all of the countries in Trinational. We sent letters to the president demanding that the students be returned alive. Although the 2021 Zoom conference was attended by a much larger number of participants than ever before, we were happy to once again return to in-person conferences in 2022. The school visits, the informal discussions, and camaraderie among members, the celebration of our victories, and the collectively written final resolution and action plans shared during conferences are such a special part of the Trinational Coalition. It is so exhilarating to not feel alone in our commitment to fight for public education, to acquire a deeper understanding of the global scope of the struggle we are in together and the transnational capitalism agenda underlying it. Over the years, we have all learned a lot about our union organizations and respective education systems, which allows us to refine our strategies and improve our actions to counter neoliberal policies.

> The first joint action of the Coalition was a letter-writing campaign in support of Mexican teachers during a major conflict. In return, the Mexican teachers got their local union sections to support a strike by Ontario teachers and, later, to support British Columbia teachers fighting against anti-union legislation put forth by the provincial government. We have also held forums on issues like standardized tests and the struggle of Mexico City's Section 9 teachers, among others. We also learned that we could quickly mobilize Coalition forces during an emergency. Two months after the 1998 Queretaro conference, the Mexican government jailed the leadership of Mexico City's Section 9 that represents primary school teachers. They protested in the Mexican Senate and were threatened with sedition and mutiny charges, which did not permit bail and led to long jail sentences upon conviction. The Trinational Coalition, led by the president of the Canadian Teachers' Federation, mobilized an international protest of letter writing, press conferences, consular visits, and various legal representations. Within two months, all jailed professors were free and the charges against them dropped. One of the reasons for the great success of this mobilization was that, a few months prior, these same jailed teachers were the ones who had given guided school tours during that conference in Mexico City! (Leahy, 2010, p. 6)

The Trinational Coalition also helped raise awareness in Canada and the United States about the incredible strike led by students at the National University in Mexico City (UNAM) in 1999. With over 300,000 students and a 3,000-member faculty, this university is a city within Mexico City. The students protested against proposals that would lead to privatization of the university, and the strike lasted 1 year. Some proposals the students opposed were, a plan to charge tuition and a plan to entrust university entrance and exit exams to private firms using standardized tests.

We promoted participation in the Hemispheric Forum on Education, organized as part of the People's Forum, which was kept on the sidelines of FTAA negotiations in Quebec City in 2001. The participation of the Mexican section and Latin American organizations, along with the Red SEPA (Civil Society Network for Public Education in the Americas), substantially enriched this forum's final declaration.

In January 2002, the Trinational Coalition joined forces with the Red SEPA and the Continental Alliance to ensure that education was formally placed on the agenda at the World Social Forum in Porto Alegre, Brazil, which exists to counter efforts of global economic governance directed by transnational corporations. Following the conference in Toronto in 2003, the Trinational Coalition became more involved in the issue of part-time workers in higher education.

> Organizing the 2006 conference in Oaxaca helped to forge close links with the teaching community in that state, which came on the radar shortly after, when a popular uprising was violently suppressed. The network of contacts—woven into and around the Trinational—has enabled trade unions to support them; the AFT, NEA and many of their affiliated organizations have passed resolutions supporting the teachers' struggle in Oaxaca and offered financial assistance. In December 2006, an international delegation pushed for and won the release of thirty people unjustly arrested during the uprising. (Leahy, 2010, p. 7)

The Los Angeles conference was a great success. Almost 200 education activists at all educational levels took part. Participants came from British Columbia, Ontario, Quebec, Mexico City, Oaxaca, Chiapas, Guatemala, and Puerto Rico.

The President of Federation of Puerto Rican Teachers (FMPR) attended shortly after they won a strike outlawing charter schools in 2007. FMPR continues to participate in the Trinational Coalition.

Members of UTLA were joined by activists from New Orleans CUNY, members of CFT locals at various California Community Colleges including Dean Murakami and Gabriel Torres (Los Rios Community College), and several faculty members and students from California State LA, Steve Miller from Oakland Educators Association, Peter Brown from Laney Community College in Oakland, the Association of Raza Educators of California (ARE), and Jackson Potter from Chicago Teachers Union. Many of the participants have continued to be part of the Trinational Coalition over the last 15 years; participating in our conferences, in exchanges and solidarity with our brothers and sisters in Canada, Mexico, and Puerto Rico, and above all, reaching out to members of our own and other education unions to take part in the defense of public education.

I think the role that Jackson Potter and CTU, under the leadership of CORE, play in the Trinational Coalition is an outstanding portrayal of how our organization functions. Many other organizations in this book know Jackson for his tireless dedication to educational and human justice; and CTU has become the leading U.S. union in building the Trinational Coalition and inspiration to other education activists in the United States.

When Jackson came to the LA Trinational conference, under the old leadership, CTU was not doing anything to stop school closures. He was hoping to find different models about unions that were fighting funding cuts and privatization of schools. At the conference, he met the newly elected progressive UTLA caucus, Mexican teachers from Oaxaca Seccion22/CNTE who had risked their lives in the 2006 Oaxaca uprising, and Mariluz Arriaga, coordinator of the Mexican Trinational who welcomed him into the Coalition. He also met with Jinny Sims, who as BCTF president, led their successful illegal strike against the Liberal government that refused to meet the teachers' demands for improved classroom conditions, the ability to collectively bargain, and a fair pay increase. Once he returned to Chicago, Jackson invited Jinny to meet with a group of 35 teachers, including Karen Lewis, to discuss forming a progressive caucus. The activists formed CORE and, with guidance provided by Jinny and the BCTF, organized the historic 2012 strike. As many of the readers know, CTU has gone on to share information and strategies with other teacher unions and caucuses to take up versions of its approach and took a leading role in forming a national network.

Organizational Structure of the Trinational Coalition in Defense of Public Education

We have continued to use an informal structure. There are no requirements or fees to become a member of the coalition. To plan our conferences, forums, campaigns, and smaller events, a group of about six to eight people meet online. While the original coordinators, Domenic Bellisimo from OSSTF/FEESO and Larry Kuehn from BCTF have retired, and Dan Leahy from Evergreen College has passed on, Mariluz Arriaga continues to dedicate her steadfast commitment and work to the Trinational Coalition. Currently, Mariluz Arriaga represents Mexico, representatives from BCTF and OSSTF/FEESO, and Steve Stewart (Red SEPA) represent Canada, Gabriel Torres and Jason Newman from the Los Rios Community College Federation, and Rosemary Lee and Jackson Potter represent the U.S. section. We discuss, debate, and decide what the theme will be for an upcoming conference based on the predominant challenge to public education in the three countries, the workshop topics, panelists, facilitators, plenary speakers, delegates, and the multitude of other tasks for organizing an international conference of 200 people.

Each section is organized differently and decides upon their own delegation. The Mexican section has long been organized with a coordinating group and monthly meetings. They hold a preconference for the section before each Trinational Conference. The Mexican trinational section includes different sectors of the CNTE (National Coordination of Education Workers of Mexico), which is the progressive, democratic movement within the notoriously corrupt, undemocratic SNTE—the state-sponsored "official" teachers union of Mexico. The CNTE focuses on empowerment of local bases, democratic rights of educators and community members, opposes standardized tests for students, and standardized evaluations of teachers. The Mexican Trinational also includes university faculty and students. Conference delegates are decided upon at a preconference of the Mexican Trinational.

The OSSTF/FEESO (Ontario) and the BCTF (British Columbia) both have international solidarity programs. They have consistently funded the Trinational Coalition conferences and other projects for 30 years. A small percent of each BCTF member's monthly dues has gone to their solidarity project and fund since the 1920s. Their projects are always for solidarity and not for charity. The unions post an announcement for their members about upcoming conferences so that they may apply to attend. The Canadian section also reaches out to other education unions in Canada to send their own members. The U.S. section has not had a national Trinational sector, per se. We had a Trinational committee in Los Angeles for about 6 years, which included education workers and students from CSU-Los Angeles and several UTLA members. Steve Miller (OEA, Oakland) has actively worked with us in the Bay Area. Outreach by the California Federation of Teachers, in particular the Civil, Human, and Women's Rights Committee, has been responsible for attendees from their locals in San Francisco, Oakland, and Pajaro Valley.

The Chicago Teachers Union sends the largest number of delegates. Like the Canadian unions, they send out an announcement to their members and interview applicants. Finally, there is an informational meeting about the Trinational for those who are selected to be delegates. As CTU is involved in national coalitions of education activists, they have been responsible for delegates being sent from different parts of the United States, which includes the San Antonio Alliance of Teachers and Support Personnel. They will host the 16th Trinational Conference in 2024. The FMPR of Puerto Rico regularly sends delegates. We also have had participants from various countries in Latin America, the Caribbean, Japan, and Great Britain.

Our organization is set apart from educational activist organizations in that we clearly understand the onslaught on public education is part of the agenda of transnational capitalism for North America. The ensuing attacks may take different forms at different times in different regions. Consequently, we believe that solidarity, sharing strategies, and information across borders is essential to bring about the educational transformation for which education activists are fighting in the interest of our future societies. We also have an informal structure for membership, funding, and leadership, which has been our strength and also a weakness. The Coalition has depended on the activists who see the value of solidarity work across borders. Although unions like the BCTF were always committed to work with activists, most are not. Both NEA and AFT have had quite rigid boundaries when it comes to solidarity work. In Mexico, the CNTE was formed as a democratic body initially by the poorest and most Indigenous states because SNTE, the government-controlled union, has a history of often violently repressing their progressive members. The Trinational's structure allows us to reach out across boundaries of both unions and countries to education activists, some of whom have since gone into leadership. The Trinational also includes groups outside of unions, such as student, parent, and community groups.

Members aren't committed to an official statement, nor do we need absolute unanimity. Debate is welcomed. We then follow up with the agreed-upon plan of work. Not only has internet technology given us a huge boost in communication for planning and coordination, we held the 2021 conference and several events on Zoom. Each section has a Facebook group; the Coalition now has a bilingual website (coaliciontrinacional.org) for sharing information including videos. The website is staffed by the Mexican section and funded by the BCTF Solidarity Program.

Our informal structure has its limitations. Organizations may commit to sending a member to a conference but not to joining the Trinational. Being on the margins of the large national unions, we don't have their clout or resources. For the Trinational, it's a question of who makes an appearance and who does the work. They have proven to have a deeply felt commitment to defend public education via mutual aid and cooperation (Mariluz Arriaga, Larry Kuehn, Domenic Bellisimo, Steve Miller, personal communication, June 2023).

> Nonetheless, with all its limitations, the Trinational Coalition in Defense of Public Education has continued to exist for much longer than any of the many trinational activities that sprouted up when NAFTA was new. One feature of this three-country solidarity movement has been the creation of trinational networks. A conference hosted by the UTLA Labor Center looked at their development in several sectors; these included the Trinational Solidarity Alliance, the Trinational Coalition to Defend Public Education, the Trinational Telecommunications Alliance, and the Trinational Energy Workers Network. (Bacon, 2014, p. 4)

Thirty years ago, we were ahead of our time in identifying the commodification of education for the world market. Bringing union activists together to share information about the attacks educators were experiencing across North America and the global agenda underlying them has allowed us to learn so much from concrete examples we share with one another. We recognize that their formulations often look different depending on where we are living and at what level of education we work. By the same token, we recognize that just because something works in one area doesn't mean it is automatically transferable. While the attack on public education continues, its forms and intensity changes as the crisis of global capitalism intensifies.

Some of the newest participants in the Trinational Coalition shared their thoughts on our work:

Aaron Goodwin, University of California, Riverside (2021 Zoom conference)

As a graduate student teaching assistant, I have just recently begun my career in education. At the Trinational, I met wonderful teachers whose diverse range of experiences showed that the fight for public education, against capitalist privatization, is very real, that it cuts across continents, and that victories can be won when we work together and learn from each other.

Janette Corcelius, Community organizer for Minneapolis Federation of Teachers, Local 59 (2022 conference)

The Coordinadora Nacional de Trabajadores de la Educación (CNTE) had us as guests in the city and state of Oaxaca. They welcomed us into their schools and not only taught us the importance of community support—they showed it to us.

Jessica Suarez, Chicago Teachers Union (2022 conference)

I was fortunate to have been able to meet folks internationally and nationally, resisting and building a counter narrative against school privatization and what folks proposed as alternative learning spaces. The need for us to not just deal with it city by city, but rather learn and support one another was key, along with the historical and political context school privatization brings into the shaping of our young people and the community.

Linda Perales, Chicago Teachers Union (2018 and 2022 conferences)

I attended the Trinational Conference in Orizaba, Veracruz in 2018. The celebration of culture and the deep commitment to organizing against privatization are the parts of the conference that stayed with me the most. The key beliefs that lead this work bleed into every aspect of life. The fact that some folks have given their life for this struggle, reaffirmed my belief that this work is absolutely necessary and that I must return to my school, to my union, and to my country with an even deeper desire to continue to advocate and organize in defense of public education. I also attended the Trinational Conference in Oaxaca, Mexico in 2022. The takeaways from members (who attended) included the impact of technology on education, especially during the height of COVID-19, the importance of solidarity amongst rank-and-file members, the need to learn from each country, and the importance of continuing in the struggle. The delegation helped identify and build a new layer of leadership in our union of educators deeply invested in this fight.

Adam Geissler, Chicago Teachers Union (2022 conference)

Together, we shared the impacts of privatization across different aspects of our work in schools and communities. New participants like me learned from a broad swath of others, some of whom have been attending these conferences since their inception. Teachers, professors, and other educators would share stories of building solidarity within their own rank-and-file, while also extending their network to learn effective strategies from each other. There was one individual who I met early in the conference and we exchanged contact information to continue our sharing of ideas and insights. Since that weekend, Mauro and I have met online almost every week to discuss our experiences in public education and the broader resistance movement. Without attending the Trinational Conference, this connection may have never been made.

Elise Knaub, Chicago Teachers Union (2022 conference)

It was an honor to attend the Trinational conference, to link up with other teachers and educators from around the continent, and connect with those militant teachers who share an understanding of the central role of education in society, having been on the front lines of fighting the corporate privatization agenda. At the conference, I learned that this fight is universal. The fight for education is truly global, and events like the Trinational Conference help us learn from each other and build mutual support. Those of us in the United States, where these tech vultures are based, have a special responsibility to join the fight to ensure that technology is implemented in service of the people and not for profit.

Kevin Cosgrove, Chicago Teachers Union (2022 conference)

I went to Oaxaca for the Trinational Conference in Defense of Public Education in October 2022, bringing together educators from North America and beyond. It quickly became evident that the aggressive moves toward privatization and demonization of unions were far from unique to Chicago. We heard about violent—and sometimes even fatal—crackdowns against union-aligned protesters. We heard about the ever-growing influence of private corporations taking over public education one massive contract at a time, promising a sort of automation of education with the not-so-subtly hidden agenda of collecting data on millions of children and making teachers redundant. But the conference struck an ultimately heartening tone thanks to the extraordinarily dedicated and deeply principled educators in attendance, unwilling to settle for the status quo or allow further corrosion of public education. We formed friendships and learned from each other. With so many like-minded educators communing together, it is a rejuvenating balm to know that we are not alone and against so many efforts; we have not given up and will keep working toward fulfilling the promise of just and equitable public education for all.

Rogelio Aguilar, Chicago Teachers Union (2018 conference)

It was only my second year teaching for Chicago Public Schools when I was able to attend the Trinational Conference in Orizaba, Veracruz (2018). I had previously learned about the struggles against privatization of schools in Chicago, but I had no idea that so many other places in the world were in similar situations. It was an invaluable experience to learn how teachers in other countries are defending public education and it was inspiring to see how solidarity can help us win what our students deserve.

Next Steps for the Trinational Coalition In Defense of Public Education

The Trinational Coalition will continue our work with adjustments to address the intensification of challenges to public education. Although the pandemic has had a severe impact on education, we must not lose sight of the ratcheting up of the privatization of education under transnational capitalism. The privatizers were quick to employ "disaster capitalism" to further their agenda, just as they did when New Orleans and then Puerto Rico were hit by disastrous hurricanes. The electronic technology that allowed us to communicate and teach during COVID-19 was quick to develop advanced electronic information and AI systems for surveillance and collecting data on all aspects of our lives. Corporations also push to keep online education because of its "success" during the pandemic while cutting the cost of education workers.

Today we live in a world where labor-saving technology is costing people their jobs, or reducing them to "gig workers." Services that governments provide to meet human needs have become priced out as they are taken over by greedy privatizers, while climate change is wreaking havoc throughout the world. There has also been a huge growth in what William Robinson calls the "global police state," which both is tremendously profitable to corporate investors and also used to repress popular uprisings and protests. Fascism is rising in a number of countries, including the United States, where democracy and our constitutional rights are under a massive, coordinated attack.

Of course, education is a key target for the right-wing agenda. In "U.S. Fascism is Growing Under the Guise of 'Patriotic Education,'" Henry Giroux (2023) observes:

> It's clear that the far right GOP has deemed education to be the most powerful tool for creating a public that is neither informed nor willing to struggle to keep a democracy alive. This is particularly evident in the right-wing war on education, which aims at replacing public education with charter schools, fashioning public and higher education into centers of far-right indoctrination, and destroying higher education as a democratic public good. Central to such an attack is a war on critical thinking, troubling knowledge, historical memory, and any form of education that address social problems. . . . What they would also like to see disappear in their reign of domestic terrorism are the educators, institutions, and other public spaces that resist this ongoing tsunami of authoritarian ideas, acts of repression, and war on critical intellectuals, dissidents, and educators. (para. 4)

People across the world continue to unite against the global capitalists' vision of the future. As Steve Miller (Oakland Education Association/retired) said: "The battle for free, quality public education is one of the major fronts in the war for the future that is consuming the United States and the entire planet" (S. Miller, personal communication, n.d.). Battles to defend and improve education in our member's countries include the November-December 2022 statewide strike by graduate education workers at the University of California;

in 2023, a Community Day of Action Against Displacement by the Multisectoral Board in Defense of Public Education in Puerto Rico, the militant protest by members of CNTE/SNTE section 9 in Mexico City against the corrupt SNTE leadership trying to invalidate section 9's elections, and the continuing fight by OSSTF/FEESO about their bargaining rights and against funding cuts in Ontario. In the United States, we have seen two important victories when our unions actively organized with other unions and community organizations.

In Los Angeles, UTLA went out in solidarity with striking members of SEIU Local 99, which represents support staff in schools, in March 2023. SEIU was able to win a 30% pay raise and other key demands. In Chicago, CTU was in a broad coalition of organizations and union members which won a tremendous victory in getting a progressive mayor elected in a race against a notorious, reactionary candidate, in April. The new mayor, Brandon Johnson, was both a former teacher and a CTU staff member. An outstanding member of CTU, Jennifer Johnson, was appointed to be the Deputy Mayor of Education. An unprecedented movement in defense of public schools, primarily led by youth with a different vision of the future, is rising in the United States in opposition to fascism.

Members of the Trinational Coalition in Defense of Public Education believe that our persistent 30-year fight for a free, quality public education has much to offer to activists. First, our work has always been based on connecting people as human beings across borders, including diverse cultures, identities, ages, and experiences. Participants have shared a wealth of information about how they have organized broadly with parents, students, and community organizations to win victories in their battles. Given the scope of the fight for a sustainable future for all, there is a growing understanding of the necessity of forming broad-based coalitions that value working collectively. We have also made an important contribution in demonstrating the global capitalist agenda that underlies the attacks on education and other necessities of life. This analysis can guide us in selecting the best strategies and tactics for the battles ahead. Presently, our coordinators are planning the XVI Conference in San Antonio, Texas, for November 2024. We look forward to you joining us there and in future conferences and activities!

Editor's Note: You can follow Trinational Coalition on Facebook and X.

References

Bacon, D. (2014). *Trinational perspectives on the future of labor: The state of labor twenty years after NAFTA*. UCLA Labor Center. https://escholarship.org/content/qt4x1871bt/qt4x1871bt_noSplash_986e77a28840fba6cf038a9355d46cd5.pdf?t=ny9nnb

Giroux, H. A. (2023). *U.S. fascism is spreading under the guise of 'patriotic education.'* Truthout. https://truthout.org/articles/us-fascism-is-spreading-under-the-guise-of-patriotic-education/

Leahy, D. (2010). *A brief history of the Trinational Coalition*. Fédération Nationale des Enseignantes et des Enseignants du Québec and Céntrale des Syndicates du Québec.

CHAPTER 13

USOS: Our Part in the Struggle to Save the Public's Schools

Becky L. Noël Smith

The Ideological Landscape Out of Which We Came

The work of Uniting to Save Our Schools (USOS) was born, ultimately, in response to the systematic standardization and dehumanization of children, communities, and educators. During the 1990s and up through our first public action in 2011, the public schools were subjected to a relentless oscillation of neoliberal and neoconservative ideologies, each of which foisted significant changes onto the policies, practices, and expectations of public education. As is always the case with public education, though, such changes are produced and enacted in countless, unique ways: they ripple differently through community discourses, classrooms, and statehouses across the country, and they are as complicated as they are regionally nuanced. It is difficult, therefore, to capture the multitudinous reasons why many of us came to this work. But the problems of that era can be read broadly, perhaps, through the lineage of federal education policies from Clinton's Goals 2000, to Bush's No Child Left Behind (NCLB), to Obama's Race to the Top, and the Every Student Succeeds Act (ESSA).

I provide a very brief depiction here of some of the specific ways these two dominant ideologies led to a breaking point and, hence, our collective action. However, if readers want an extensive ideological analysis that is as instructive today as it was 20 years ago, I highly recommend Michael Apple's (2001) *Educating the 'Right' Way: Markets, Standards, God, and Inequality*. I rely heavily upon Apple's work in this chapter because he so accurately describes the complex and contradictory landscape out of which USOS's organizing efforts sprang, one where neoliberalism and neoconservatism built off of and converged with one another in increasingly inhumane and unjust ways.

Neoliberalism, Apple explains, is comprised of the following characteristics:

> ... the dramatic expansion of that eloquent fiction, free market; the drastic reduction of government responsibility for social needs; the reinforcement of intensely competitive structures ... the lowering of people's expectations for economic security; the "disciplining" of culture and the body; and the popularization of what is clearly a form of social-Darwinist thinking. (Apple, 2004, p. 15)[1]

In effect, the neoliberal rationale constructs schools as "markets" that must be measured and manipulated so they can then be marketed to families. The humanity of the children is wiped away within this framework as they come to be viewed as raw materials to be exploited, eventually turned into the assets to be invested in and leveraged. The focus turns to human capital, meaning that the main purpose of education is to prepare children for the job market. Thus, education is not viewed as an endeavor that benefits the good of the child, the community, and a democratic mode of being. Instead, learning and public schools are retooled to serve the economic system and the individuals who wish to profit off education at the same time that they intensify existing inequalities.[2]

Neoliberals believe that in order to effectively measure and manipulate said markets and products of schooling, data must be created so that everything in the chain can be monitored, or surveilled, from afar. Thus, just as we saw following the signings of both NCLB and ESSA, an unconscionable emphasis is placed on the quantification and datafication of everything that ensures neoliberal ends. This is evident in the creation of high-stakes assessments, for instance, which then generate test scores that are used to place "value" on everything from students to teachers to schools and entire communities (Au, 2009; Nichols & Berliner, 2007). As a result, the very human process of learning is converted into a commodity so it can be bought, sold, and consumed, a mentality that is reproduced in discursive phrases that tell us we should be getting *an* education.

In addition to datafication, another characteristic of the market mentality are policies and discourses that aim at "school choice," especially those that permit vouchers, the creation of charter schools, and the use of privately owned educational management organizations. Importantly, such programs atomize the individual schools within a larger public system by placing them in competition with one another for vital resources that can only be secured once a school "wins the favor" of a family's choice and a child's enrollment. As one might expect, this also puts families in competition with one another as they shop and compete for their choice to secure the good of their individual child. In effect, it is a classic divide-and-conquer strategy, one that favors privileged families while simultaneously weakening institutional supports for our students of greatest need.

A tenet of neoliberalism is the belief that things work best when they are managed by or run like a business. Essential to this claim is that there must be an absence of regulation so the market can "work its magic," and therefore neoliberals tend to desire a weakened state. However, this weakening of federal and state oversight allows for a proliferation of spaces that are rife with public/private conflicts of interest. For instance, testing corporations, educational management organizations, and corporate charter schools receive and profit off public tax dollars. Though they are publicly funded, and thereby should be held accountable to the public, their private nature allows them to avoid the public's scrutiny and, at times, the federal protections that are designed to oversee equity, especially for our students of color and those with special needs.[3] In this way, neoliberals not only open schoolhouse doors to corporate involvement and private interests that exacerbate inequities (Dixson et al., 2015; Lipman, 2011) and corruption,[4] but tragically, they lure their entrance by placing large financial incentives on the welcome mat (Boyles, 1995, 2000; Hewitt, 2009).

Neoconservatism is equally damaging, of course, though it comes at schools from a different angle. Whereas neoliberalism is framed around the myth of "the free market," neoconservatives stake their claims on the fairytale of "a golden age" in American society. Apple explains this ideology as follows:

> It is largely, though not totally, based in a romantic appraisal of the past, a past in which 'real knowledge' and morality reigned supreme, where people 'knew their place,' and where stable communities

> guided by a natural order protected us from the ravages of society. (Apple, 2001, p. 47)

With its emphasis on schooling practices that get us "back to basics" and focus on "tradition" and "the classics," it goes without saying that this harkening back to a golden age is little more than a yearning for points in time when power, popular narratives, and curricular discourses were rooted in Eurocentric, masculinist, heteronormative, patriarchal perspectives. A hallmark of neoconservative ideology is the desire to retain control over what counts as "knowledge, values, and the body." These mechanisms of control are no doubt forced upon the general public in countless ways, but with the public schools, Apple explains they tend to manifest in the push for "national curricula, national standards, and national systems of assessment" (Apple, 2004, p. 23). The primary emphasis here is one of standardization, which simultaneously implies attacks on bilingualism, multiculturalism, and immigration, in addition to the squelching of the rich cultural, historical, and experiential perspectives that counter the narrowness of neoconservative values and resist white supremacy.[5]

In order to effectively force their ideology on the minds and bodies of the people, neoconservatives require a strong state. This was made evident, for instance, in NCLB's federal mandate for high-stakes testing and, at least in part, with the creation of Common Core State Standards and the Next Generation Science Standards.[6] However, it warrants mentioning that neoconservatism is surging vehemently right now in the most current fights to ban AP African American history, critical race theory, and gender studies, as well as all children's books that express empowering views of marginalized peoples.[7] Again, neoconservative discourse and policies make it very clear that anything reflecting the knowledge and experience outside the realm of a white, straight, masculinist view is to be eradicated.

These are the two dominant ideological machines that were at play in the lead up to the first convening of our organization in 2011. One thing that made this period confusing, particularly for someone like me who was just finding her way into the realm of education activism, was the contradictory aspects of these two ideologies created. Apple articulates the felt contradiction this way: "At the same time the state appears to be devolving power to individual and autonomous institutions . . . the state remains strong in key areas" (Apple, 2004, p. 23). This often made it feel like the national education policy discourse was talking out of both sides of its face, which it was, and this was primarily because there were converging points of interest between the two ideologies. Clearly, these were not the only ways of viewing public education at the time, otherwise there would never have been a movement to resist them. But, as USOS cofounder Rick Meyer explains, these only became the dominant belief systems "by systemically and systematically silencing, marginalizing, dismissing, oppressing, and repressing those deeply interested in disrupting the binary in order to create a more equitable democracy or even a social democracy." By controlling the narrative with two bad options, people too easily get wrapped up in arguments of either/or, further distracting the public from critical questions about power and humane alternatives. The common outcome of this tactic, Rick says, is that "we forget to ask: who's gaining from this binary? Who's losing? Why? How? Who's served? Who's neglected and left to perish? At whose expense and for whose gain?"

Over the course of a little more than a decade, we had witnessed neoliberal dehumanization through the Clinton and Obama administrations as well as neoconservative standardization from Bush's No Child Left Behind. We came into this work, and have remained committed to it, because we know that neither of these options is ever going to be good for the well-being of children and communities. USOS's fight has not been one related to partisan politics, but it is instead against ideologies that prevent people from freely learning about, and subsequently acting upon, the many ways of being in the world: culturally, linguistically, experientially, sexually, and in terms of gender and varying abilities.

From One Man Walking to Thousands of People Marching

Seven years of NCLB's increasingly inequitable and punitive consequences left many educators and families feeling utterly frustrated and exasperated, such that in the lead-up to President Obama's inauguration, there was some optimism that his administration would bring some humanity to federal education policy. That confidence quickly started to wane, first with his appointment of Arne Duncan as Secretary of Education and then again with Race to the Top in 2009. For so many of us, there was a palpable feeling that each new policy had only grown increasingly worse than the previous. Anthony Cody (2009), an educational blogger and activist from Oakland, shared some of this letdown publicly in November 2009 with his "Open Letter to President Obama." This precipitated a Facebook page called "Teachers' Letters to Obama" where over 1,500 people would soon post their own concerns.

During this same time, Jesse Turner[8] attended the National Council for Teachers of English (NCTE) conference in Philadelphia. He and Ruby Clayton[9] were sharing stories of resistance to NCLB with a few other attendees, when one of them finally asked of the disheartening state of affairs: "What are we gonna do, Jesse?" Maintaining an intent focused on his lunch of hoagies and Philly cheesesteaks, Jesse said to them, "Well, maybe we should just start doing what we used to do: start marching." Though Jesse grew up a working-class kid from New Jersey, he speaks of justice and activism with such energy that, if it were not for his thick accent, one might mistake him for a southern preacher. Soon after this conversation, he wrote a letter for Cody's Facebook page, explaining that he was going to walk from his home in Connecticut to Washington, DC in an effort to empower and to drum up support because something just had to be done. Drawing upon the narratives of his mother and the lifelong lessons he learned of human movement and resilience in the face of brutality, he recalled:

> Mom told us the story of the Hebrews, and how they walked for 40 years in the desert. We grew up watching Dr. Martin Luther King, Jr, walk all over this nation of ours on television. I learned about the Cherokee Nation and their "Trail of Tears" in school. Years later on the Navajo nation I would learn about the Navajo "Long Walk" from my friend Tony Gatewood on the third mesa. I have no illusions about walking. I only know somehow it keeps us warm. It starts things moving, and it is so much better than standing still. Plus I have some other feet stepping beside me to help pull it off. (Cody, 2010)

Jesse was right in that he didn't walk alone that summer. Many resisters met him along the way: joining him, feeding him, and providing places to rest on his journey. Among the folks who supported him were his friends and colleagues, Bess Altwerger[10] and Vivian Vasquez.[11] During Jesse's stopover at Bess' house in Maryland, she told him, "Well, you're walking this year, but next year, we're *all* walking!" This, of course, was a foreshadowing of the large task ahead, but in the interim, Vivian started making plans to host a welcome reception at American University in DC to mark Jesse's arrival and the culmination of this dedicated act of resistance. Before making his way back home, Jesse, Bess, Vivian, and Sabrina Stevens,[12] an activist who had followed Jesse's journey online, gathered for a smaller celebration at the renowned café, Bus Boys and Poets. The 350+ mile, midsummer walk in 2010 earned him the nickname Jesse "The Walkin' Man" Turner. Most importantly, though, his action resonated with the angst that had been building in so many folks for a decade or more, and he inspired this small group to start planning a teachers' march on Washington.

Before long, Bess contacted Laurie Murphy,[13] an educational activist and strategist in Florida who had been working on a similar, though virtual, idea for a large-scale demonstration with Chris Janotta.[14] Laurie agreed to join the effort and eventually became the Executive Director of the Organizing Committee. Bess also brought along the support of the Center for Expansion of Language and Thinking (CELT), a nonprofit organization dedicated to "the principles of education for democracy with a focus on natural language learning and inquiry" (Center for Expansion of Language and Thinking, n.d.). CELT's support was instrumental to our formation for many reasons, but a vital factor was that its members share a progressive view of literacy that includes the philosophy of Paulo Freire (1997) and the research foundation of Ken and Yetta Goodman (2014). Specifically, literacy should serve the purpose of liberation, such that reading, writing, listening, speaking, viewing, and visually presenting should help us create and maintain our identities. This liberatory and humanizing tenet runs entirely counter to the controlling mechanisms of both neoconservatism and neoliberalism and has remained foundational to how those of us in USOS conceive of our work as well as the purposes of public education in our society. As Bess said in a recent conversation with me, from the start, USOS's work has been rooted in literacy and the fight over power within and engagement in a democratic society: "Control literacy, control the masses." Among the members of CELT who joined onto the effort through Bess were Rick Meyer,[15] another one of USOS's cofounders, and Michael Shaw.[16]

As the network of organizers grew, folks brought their nuanced perspectives on localized problems, along with their stories of resistance and their varied connections. While there are too many people to recount in detail here, I provide four examples of how the national coalition was built around regional concerns and personal networks. Rita Solnet is a cofounder of Parents Across America who contributed to USOS through political outreach. In addition to sharing her expertise regarding the problems occurring in Florida at the time, she brought the support of her national advocacy network, which included education historian, Diane Ravitch (Strauss, 2011b; Solochek, 2011). Diane's support was pivotal, as she helped us fundraise and broadcast our message through blog posts and webinar series.

Two other people who were important to our organization's early development are Ceresta Smith,[17] a National Board Certified Teacher, and Bob George,[18] a lifelong peace activist. Prior to joining USOS, Ceresta had done transformative work in Miami-Dade Public Schools, with her local union, and with BAMN (By Any Means Necessary, n.d.). She was essential to keeping our earliest efforts conscious of issues related to race, and she also helped connect our work with that of Rose Sanders at the Selma Bridge Crossing Jubilee[19] in Alabama, who we collaborated with for several years. Bob, on the other hand, had deep connections in Chicago from years of collaboration with KOCO (Kenwood Oakland Community Organization, n.d.), the Journey 4 Justice Alliance (Journey 4 Justice Alliance, n.d.), and the Chicago Teachers Union. Though Ceresta and Bob came at this work from different perspectives and regions, they both facilitated long-standing alliances between USOS and some of the crucial groups who continue to make history through their support and advocacy for Black and Brown communities.

Finally, the organization established a countrywide network of Information Coordinators (ICs) that was essential in developing the growth, connection, and awareness of our organization. This network was originally intended to share the details about webinars and events as they developed.[20] However, a great many of the ICs were educators and unionists, meaning that all of them were actively immersed in their communities and were knowledgeable about the intricacies of regional education politics. Thus, the ICs were not only incredible organizers of the localized membership, but through virtual meetings and monthly newsletters, they effectively educated our national network on the nuances of the struggles and developing actions that were occurring all around the country.

Thanks to the efforts of many folks, the movement grew to include parent and community organizers, student activists, grassroots and educational organizations, aspiring and lifelong educators, academics, legislators, and local and national unions. So many communities had already been engaged in powerful actions and organizing efforts, both on the ground and via social media, such that a national convening felt immanent. The Save Our Schools March & National Call to Action was nothing short of timely, and it became a galvanizing focus that urged people to take their collective concerns to the President's backyard. The event was held July 28–31, 2011, and it consisted of an impressive conference for educational activism that was hosted by the College of Education at American University, a weekend-long film festival on contemporary and historical acts of resistance, a culminating congress to discuss future actions, and a rally at and march on the National Mall. The march drew as many as 8,000 protesters from all across the country and provided a lineup of speakers, artists, and rock stars in the education world[21] that has likely gone unmatched in recent history (Strauss, 2011a). For a more extensive study on the discursive dynamics surrounding this event—including historical documents detailing the participants, schedules, and topics explored therein—I recommend the work of Troy Spencer Grant (2013),[22] a veteran educator who served as an organizer and emcee for the march and rally.

This national event became a powerful reason to unite in solidarity at the capitol and to channel years of frustration into sharing, learning, and building together. As Jesse recalled, it had developed into "a movement Howard Zinn would be proud of" (Turner, 2011). While much of the national network was built over distance and via technologies (social media, teleconference, email, webinars), it was the human-to-human connections made on the Ellipse and in the conference rooms at American University that seemed to be most catalyzing and transformative. Through concerted, face-to-face time with one another, people from all over were able to discover and bond with kindred activist spirits, thereby opening up space for folks to develop relationships, share ideas, and build new coalitions around the many different tactics that are necessary in the demand for change. United Opt Out,[23] the Badass Teachers Association, and the Network for Public Education are a few of the influential groups that emerged from the interactions and collaborations that occurred before, during, and after that weekend.

Uniting Now & In the Years to Come

Since the march and rally in 2011, we have continued the work of organizing conferences, campaigns, webinars, and rallies aimed at raising awareness, educating ourselves about the ever-present problems facing school communities, and bringing people together to discuss collaborative action. A couple events that stand out as moments of accomplishment are the National Campaign for Artful Resistance in 2013 and The Save Our Schools Activists Conference: New & Experienced Organizers Working for Public Education & Communities in 2016. The art campaign was a collaboration with artist, educator, and fellow activist, Morna McDermott.[24] Throughout the art campaign, we encouraged children, educators, and communities to creatively express their critiques of "reform of public education" and their hopes for it. The collection of artworks (inclusive of paintings, drawings, videos, poetry, and sculptures) was curated in an online gallery and in a series of portfolios that were displayed at numerous grassroots actions and conferences around the country (McDermott & Noël Smith, 2014; Noël Smith & Shaw, 2014). The Save Our Schools Activists Conference was another amazing collaboration that culminated in a demonstration at the Lincoln Memorial. Hosted at Howard University, thanks to significant work on the part of Denisha Jones (Defending the Early Years, n.d.),[25] this event moved us into a decidedly specific focus on the intersection of race and social class. In addition to learning from the amazing grassroots wisdom of Rev. Dr. William Barber II and Bishop John L. Selders Jr. of the Moral Mondays Movement,[26] this conference and rally highlighted the dedication and triumphs of youth organizations, urban community organizers, and unionists from Boston, Chicago, Detroit, Newark, and Washington. These participants provided lasting inspiration for the work of our organization and served as a reminder that the health of our public education system: 1) always stands in direct relation to the broader social, political, and economic dynamics of our society and 2) can only be measured by the well-being of our most marginalized populations.

At the beginning of 2020, we reorganized under the name, Uniting to Save Our Schools. This provided us the opportunity to place particular emphasis on the act of "uniting." Again, we are keenly aware that there are groups of people all around the world who are constantly engaging in creative and powerful acts of resistance to dehumanization and standardization. Thus, the primary though complex question driving the work of USOS is: how can we come together, learn from one another, amplify each other's efforts, and create the change that our children and communities deserve? This shift served as a rejuvenation of our roots, in many respects, in that it brought us back around to the foundational belief that moved Bess, Jesse, and Rick—our organization's most enduring leadership—to act in the first place. Quite simply, all fights over public education are fundamentally about power over literacy (broadly conceived) and how we construct knowledge and our identities. It all comes down to battles over control and liberation.

The paradox of critique, Apple (2001) reminds us, it that the "analysis of what is [leads] to a neglect of what might be," which in turn necessitates "substantive large-scale discussions of feasible alternatives to neoliberal and neoconservative visions, policies, and practices that would move well beyond them" (p. 95). Critique is essential but never enough. We have to understand the dominant ideologies that are surging through discourses and driving policies, and we have to work to enact something different, something better. This requires clarity and focus. Upon our reorganization, we created an alternative framework to counter systematic standardization and dehumanization. This is detailed in the *USOS Platform for Public Education,* a living document that we update accordingly to meet the changing dynamics and problems forced upon the public's schools. The primary components of the platform are as follows:

- Public Education as a Human and Civil Right
- Fair and Equitable Funding for Public Education
- Safe, Socially and Racially Just Public Schools
- Strong School Communities and Families
- Educator and Community Leadership
- Professional, Diverse Educators in Every School
- Engaging and Comprehensive Classroom Instruction for Every Student
- An End to Mandated Standardized Testing

I recommend that readers refer to the version we have posted on our website because we provide additional suggestions and conditions for how we might come to realize each tenet (Uniting to Save Our Schools, n.d.).

Our mission is to join diverse organizers, groups, and activists at the international, national, and local levels to build a movement and strategize actions that challenge and transform our political, economic, and educational systems in an effort to build a more equitable future for all our children. USOS seeks to sustain and build upon the long-held conversation that educational equity only becomes possible when we simultaneously act to dismantle racialized capitalism and work towards a new economic order sutured to deep principles of justice. Our vision is quite straightforward: we want a public education system that is equitable, democratic, humane, and nurturing.

Lessons Learned and a Few Considerations for Our Future

There have been two aspects of this work that have been especially difficult to navigate since our inception over a decade ago: fluidity and distance. First, we are a national organization made up of leaders and members from all regions and backgrounds, most of whom have great physical distance between them. Because of this, technology has been essential to our survival and collaboration. Since the very beginning, our organizational meetings have been held via web conference. It's not a stretch to say that many of the organizers for the 2011 event met one another for the very first time when they arrived in DC, despite the fact that they had logged countless hours together in online formats. It is a strange thing to realize that you can do so much with someone and feel like you know them so well, even though you have never seen or hugged them. But, technology and distanced connection has its limits. What I have realized over my 11 years with USOS, and especially in light of our experience with the pandemic, is that more often than not, these technologies are most effective at *maintaining relationships* that we have *already cultivated* with people.

For instance, with the onset of the pandemic, we obviously had to put a hold on all grassroots efforts and in-person collaborations as we transitioned into online formats. We, like many other groups, channeled our energy into a series of webinars that we called Action Dialogues. This became our primary mode of interaction for 2 years, and they were wonderfully educational as well as good for morale. We were able to address an assortment of topics, from the school-to-prison pipeline, to high-stakes testing, to the attacks on critical race theory, to demoralization and moral injury, to the impacts of COVID-19 on the mental and physical well-being of schooling communities. In most cases, our organizers drew upon established connections in the planning of each webinar. This in itself is not a bad thing, but what I can see upon reflection is that, while we continued to engage in actions to the best of our ability under the constraining circumstances, neither the membership of our organization nor our connections with other groups showed noticeable growth. As Rick recently pointed out, the takeaway is, "We need to have a regular presence that is not just online; it needs to be face-to-face." This is vital, especially given our national span. If we do not grow, or at best maintain, then our story comes to a close.

This brings me to the point about fluidity: a trait that has been consistent since our organization's inception and one that has also complicated the ability to write about our history here. We have been around since 2010, and it goes without saying that this movement and our momentum have been created by countless people. Many of those people have been activists who have traversed across and worked within numerous organizations, taking part in one another's actions, moving onto other projects, or becoming entirely dedicated to localized needs. Surely, some folks have left over political differences, something that often comes with the territory of this type of work. But also, most of what we do is unpaid, and so fatigue is a real concern, especially when people are balancing families, careers, graduate school, health, and the simple yet profound realities of what it means to live a human life. Sadly, we have seen some beloved people within our networks depart this life altogether. USOS's own José Soler (Larson, 2017) and CTU's Karen Lewis (Perez et al., 2021) are two beautiful powerhouses who come to mind, two folks who dedicated their lives to justice and liberation in education. There have been other people too, like Donna Mace, for instance (Stenoff, 2022). She was someone I knew exclusively through our interactions on social media, and I felt a profound sense of loss when I heard that I would no longer see her thoughts and stories posted in my feed. It all underscores how deeply meaningful, humane and, dare I say, intimate these connections can be.

The people and the energy that comprise activist movements will naturally wax and wane, and just like any living, breathing organism, some things will change, and some will stay the same. But, Jesse offers a very pragmatic way of looking at this ever-evolving nature of USOS and the push toward justice in general. He tells the story of a time when he heard Reverend Ralph Abernathy speak when he was in college, and drawing reference to the enduring success of the Freedom Riders, Jesse says, "It didn't matter when you got on the bus, when you got off the bus, or if you stayed on the bus. What mattered is that you *got on* the bus. . . We have been a bus for people to come, stop, and grow. . . People can get on, and jump off wherever they want, and become whatever they want. . . This is a movement to take back our schools, the schools we never had."

As I was preparing to write this chapter, I had to consider how I became part of this movement. The funny thing is, I honestly have no clue; even after digging through archived emails, I can still find no hint. The best I can surmise is that I may have received an email from the American Education Studies Association in the spring of 2011. The most important detail, I believe, is that I was so angry at what was being done to public schools at the time and so desperate for change that I bought a plane ticket, packed my backpack, and went entirely alone to DC. Knowing not a soul when I touched down, my only hope was that I would meet someone who could help me put my energy to good use. The march was powerful enough that I returned the following spring for United Opt Out's (n.d.) Occupy the DOE, where I met many of the people written into this story. My work with USOS began the moment I returned home.

It has been nothing short of an absolute honor to ride alongside everyone who has gotten on and off this bus. Postpandemic and given the surging convergence of neoconservatives and authoritarian populists, though, it seems terribly evident that we still have a long ride ahead of us, and we are gonna need a lot of company to keep this thing fueled and moving, so that its wheels can keep turning toward our vision. We can maintain some of our connections via distance and technology, but it is clearly time to start building relationships again so we can revitalize for the long haul, and that is only going to happen through the close human interaction that comes from putting our butts in the seats next to those who are intent on traveling to similarly just places.

Editor's Note: You can follow Uniting to Save Our Schools on Facebook and Instagram. Their website is https://www.unitingtosaveourschools.org/

References

Acosta, C. (2014). Dangerous minds In Tucson: The banning of Mexican American Studies and critical thinking in Arizona. *Journal of Educational Controversy, 8*(1), Article 9. https://cedar.wwu.edu/jec/vol8/iss1/9

American University. (n.d.). *Vivian Vasquez*. https://www.american.edu/soe/faculty/vvasque.cfm

Ames, B. (2014, May 13). Towson education professor seeks seat on Howard School Board. *The Baltimore Sun*. https://www.baltimoresun.com/maryland/howard/ph-ce-altwerger-boe-candidate-0515-20140515-story.html

Apple, M. W. (2001). *Educating the 'right' way: Markets, standards, god, and inequality*. Routledge.

Apple, M. W. (2004, January and March). Creating difference: Neo-liberalism, neo-conservatism and the politics of educational reform. *Educational Policy, 18*, 12-44.

Au, W. (2009). *Unequal by design: High-stakes testing and the standardization of inequality*. Routledge.

Beyond Rhetoric. (n.d.). *About us*. https://beyondrhetoric.org/about-us.

Boyles, D. R. (1995). The corporate takeover of American schools. *The Humanist*, May/June, 20–24.

Boyles, D. R. (2000). *American education and corporations: The free market goes to school*. Routledge.

Bridge Crossing Jubilee. (n.d.). *Founders Hank & Rose Sanders*. https://www.selma-jubilee.com/founders

Buras, K. L. (2008). *Rightist multiculturalism: Core lessons on neoconservative school reforms*. Routledge.

By Any Means Necessary (BAMN). (n.d.). *Home*. https://www.bamn.com

Center for Expansion of Language and Thinking. (n.d.). *About*. https://www.celton-line.org/about

Central Connecticut State University (n.d.). *Jesse Turner, Ph.D.* https://directory.ccsu.edu/person/jesse-turner-phd.

Cody, A. (2009, November 2). Open letter to President Obama. *Education Week*. https://www.edweek.org/education/opinion-open-letter-to-president-obama/2009/11

Cody, A. (2010, March 15). Jesse is walking to Washington, D.C. *Education Week*. https://www.edweek.org/education/opinion-jesse-is-walking-to-washington-dc/2010/03

Cortez, J. (2021, October 12). The scars from Tucson Unified and the fight for Ethnic Studies. *City College Times*. https://sjcctimes.com/15856/social-justice/the-scars-from-tucson-unified-and-the-fight-for-ethnic-studies-programs/

Defending the Early Years. (n.d.). *About*. https://dey.org/.

Dixson, A. D., Buras, K. L., & Jeffers, E. K. (2015). The color of reform: Race, education reform, and charter schools in Post-Katrina New Orleans. *Qualitative Inquiry, 21*(3), 288–299.

Dudley-Marling, C., & Baker, D. (2012). The effects of market-based school reforms on students with disabilities. *Disability Studies Quarterly, 32*(2). https://doi.org/10.18061/dsq.v32i2.3187

Freire, P. (1997). *Pedagogy of the oppressed*. Continuum.

Goodman, K. S., & Goodman, Y. M. (2014). *Making sense of learners making sense of written language: The selected works of Kenneth S. Goodman & Yetta M. Goodman*. Routledge.

Grant, T. S. (2013). *"Stop the lies. Let the truth be told!": Education reform and the Save Our Schools March and National Call to Action (SOS)* Publication No. 3563328 [Doctoral dissertation, University of Maryland]. ProQuest Dissertations and Theses Global.

Hewitt, R. (2009). Priming the pump: 'Educating' for market democracy. In D. R. Boyles (Ed.), *Schools or markets?: Commercialism, privatization, and school-business partnerships* (pp. 47–58). Lawrence Erlbaum Associates.

Journey 4 Justice Alliance. (n.d.). *Home*. https://j4jalliance.com/

Kenwood Oakland Community Organization. (n.d.). *Home*. https://kocoonline.org/

Labaree, D. F. (2010). *Someone has to fail: The zero-sum game of public schooling*. Harvard University Press.

Larson, E. (2017). José Soler: A life working at the intersections of nationalism, internationalism, and working-class radicalism. *Radical History Review, 128*, 63–76.

Lipman, P. (2011). *The new political economy of urban education*. Routledge.

McDermott, M. (n.d.). *Home*. Education Alchemy. https://educationalchemy.com/home/

McDermott, M., & Noël Smith, B. L. (2014). Imagining alternatives to education reform: The Save Our Schools Campaign for Artful Resistance. In B. L. Noel Smith, K. L. Becker, L. R. Miller, N. S. Reid, & M. D. Sorenson (Eds.), *Collective unravelings of the hegemonic web* (pp. 209–226). Information Age Publishing.

McDermott, M., Robertson, P., Jensen, R., & Smith, C. (Eds.). (2015). *An activist handbook for the education revolution: United Opt Out's test of courage*. Information Age.

McGuinn, P. J. (2006). *No Child Left Behind and the transformation of federal education policy, 1965–2005*. The University Press of Kansas.

Meyer, R. (2020). A series of (mostly) fortunate events & relationships. In B. L. Noel Smith & R. Hewitt (Eds.), *Love in Education and the Art of Living* (pp. 113–132). Information Age Publishing.

National Council of Teachers of English. (n.d.). *Awards*. https://ncte.org/awards/affilicate-ncte-intellectual-freedom-state-regional-provincial/

Network for Public Education. (n.d.). *Chartered for profit II: Pandemic profiteering.* https://networkforpubliceducation.org/chartered-for-profit-ii-pandemic-profiteering/

Nichols, S., & Berliner, D. (2007). *Collateral damage: How high-stakes testing corrupts America's schools.* Harvard Education Press.

Noël Smith, B. L. (2018). Public transparency, student privacy, and technological persuasion in education: Refining some concerns of Opt Out. *Thresholds in Education 41*(3), 201–219.

Noël Smith, B. L., & Shaw, M. L. (2014). Art as resistance: Creating and collecting content for a public lesson on standardization. *Journal of Curriculum & Pedagogy 11*(1), 5–17.

Owens, D. (2015). *The origins of the Common Core: How the free market became public education policy.* Palgrave MacMillan.

Perez Jr., J., Rosenberg-Douglas, K., Byrne, J., & Pratt, G. (2021, February 8). Legendary former Chicago Teachers Union President Karen Lewis has died. 'She was a fighter and a treasure for this city.' *Chicago Tribune.* https://www.chicagotribune.com/news/breaking/ct-karen-lewis-chicago-teachers-union-leader-dies-20210208-qruqfcggurcqjaw62r4f5ppoeq-story.html

Poor People's Campaign. (n.d.) *Home.* https://www.poorpeoplescampaign.org/

Ravitch, D. (2013). *Reign of error: The hoax of the privatization movement and the danger to America's public schools.* Basic Books.

Reckhow, S. (2013). *Follow the money: How foundation dollars change public school politics.* Oxford University Press.

Rosa, R. D., Noël Smith, B. L., Smith, C., & Campos-Martinez, J. (2015). The advancing endgame revolt! Dialogues with activists & community organizers in the trenches. In R. D. Rosa, & J. J. Rosa, (Eds.), *Capitalism's educational catastrophe and the advancing endgame revolt* (pp. 121–160). Peter Lang.

Shaw, M. (n.d.). *Michael Shaw.* ResearchGate. https://www.researchgate.net/profile/Michael-Shaw-14

Smith, C. (n.d.). *Ceresta Smith.* Academia. https://independent.academia.edu/CerestaSmith

Solochek, J. (2011, August 6). A weekend interview with Rita Solnet, Florida co-founder of Parents Across America. *Tampa Bay Times.* https://www.tampabay.com/archive/2011/08/06/a-weekend-interview-with-rita-solnet-florida-co-founder-of-parents-across-america/

South Florida Sun Sentinel. (2010, July 30). Teachers and parents protest at 'Million Teacher March.' https://www.sun-sentinel.com/2010/07/30/teachers-and-parents-protest-at-million-teacher-march/

Stenoff, S. (2022, December 18). *For Donna Mace with gratitude.* The Opt Out Florida Network. https://theoptoutfloridanetwork.wordpress.com/2022/12/18/for-donna-mace-with-gratitude/

Stevens, S. J. (n.d.). *About.* Sabrina Joy Stevens: Awakening Liberation from the Inside Out. https://www.sabrinajoystevens.com/.

Strauss, V. (2011a, July 30). The Save Our Schools March. *The Washington Post.* https://www.washingtonpost.com/blogs/answer-sheet/post/the-save-our-schools-march/2011/07/30/gIQAhf71jI_blog.html

Strauss, V. (2011b, May 19). Why teachers, parents are planning 'Save Our Schools' March," *The Washington Post.* https://www.washingtonpost.com/blogs/answer-sheet/post/why-teachers-parents-are-planning-save-our-schools-march/2011/05/18/AFEqMD7G_blog.html

Thompson, K. (2012, April 1). Backers of national 'Million Teacher March' hope locals will join protest July 30 in Palm Beach County. *The Palm Beach Post.* https://www.palmbeachpost.com/story/news/education/2012/04/01/backers-national-million-teacher-march/7873799007/

Turner, J. (2011, June 26). *A walking man resistance story.* Children Are More Than Test Scores. https://childrenaremorethantestscores.blogspot.com/2011/06/walking-man-resistance-story.html

United Opt Out. (n.d.). Occupy the DOE in DC schedule March 30th to April 2nd, 2012. http://unitedoptout.com/archived/occupy-the-doe-march-30-april-2-2012/

Uniting to Save Our Schools. (n.d.). *Uniting to Save Our Schools: Platform for Public Education.* https://www.unitingtosaveourschools.org/usos-platform

Weber, M. C. (2010). Special education from the (damp) ground up: Children with disabilities in a charter-dependent educational system. *Loyola Journal of Public Interest Law, 11*(2), 217–248.

Endnotes

1 McGuinn (2006), Labaree (2010), Ravitch (2013), and Reckhow (2013) provide context on the history of this bipartisan convergence.

2 This group has included venture philanthropists, corporations, and also a group of people Apple (2001) calls the professional and managerial new middle class (p. 48). He also explains, "The entire project of neoliberalism is connected to a larger process of exporting the blame from the decisions of dominant groups onto the state and onto the poor people" (p. 39).

3 Post-Katrina New Orleans is a comprehensive example of the way systematic damage was done to working-class communities of color and especially to disabled students. There are countless stories of charter schools engaging in selective admissions (i.e., cherry picking) that prohibited enrollment of students with special needs (Dudley-Marling & Baker, 2012; Weber, 2010).

4 See the Network for Public Education (n.d.) for their ongoing analysis of the corruption in charter schools across the nation.
5 The attacks on ethnic studies in Tucson Unified School District provides a case study for how these ideological dynamics came together, though similar attacks occurred in other conservative states as well (Acosta, 2014; Cortez, 2021; and Apple, 2004, p. 15).
6 I say neoconservatism was "in part" responsible for these national standards because the foundation is ideologically consistent with their camp (Buras, 2008). However, the creation of these programs represents a space of convergence with the neoliberals (Owens, 2015).
7 The current politics in Florida and the base of Governor Ron DeSantis is a case in point. There we can see the way neoconservatism has converged with a third ideology that Apple (2001) addresses, which is authoritarian populism (pp. 44–47).
8 Jesse Turner is a professor of literacy, elementary, and early childhood education as well as the Director of the Literacy Center at Central Connecticut State University (n.d.).
9 Ruby Clayton is a teacher from Indianapolis Public Schools and a recipient of the 2010 NCTE Affiliate Intellectual Freedom Award Winners (National Council of Teachers of English, n.d.).
10 Bess Altwerger is a professor emeritus at Towson University who has dedicated her career (as well as her retirement) to the study of critical literacy pedagogies and advocacy for the good of public schools. She is a cofounder of USOS and also served as a school board member of Howard County Board of Education in Maryland (Ames, 2014).
11 Vivian Vasquez is a professor at American University and the recipient of NCTE Outstanding Elementary Educator in the English Language Arts Award, among many others (American University, n.d.).
12 Sabrina Joy Stevens (n.d.) created the Failing Schools Project in 2010, served on the planning committee for the 2011 march, and has remained an advocate and strategist on issues related to education and justice.
13 Laurie Murphy was instrumental in the planning of the 2011 march and conference, and she became a co-founder for United Opt Out (McDermott et al., 2015).
14 Chris Janotta agreed to join on but left shortly after for political differences (Thompson, 2012; South Florida Sun Sentinel 2010).
15 Richard "Rick" Meyer (2020) is a professor emeritus of literacy at the University of New Mexico who also has extensive experience as a community organizer, something he credits to his mother's commitment to justice, education, and her Jewish faith.
16 Michael Shaw (n.d.) retired from being a professor of literacy at St. Thomas Aquinas College and would eventually serve as a Steering Committee member for our organization.

17 Ceresta Smith (n.d.) served on our board for several years and co-founded United Opt Out. It is important to note that she was not only a speaker at the 2011 march and rally, but some of the organizers at the time, who were white, were uneasy because of her message about racism and her connection to BAMN.

18 Bob George contributed to the Fundraising Committee for our first event and stayed on to serve several years as the National Director of the organization.

19 Rose Sanders has built a legacy of activism, especially in political and legal realms of Alabama (Bridge Crossing Jubilee, n.d.). She contributed to several of the actions organized by USOS and was a keynote for our People's Education Conference 2012. In turn, we collaborated on several education-related panels at the Selma Bridge Crossing Jubilee.

20 The ICs were led by Katherine McBride Cox the first year, and then Becca Ritchie served as their lead organizer through 2013.

21 This included scholar activists such as Jonathan Kozol, Deb Meier, Pedro Noguera, and Angela Valenzuela.

22 Troy Spencer Grant is a full-time public school teacher, an adjunct professor, and the Founder and President of the organization, Beyond Rhetoric (Beyond Rhetoric, n.d.).

23 Peggy Robertson, Morna McDermott, Ceresta Smith, Tim Slekar, Shaun Johnson, and Laurie Murphy each resided in different parts of the country, but they met one another through the social networks that grew out of the Save Our Schools March. Eventually, Rosemarie Jensen would also join their ranks. For the written work of some of these founders, see *An Activist Handbook for the Education Revolution: United Opt Out's Test of Courag*e (McDermott et al., 2015). Noël Smith (2018) and Rosa et al. (2015) provided analyses of some of the overarching concerns of the opt out movement as well as a brief history.

24 Morna McDermott (n.d.) is a professor at Towson University and a cofounder of United Opt Out. One of her many creative approaches to activism was displayed at the 2011 march. It was an art installation of gravestones paying homage to the beautiful aspects of education that had been lost (and killed) under NCLB.

25 Denisha Jones is a board member of USOS and the Executive Director of Defending the Early Years, in addition to serving with several other educational advocacy groups. She was a professor at Howard when we planned this event, and she is now teaching at Sarah Lawrence University (Defending the Early Years, n.d.).

26 The Moral Mondays Movement developed into the Poor People's Campaign (n.d.).

Part 3:

Opportunities for Preparing Preservice and Current Teachers

CHAPTER 14

Aspiring Educators as Aspiring Organizers and Activists: A Blueprint for Action[1]

Gerald K. Wood, Kimo Homer, Erin Hiebert, Jeff Lang, Michelle Novelli, and Christine Lemley

Introduction

#RedforEd was a catalytic moment in the resurgence of teacher activism in Arizona in 2018 (Karvelis, 2019). Started as a grassroots effort by rank-and-file members, #RedforEd pushed teacher unions to stand behind educators who were willing to risk their jobs and their livelihoods to advocate for better working and learning conditions for students, colleagues, and community members. Pro-public education community members lined busy streets shoulder-to-shoulder with striking teachers—all with the same message—urging the state of Arizona to increase teacher pay by 20%, along with an increase of pay for classified staff, and to restore school funding to 2008 prerecession levels. The mobilization of large-scale community support played a crucial role in the formation of a new consciousness among our aspiring educators, many who participated in walkouts and realized the power of grassroots organizing. Kimo Homer, a coauthor who was a freshman, joined community members, professors, aspiring educators, students, and educators in the Flagstaff community for marches and rallies at city hall.

The purpose of this chapter is to provide a road map for Aspiring Educators across the United States who seek to understand how student chapters can both organize and activate in ways that reflect new articulations of social justice unionism (Peterson, 2021). In one of the recruitment events for our AE chapter, as Joe Thomas, then president of the Arizona Education Association

(AEA), invited, "I don't want you to join the union. I want you to take it over" (personal communication, January 29, 2020). By documenting what we have done, where we hope to go, and the possibilities/tensions of shifting our student chapter towards a social justice union-model of organizing, we highlight our framework to provide a road map to build power in ways that align as union organizers and activists. We focus on three areas: 1) identifying member interests and concern to build membership and address traditional union roles; 2) activating and mobilizing campaigns to address legislation that impact the teaching profession and communities; and 3) interfacing with local unions to build solidarity and deepen social justice unionism. In the last part of the chapter, we identify challenges and provide a vision for focusing on communication, consciousness-raising, and community-based accountability.

In this chapter, we began with an introduction, inviting a former AE student member to share how and why he became involved with the union. We then move to positioning selves, again intending to provide background and foundational knowledge of who we are and who we are becoming. We then move to History of Aspiring Educators within the NEA, History of NAU AE, and present our Theoretical Framework, Social Justice Unionism, in order to underscore the importance of how historical foundations shape our work and then present a framework to guide our analysis of our engagement thus far. We then present Social Justice Unionism using the Four Pillars for Action to highlight the importance of considering AE's framework and then provide a blueprint for action for other chapters to consider integrating into their work. We finally end with closing thoughts from a former AE student member to complete a circle begun by the former AE student member in the introduction, intentionally underscoring the importance of member voice and accountability to self and others.

Positioning Selves

The structure of aspiring educator members and advisors are all interconnected. As coauthors of this chapter, we have interdisciplinary expertise to offer to the students, community members, and ourselves. We chose to position ourselves through the following questions in order to provide a glimpse of us to our readers:

1. What are our identities? Where are we from? How did we get involved in union work?
2. What is our connection to AE? What do we contribute to AE?
3. What is the future of AE? What do we hope for with our engagement?

Gerald Wood, Founding and Former AE Co-Advisor

As a United Statian, Latiné and white, bilingual, cisgender, and an able-bodied male, Gerald Wood grew up in Latin America and the United States. Since 2014, he has advised the AE chapter moving from social justice to political action to social justice unionism as different members have brought forward different strengths and issues, as well as his own shifting knowledge. For the future, Gerald hopes to see AE develop a more grassroots organizing model that prepares union members to become building reps while putting pressure on more traditional union organizing.

Kimo Homer, Former AE Student Member

Kimo Adriano Homer is a queer, biracial, early-career educator born and raised in San Diego, California. He graduated with a Bachelor of Science in Education–Secondary Education, History, & Social Studies from NAU in 2021. Born into a family of union members who were inactive within their local organizations, he found a proactive space to organize at NAU. Drawn to organize by the #RedforED movement, he actively worked as an aspiring educator with NAU AE in Flagstaff, at the state level with AEA, and nationally with the NEA. He held a plethora of executive positions with NAU AE including president at the state level. He was also elected to the NEA Representative Assembly from 2019 until 2021 and served nationally as a zone director for the NEA's Aspiring Educators caucus. Upon his departure, he was awarded the National Education Association's 2021 #AspiringEdLife State Leader award for his union work in political action within the state of Arizona. Kimo hopes to create a new vision and space for future educators to organize and advance social justice unionism through political action.

Erin Hiebert, Former AE Student Member and Community Schools Organizer for AEA

As a queer, feminist, cisgender white woman, Erin Hiebert is a community organizer and abolitionist educator who was born and raised in Yuma, Arizona. Her paternal ancestors—beekeepers, field workers, and farmers—have lived throughout the ancestral homelands of the Cocopah, Yaqui, and Quechan peoples since the early 1800s. Her maternal ancestors—teachers, caretakers, and homesteaders—have occupied the Pacific Northwest since they immigrated to the United States from Germany in the late 1800s. She is a former organizer for the University Union of Northern Arizona (UUNA-AFT). She currently works as a Community Schools Organizer for the Arizona Education Association. Erin is a proud product of Arizona public schools and a 2019 graduate of Northern Arizona University's Secondary Education of History and Social Studies Program and Community Engagement Program. NAU's Aspiring Educators program ignited Erin's passion for social justice work and labor organizing as she engaged regularly as a preservice teacher through AE, with various localized advocacy campaigns related to Arizona's school voucher expansion, school investment ballot initiatives, and school board elections.

Jeff Lang, Union Organizer, AEA

Jeff Lang identifies as a white, gender-conforming, and able-bodied male. His work as a union staff member focuses on providing organizing, advocacy, and bargaining support to union leaders. He is motivated to work with aspiring educators because he believes they are the future of the profession, as well as the future of the labor movement. He keeps an old picture on his desk of his grandpa walking a picket line that serves as a constant reminder of the importance of worker solidarity in our movement to raise wages and improve the lives of all working people.

Michelle Novelli, AE Advisor

Michelle Novelli is a 23-year NEA member who started as a P-12 classroom teacher in a local Title I elementary school before beginning work at NAU in 2015. Michelle has worked with a team of faculty advisors for the student Aspiring Educators program and is dedicated to supporting the next generation of world-changing teachers. Michelle hopes to grow the student organization, secure pay for student teaching, and see Aspiring Educators as central participants in the union.

Christine Lemley, Former Aspiring Educators (AE) Co-Advisor

Christine Lemley is a white, bilingual, visually impaired, cisgender, female scholar activist committed to equity, justice, and solidarity. She served as AE co-advisor for several years, wanting to support students building skills at the university they could then transfer to their teaching professions. She remembers how informational her union representatives were when she first started teaching and wants students to realize they have resources for leadership and support opportunities, as well as ways to engage social justice and equity issues when they begin to teach.

History of Aspiring Educators within the NEA

On August 26, 1857, Zalmon Richards called upon "fellow-educators throughout the United States to assemble . . . for the purpose of organizing a National Teachers Association" (Butler, 1987). Teachers from state associations in the North, South, East, and West answered the call by merging with what would eventually become the National Education Association (NEA). Our NEA union has served a pivotal role in our nation's history and the creation of its public education system.

NEA student chapters have gone through various names and iterations. In 1937, Joy Elmer Morgan, who edited the NEA Journal, was influential in starting the student program known then as Future Teachers of America to encourage high school and college students to become teachers. During the 1950s, the NEA moved to create a separate structure for college students, establishing the Student-NEA program (Aspiring Educators Chapter Toolkit, 2021). In 2018, at the NEA Representative Assembly, members voted to change the Student-NEA name to Aspiring Educators. This change was seen to reflect the diversity of its membership (Aspiring Educators Chapter Toolkit, 2021, p. 8). Today 40,000 NEA Aspiring Educators across the United States collectively make up the future of the teaching profession, as well as the future of our union—the NEA.

History of NAU AE

In 2014, Matt Nichols, an organizer with AEA, approached the Associate Dean of the NAU College of Education to see about the possibility of starting an NEA student chapter. After going to lunch and discussing how to move forward with Matt and his Associate Dean, Gerald worked to identify interested students through several Educational Foundations classes—Introduction to Education and School and Society. To launch the chapter, Gerald and the students worked with AEA to host a recruitment night, inviting over 400 teacher candidates to the event. The students coordinated a breakfast to invite interested faculty to hear about AE and to also advertise the event. The NEA helped coordinate this event, bringing in the president of the AEA, the NEA Student Chair, our local Flagstaff Education Association president, and the AEA attorney to address the dos and don'ts of social media to invite students to consider intentional ways forward.

Successes and Challenges: A Chronology

During the initial years (Phase 1: 2014–2019), advisors worked hard to ensure AE was substantially different from other student organizations in the College of Education, both through its focus on social justice and in terms of its college-wide impact. With this launch, our fledgling chapter started with a cadre of motivated members to emphasize social justice. In its early iterations, Aspiring Educators adopted the four pillars of the NEA's Aspiring Educators' Program—Teacher Quality, Community Engagement, Political Action, and Social Justice. Through various iterations, the student chapter addressed a range of issues—teach-ins, political action, and #RedforEd mobilizations. During these years, the AE Executive Board (EB) developed skills in writing grants and organizing college-wide events. Beyond large recruitment events, the EB geared events towards topics identified by the NEA (e.g., school-to-prison nexus) or heritage months. This required communicating with NEA and AEA, who would fly in speakers for our events as needed. We would also outreach to educators in local schools to serve as presenters and create connections.

Amidst the 2020 COVID-19 pandemic, NAU's AE was moved fully online and was forced to come up with new effective ways to organize (Phase 2:

2019–2021). As the world came to a halt due to mandated lockdowns, NAU's Aspiring Educators Chapter continued to hold executive board and chapter meetings weekly on Zoom. Since 2020 was an election year, coming off the back of the 2018 #RedforEd movement, the EB felt the urgency to carry the pro-public education momentum from #RedforEd to make changes up and down the ballot. The EB focused on passing Arizona Proposition 208, which would raise taxes for the wealthiest Arizonans and bring that money back to our public schools. In our virtual EB meetings, we brainstormed and discussed what would be the best course of action to ensure that Prop. 208 passed. While Prop. 208 was approved by Arizona voters during the 2020 election to boost public education funding, it was ultimately criticized by GOP lawmakers and was shot down by the Arizona court system, which was a catastrophic blow to the #RedforEd movement.

The next board shifted away from political action to hone in on important social justice topics. The conversations were timely (e.g., critical race theory (CRT), lesbian, gay, bisexual, transgender, queer + (LGBTQ+) attacks, and climate justice), and the meetings were well-attended. These conversations were usually led by EB members or other students knowledgeable in their respective fields. While the weekly conversations were brilliant, these conversations remained far removed from the realities educators face every day and existed in a political bubble because these events failed to underscore how educators navigated this political terrain. By remaining separate from the struggles of educators in classrooms, our EB lost the ability to enact "solidarity networks" (Smith, 2009). While we tried to generate more substantive relationships with core FEA members by standing with them at rallies to support union certification or hosting a dinner for FEA members, we needed a different organizational model that could be more flexible and offer more long-term planning.

Shifting Towards Social Justice Unionism

Over the last 3 years, advisors have pushed to shift the chapter towards models of social justice unionism. We advocated for new, specific board positions with a focus on recruitment, campaigns, and direct connections to local unions. In the fall of 2022, we developed a mission statement to be part of the recruitment strategy. The board seemed to be split between wanting to be more focused on action and being more of a social organization. After multiple conversations discussing how the mission statement aligned with our goals, the board voted to adopt the following statement:

> As an Aspiring Educators chapter, we are a union dedicated to educating and preparing teachers and other education candidates to understand the value of unions in supporting the work of public schools, educators, families, and communities. Our mission is to ensure educators aspire to join their local unions as active and engaged members by advocating for: 1) the profession, 2) better working and learning conditions, 3) more equitable and just communities.

Drafting a mission statement created a tool for the EB to use when leadership decisions needed to be made on how the chapter would allocate time and resources, while also prioritizing topics. Advisors also hoped it would help restructure the work and how the EB prioritized weekly meetings and other kinds of organizational spaces (e.g., training for EB or general membership, EB meetings, business meetings, running campaigns). Ideally, the mission statement reminded the EB of the significant responsibilities they have to lead an organization reliant on them.

Theoretical Framework: Social Justice Unionism

Traditionally, labor unions have addressed bread and butter issues in what has been termed industrial unionism (Peterson, 1999). Within the context of teachers unions, this has been reflected in calls for increased educator pay, better hours, and representation of members regarding working conditions. This work relies on building site reps to bring attention to working conditions when educators may not have time for lunch, negotiate professional development time with principals, or ensure due process rights. The focus revolves around an adversarial relationship between labor and management. Internally, industrial unions tend to emphasize decisions made by the executive board with little participation or engagement from the broader membership (Editors, 2021). In the context of our student chapter, this has meant (or more accurately could mean) representing teacher candidates in disputes with faculty and sending out surveys to ensure field placements in order to allow teacher candidates to develop the skills needed to be successful in the university and beyond.

Building off of industrial unionism, professional unionism has also been a cornerstone of unions like the NEA, focusing on teacher quality and accountability (Peterson, 1999). The ability to provide ongoing professional development to teachers and help support the exit of teachers who are not the best fit have been central pillars. Members are able to participate in webinars, workshops, and other blended learning opportunities that advance the teaching profession. These opportunities are also available to aspiring educators just starting their teaching journey. Unlike industrial unionism, this model tries to establish more cooperative relationships with management by encouraging greater teacher leadership at the school building level.

In 1994, teacher union activists called for changes to approaches to union organizing. In the document, Social Justice Unionism: A Working Draft, educators stated:

> Without a broader conception of the interests of teachers and of teaching, our unions will find themselves on evermore shaky ground defending fewer jobs and shrinking privileges against repeated attacks. Without a better partnership with the parents and communities that need public education most, we will find ourselves isolated from essential allies. . . Without a new model of unionism that revives debate and democracy internally and projects an inspiring social vision and agenda externally, we will fall short of the challenges before us. (cited from "The 1994 Call for Social Justice Teacher Unionism," Charney et al., 2021, p. 74)

This shift has led to the recognition that educators must work hand-in-hand with families and communities to develop more extensive agendas that reflect the needs and aspirations of a broader public. Social justice unionism may tackle broader issues such as the privatization of education or might engage with social movements that may not seem to directly impact schools (Editors, 2021). In addressing paid student teaching, this campaign organized by EB members and coordinated with teacher candidates at NAU and statewide has also sought to expose the exploitation of unpaid labor and the financial challenges many student teachers face when not allowed to work while having to pay for school.

Social Justice Unionism Using the Four Pillars for Action

As we continue to evolve as a chapter, we have worked to shift our work to more deeply engage social justice unionism to be ready to change with the times and needs for equity outcomes. Since the EB has consistently expressed an interest in social justice, we have sought to develop a framework for more directly preparing aspiring educators to engage in union organizing. Our chapter has been successful in having our graduates, who have been members and generally on the EB, go on to take leadership roles in their locals. Therefore, we are hoping to better reflect what unions do, while also amplifying the social justice component that is often not part of locals. As a chapter committed to social justice unionism, we are working to better represent education candidates and the working conditions they face, becoming much more active in organizing local, state, and national campaigns, and better interfacing with our local unions and educators.

Becoming More of a Traditional Union

In order to model ourselves more like a traditional union, we are crafting ways to better represent the needs and working conditions of our student members. As far as we know, few student chapters have not been involved in representing education candidates' working and learning conditions. In the first couple years of our chapter, we worked to generate a survey for teacher candidates in practicum because we heard from several students that they were not learning what they expected to learn in their placements. In some cases, teacher candidates expressed spending most of their time making copies or grading assignments, having very limited interactions with students. While the survey initially received considerable pushback from the College of Education administration, the administration would later adopt this survey, even though this information was not shared with our student chapter. More recently, teacher candidates, particularly students of color and LGBTQ+ students, have shared experiences of discrimination and/or invisibility in their college classrooms or in their practicum fieldwork placements. These conversations have often revolved around dispositions regarding professionalism, students being marked down or not passing because they had accents, or students who were not recognized for being gender fluid.

These are some questions which help inform how we might better align our students with organizing when they enter the field.

1. How can we organize in ways that align more closely with reflecting our union members' interests? (e.g., providing representation over due process issues for teacher candidates when they encounter conflicts in their workplace or developing shared concerns to address the working conditions of teacher candidates)
2. How can we develop a governance structure more aligned with traditional unionism? (e.g., creating building site reps/ reps based on majors with exec board meetings and membership meetings)

Organizing Local, State, and National Campaigns

As a way to think more concretely around political action and drawing on the momentum from #RedforEd, we are working to translate union member concerns into actionable campaigns and movements. Utilizing mobilization techniques from #RedforEd such as wearing colors to show support, walk-ins, walkouts, and the use of social media to gauge community support; we also seek to expand how unions see their work in ways that align more closely with social justice unionism.

In Table 14.1 on the following page, we provide a couple of examples of what these campaigns could center on based on our four grounding principles of: Teacher Quality, Community Engagement, Political Action, and Social Justice.

Connecting with Our Local Union

In an attempt to extend social justice unionism into our work with our local educators union, we have worked to strengthen collaboration between AE and the FEA. In 2022, the FEA invited our chapter to participate in the process of recommending school board candidates, as well as canvassing neighborhoods to support voter turnout. We hope to expand this to have more symbiotic

Table 14.1.

Examples of Campaigns Using Four Pillars

Issue	Teacher Quality	Community Engagement	Political Action	Social Justice
Expansion of vouchers through Empowerment Scholarship Accounts in Arizona	Show impact of $900M loss to public schools; higher class sizes and fewer educators	Organizing with FEA & Save Our Schools Arizona to stop the expansion of vouchers	Work to reduce vouchers to middle and upper class families to stop funneling public $ to private and religious schools	Promote high quality & equitable education to all students no matter their socioeconomic background
Paid student teaching	Understand the impacts of moonlighting on the quality of student teaching	Discuss practicum and student teaching concerns with members and stakeholders	Mobilize to secure stipends for all student teachers	Address impacts of exploitation of first-gen students of color
End period poverty	Create awareness and materials for teachers to use/ share with students regarding menstruation and identify ways to celebrate these moments (e.g., period parties, family nights to acknowledge)	Survey/interview school nurses or principals about existing policies and needs	Support legislation advocating for ending period poverty and expand to upper elementary grades	Understand the systemic inequities facing working class communities and lack of access to period products
LGBTQ+ issues	Create awareness and support for educators who use LGBTQ+ materials in their classrooms and schools	Advocate for the use of appropriate gender pronouns for teacher candidates and by extension educators and students	Organize protests and mobilize support against attacks on LGBTQ+ communities; write letters to legislators who support the inclusion of LGBTQ+ issues in the curriculum; organize mobilization to support teachers who are targeted under current bills	Collaborate with mental health professionals to address the trauma of these attacks and build coalitional support

relationships with union educators to both understand the barriers facing educators in classrooms and schools and also to serve as a sounding board for how to act in solidarity to navigate the current political climate. In an effort to create more direct links, we wrote a job description for our vice president or designee to attend FEA meetings. While we have not been successful in honoring the vote, the executive board took last semester to identify one board position to meet with FEA, and we continue to see the benefits of working closely with our local union.

Moving Forward: A Blueprint for Action

Our AE chapter has done some groundbreaking work, receiving awards from the NEA as the Emerging Chapter of the Year in 2021, and the chapter was recognized for their work in Political Action during the 2020 Representative Assembly. Additionally, our advisors received the Distinguished Advisors award in 2022. We are honored and humbled by these distinctions and continue to believe our alignment requires greater attention to social justice unionism. Through the years, we have identified some challenges, and here offer a road map to the ways in which we have tried to shift towards social justice unionism.

Challenge 1: Conservative nature of teacher education

As we grapple with the structure of student organizations in the College, we are also confronted with what seems to be a strong ability by teacher candidates to name problems, yet maintain an acceptance of the status quo. In providing possible explanations for why teacher candidates may not take on more progressive stances, Zeichner and Tabachnik (1981) argue there may be a fundamental alignment between teacher education programs and PK-12 schools where teacher candidates develop their skills with both espousing conservative understandings of the teaching profession. Another explanation may be that future teachers align with fairly conservative positions and use the language of social justice while they are in university programs to reflect this language. Could it be that teacher candidates have emerging knowledge of language connected to social justice but have not been able to practice "walking the walk"

(Olsen, 2016, p. 18)? Teacher candidates may have little exposure to faculty who envision themselves as change makers and may not see modeled what actions could look like. While teacher candidates may be exposed to the idea that teaching is always political, we venture to argue they may not always believe this to be the case, as they adopt technical solutions to the issues of teaching. Without deep experiences participating in union organizing or solidarity movements, teacher candidates may be limited to talking about issues of concern rather than viewing themselves as public actors.

Challenge 2: Private versus public relationships and the need for public accountability

Over the course of several different executive boards, we saw patterns that these boards tended to spend time together cementing friendships outside of the weekly meetings. These strong private bonds often filtered into the weekly meeting as cliques formed and board members separated themselves from the general membership. These private relationships created a wall between the EB and members of the organization, ultimately deterring folks on the outside of these cliques from organizing—weakening our communal outreach. As these private relationships became stronger, our ability to develop public accountability often faltered (Chambers, 2018). We hope more training on understanding the difference between public relationships and private relationships would allow teacher candidates to initiate their education into politics.

Challenge 3: Creating norms for democratic governance

As a way to develop more public accountability, we worked to reframe positions and develop norms that were more aligned with social justice unionism. By having more clear expectations about different board member positions and eliminating co-presidents and other shared positions, this allowed us to ensure folks would be able to report out what they had done, but also ensure everyone understood their job descriptions. We also worked to instill accountability for responding to text messages and figuring out when board members were feeling overwhelmed and needed to step away. In addition, we worked to create a structure that ran more parallel to how locals organized their meetings (exec board meetings once a month and general membership meetings once a month). While not always possible, the EB meetings would encourage the board to conduct their business, consider other kinds of actions outside of weekly meeting topics, and practice running meetings with *Roberts' Rules of Order*. By providing trainings and conducting a book study of *Rules of Order*, the EB was able to start changing the nature of how they conducted business by acknowledging the need to make motions, second motions, have discussion, and vote on particular issues of interest.

Beyond these structural changes to align with more traditional models of union organizing, we also sought to address underlying issues around power dynamics. How can we organize competitive elections where folks are elected on their platforms rather than friendships? What issues matter to members in how we conducted weekly meetings? How do we create feedback loops for the EB and general members to weigh in on issues and decisions? Were the meetings accessible to all students if only held in person? How were voices of students who were historically marginalized heard and acknowledged? How do we negotiate conflict and heal from conflicts when topics and conversations matter so deeply and there is so much passion and care?

Social justice unionism provides guidance on how to create more democratic governance that allows us to align with a broader constituency. How are we challenging white supremacy? What does that look like in our advising, our executive board, and our general membership? Were we openly able to deal with "racial issues internal to the union"? How do we involve "broader membership engagement and involvement in decision-making" (Editors, 2021, p. 104)? How can we align ourselves with broader social justice movements?

Challenge 4: Moving from social justice talk to concerted social justice action/solidarity

As we thought about the seemingly artificial divide between the EB and general membership, we also thought about the structure of our weekly meetings. The structure of the weekly meetings has been detrimental to being able to mobilize effectively because the different boards seemed to feel the need to address different topics each week. As we mention above, we tried to move towards agendas that required decision-making, taking votes, or developing consensus.

We also worked to create structures that required a different set of skills (e.g., voter turnout, lobbying, running campaigns such as paid student teaching).

As advisors and organizers, some ways we sought to overcome this challenge was by shifting conversations towards the subject of power and who has it. We talked about what power would look like if the chapter had it, and we set membership goals to take strides towards building more strength by inviting potential members for coffee to increase our membership by four to five students each semester. A group of like-minded individuals, for the most part, would not make change by only engaging each other in groupthink. Like a shop steward might map their worksite, we encouraged our leaders to do the same with their campus. The chapter is member-driven, but as advisors and organizers, we worked to nudge and guide the chapter along by providing opportunities for them to build union leadership skills, engage co-conspirators, and bring other potential leaders into the fold.

While speaking to profound issues confronting educators, many students were hesitant to mobilize and take collective action. Were students overwhelmed with the responsibility of planning weekly meetings, or did students need more guidance on how to take collective action? Or is there a more profound reason tying back to the conservative nature of teacher education, where students do not see this modeled?

Conceptual Elements for Shift to Social Justice Unionism

Figure 14.1.

Communication, Consciousness-raising, Community Accountability

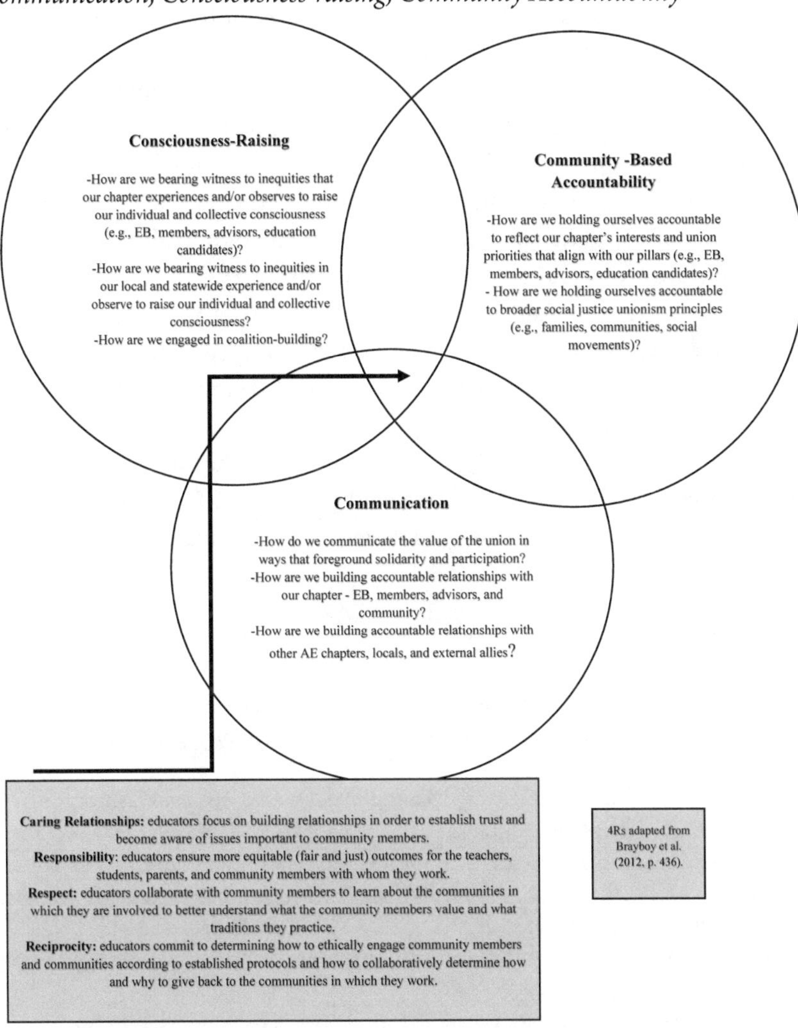

Our blueprint demonstrated in the diagram above and the conceptual elements for a shift toward social justice unionism serve as a road map to action for future aspiring educators who plan to engage in work similar to ours. In the process of unearthing the ways in which our NAU AE have both successfully and unsuccessfully organized around social justice unionism, we identified communication, community-based accountability, and consciousness-raising as the central tenets of our road map to successful chapters. Central to our vision of social justice unionism, like the Aspiring Educators, is the true attempt to behave like a grassroots organizing body rather than simply a "club" or "student organization." We also needed to enact some traditional union organizing practices and structures without being locked into a narrow set of bread and butter issues.

Building relationships within Aspiring Educators, amongst its members, and externally in our community must be at the center of AE as a union. Relational organizing is the currency with which AE could truly operate like a union to ensure more equitable workplaces for the teachers, preservice educators, students, and community members, as well as communities with whom aspiring educators work. In order to implement this blueprint for social justice unionism, a commitment to ethically engage with AE's immediate community in a reciprocal way is also needed in order to act upon the relationships that are central to this blueprint's conceptual elements. In the end, we hoped if we modeled how to engage this work, we could inspire, as Joe Thomas invited, co-owning and taking over a union, rather than just joining one.

References

Aspiring Educators Chapter Toolkit. (2021). National Education Association. https://www.nea.org/sites/default/files/2021-09/Aspiring%20Ed%20Toolkit%202021.pdf

Butler, S. (1987). *The National Education Association: A special mission*. Washington, DC.

Brayboy, B. M. J., Gough, H. R., Leonard, B., Roehl II, R. F., & Solyom, J. A. (2012). Reclaiming scholarship: Critical Indigenous research methodologies. In S. D. Lapan, M.T. Quartaroli, & F. J. Reimer (Eds.), *Qualitative research: An introduction to methods and design* (pp. 423–450). John Wiley.

Chambers, E. T. (2018). *Roots for radicals: Organizing for power, action, and justice*. Continuum.

Charney, M., Hagopian, J., & Peterson, B. (2021). *Teacher unions and social justice: Organizing for the schools and communities our students deserve*. Rethinking Schools.

Editors. (2021). Industrial, professional, and social justice unionism. In M. Chaney, J. Hagopian, & B. Peterson (Eds.), *Teacher unions and social justice: Organizing for the schools and communities our students deserve* (pp. 102–106). Rethinking Schools.

Karvelis, N. (2019). Toward a theory of teacher agency: Conceptualizing the political positions and possibilities of teacher movements. *Berkeley Review of Education, 9*(1), https://doi.org/10.5070/B89146418

Olsen, B. (2016). *Teaching for success: Developing your teacher identity in today's classroom*. Routledge.

Peterson, B. (2021). Social justice teacher unionism. In M. Chaney, J. Hagopian, & B. Peterson (Eds.), *Teacher unions and social justice: Organizing for the schools and communities we deserve* (pp. 99–101). Rethinking Schools.

Peterson, R. (1999). Survival and justice: Rethinking teacher union strategy. In R. Peterson & M. Charney (Eds.), *Transforming teachers unions: Fighting for better schools and social justice* (pp. 11–19). Rethinking Schools.

Smith, J. (2009). Solidarity networks: What are they? And why should we care? *The Learning Organization*. https://www.emerald.com/insight/content/doi/10.1108/09696470910993936/full/html

Zeichner, K. M., & Tabachnick, B. R. (1981). Are the effects of university teacher education "washed out" by school experience?. *Journal of Teacher Education, 32*(3), 7–11. https://doi.org/10.1177/002248718103200302

Endnotes

1 Aspiring Educators (AE) is the name for the National Education Association (NEA) student chapters established on college campuses to provide support to education candidates and encourage more educators to join the union. When we capitalize the term, we are referring to the student chapters. We use the following acronyms: Northern Arizona University (NAU), National Education Association (NEA), the Arizona Education Association (AEA), NAU AE Executive Board (EB), and the Flagstaff Education Association (FEA)—the local association for public school educators in Flagstaff.

CHAPTER 15

Reframing Curricular Opportunities to Nurture and Sustain Critical Consciousness

Jessica Manzone and Julia Nyberg

The Need for Critically Consciousness Curriculum

Curricular experiences must center the child, their home, and community so they develop an awareness of the cultural, ethnic, racial, linguistic, and socioeconomic diversity that exists within themselves and in others. Historically, the education system has done the opposite. It has fueled the marginalization of languages, cultures, and racial groups. This chapter proposes strategies for a critically conscious curriculum that activates *Curricular Critical Reflection* and the translation into *Instructional Critical Action* using the *Home and Community Connections* model. Freire (2000) defined this assets-focused approach to education as *critical consciousness*, or the ability to recognize and analyze systems of inequity and the commitment to take action against them. The need to reframe curricular and classroom experiences through a critically conscious lens is glaringly apparent and can be done so through *Curricular Critical Reflection* and *Instructional Critical Action*.

Reframing curriculum to nurture and sustain critical consciousness must become synonymous with the shift from traditional models that decontextualize and silo culture, race, and language into frameworks that demand the application of subject matter to world issues. Rapa, et al. (2022) define this type of educational space as an "open classroom climate," where diverse opinions and discussions of social and political issues are welcome (p. 471). The longitudinal research conducted by Seider et al. (2020) highlights how critical consciousness naturally rises in young people during adolescence. This chapter proposes that critical consciousness can be nurtured, sustained, and enhanced in *all* learners, from kindergarten through high school, through *Curricular Critical Reflection* and *Instructional Critical Action*. These shifts in the curriculum must move beyond performative and pejorative activities into authentic experiences that value learners' strengths and cultural assets. Superficial rather than authentic changes to a curriculum and ecosystem of a school site reinforces comfort and compliance, and serve the teacher rather than the learner (Cintron et al., 2021, p. 35). Authentic and culturally responsive pedagogies, on the other hand, value the child—their language, funds of knowledge, cultural wealth, talents, and interests (Flint & Jaggers, 2021; Yosso, 2005), and place them at the center of the learning experience. Table 15.1 outlines the trajectory of curricular shifts that need to occur to move instructional experiences from traditional and disconnected to culturally sustaining and critically conscious.

Engaging in Curricular Critical Reflection and Instructional Curricular Action

Today's educational and social challenges reiterate the fact that curriculum is never neutral. It espouses the values, mores, political agendas, and historical perspectives of its creators. Wegwert (2011) vividly describes the curriculum as being "steeped in the lessons of privilege, entitlement, moderation, and exclusion" (p. 93). The role of the teachers is to become active "curricularists" who question, analyze, and modify curriculum when it lacks the critically conscious frameworks described above. This work begins when teachers engage in *critical reflection* and *critical action* regarding their current curriculum and instructional practices and can be referred to as curricular activism. Diemer and Li (2011) define *critical reflection* as the ability to analyze social realities and recognize how current and historic conditions impact access to opportunities. We extend and apply this concept specifically to curriculum and instruction. Therefore, we propose that *Curricular Critical Reflection* must then translate into *Instructional Critical Action*. *Instructional Critical Action* reflects the extent to which individuals actually engage in *Curricular Critical Reflection*, modify

Table 15.1.
Moving from Traditional and Performative to Critically Conscious Shifts in Curriculum

Traditional	Performative	Critically Conscious
Align to core standards and grade-level competencies	Promote diversity generally with no clear plan to analyze current curriculum or accountability for implementation	Conduct a document analysis to recognize the erasure that exists within the standards and actively integrate historically marginalized voices and perspectives
Place real-world applications as the extension or conclusion to the original learning experience	Provide opportunities for real-world connections that focus on "building-centered" activities selected by the teacher (Luter et al., 2017, p. 2)	Place connections to real-world contexts and applications at the forefront of the learning experience in ways that promote community project-based solutions driven by the learners
Utilize current events and multicultural literature as supplemental resources or companion texts within a learning experience	Utilize the token inclusion of diverse literature while keeping the focus of the lesson or unit on a predominant view of power	Utilize current events and diverse literature as the dominant resources for a learning experience that challenges power positions
Build differentiated learning experiences around students' academic strengths and needs	Integrate differentiation that focuses on the social and emotional needs of learners in ways that are void of cultural implications and context	Build differentiated learning experiences through students' funds of knowledge and home and community assets that are transformative in nature (Nyberg & Manzone, 2022a; Jagers et al., 2019)
Center units of study around themes such as friendship, communities, and the environment	Provide opportunities for learners to make connections to larger themes such as power or change, but stops short of discussing how those themes challenge or perpetuate systems of oppression, racism, and bigotry	Weave concepts and themes that can be applied across content areas, such as change, power, conflict, and equity in every learning experience and explore how discussing how these themes challenge or perpetuate systems of oppression, racism, and bigotry
Integrate assessment measures that evaluate student learning for one moment in time	Integrate assessments that promote service learning projects with a focus on good citizenship (Westheimer & Kahne, 2004) built around a decontextualized community project-based solutions	Integrate authentic service learning assessments that critically analyze social conditions and address the impact of issues on communities and societies over time using a community project-based solutions

the curriculum, and then transfer curricular decisions to instructional action. Districts, school sites, and individual teachers are all responsible for consciously working to dismantle the racist and oppressive systems that have historically hindered access to knowledge and opportunities for historically marginalized learners. The questions in Table 15.2 form an initial set that teachers can pose to themselves, their colleagues, and their curriculum to engage in *Curricular Critical Reflection* and *Instructional Critical Action*. Follow-up questions to aid in the transfer from *Curricular Critical Reflection* to *Instructional Critical Action* are also provided and help frame the activist mindset necessary to challenge current curricular structures and instructional decisions.

Table 15.2.

Questions to Engage in Curricular Critical Reflection and Instructional Curricular Action

Questions for *Curricular Critical Reflection*	Questions for *Instructional Critical Action*
How can I place the child and their community at the center of my classroom? How can I get to know my learners as people and build authentic relationships with each student? How can I reflect on my own beliefs and recognize where my biases are impacting the equity of my instruction? How do I enact my district curriculum in ways that are assets-focused and that leverage learners' funds of knowledge? How can I create space for historically marginalized perspectives in my curriculum? How can I reframe my thinking and incorporate unbiased information into my curriculum?	Does my curriculum provide opportunities for learners to understand and engage in the world around them? What steps can I take to bring current events and global competencies into my lessons? Does my curriculum provide context to a topic in ways that challenge the dominant narrative? How can I check my implicit biases and bring multiple perspectives into my lessons? Does my curriculum celebrate identity, culture, community, and joy? How can I move through my learning arch to find and integrate diverse resources into my lessons? Does my curriculum provide opportunities for all learners to connect with the content in meaningful ways? What steps can I take to honor and leverage learners' funds of knowledge in ways that are tangible and immediate?

Teachers are socialized to believe that "professionalism" equals neutrality and that one must maintain a neutral position in the classroom on critical issues (Wegwert, 2023). To appear "unneutral" regarding contemporary and historic issues of social justice is thereby behaving in an unprofessional manner. This chapter argues the opposite; that a true professional educator is an activist, advocate, and agitator for critically conscious curriculum and instruction. The authors are former classroom teachers and current teacher educators who have written this for faculty operating in the K-12 arena. The chapter has three objectives: (a) to advocate for critical consciousness through a tangible set of prompts, (b) to provide clear access points for reframing the curriculum through the use of these prompts, and (c) to highlight a series of questions teachers can use to directly engage in *critical curricular reflection* and *curricular action*.

The authors hope this chapter stimulates teachers' creativity and confidence in making curricular modifications that reflect and respond to the lives of their students. We hope that it will explore the teacher–student, teacher–curriculum, and student–curriculum relationships at their most human level. We hope that it will help create classrooms where trust develops over time and where teachers and students are "knowledge holders who have a deeply interconnected relationship" (Osorio, 2018, p. 109). The remainder of the chapter addresses the question: How can teachers engage in *Curricular Critical Reflection* and *Instructional Critical Action* to develop a critically conscious classroom?

Critical Consciousness Curriculum through Home and Community Connections

A core feature of critically conscious pedagogy is when educators and students are recognized as equal partners. This partnership is based on an ongoing exchange of learning, listening, integrity, respect, and trust (Jack, 2020). These core features cannot be obtained without valuing, acknowledging, and integrating the lived experiences each student brings to the classroom. Once this partnership between teachers and students is built, they can begin to reframe and design the curriculum as a collective unit. Jack (2020) describes how this process transforms educators into "facilitators of learning who provide specific and personalized opportunities for students on their paths to inquiry" (p. 54).

But what do these pathways that value, acknowledge, and integrate students look like in a classroom? How can teachers and students engage in *Curricular Critical Reflection* with their curriculum to create these pathways in a concrete and authentic way that demonstrates *Instructional Critical Action*?

This chapter presents a model that strategically and purposefully reorients the learning experience so that it can be authentically accessed through the lens of students' cultural, racial, linguistic, and communal identities, in addition to their interests, needs, and abilities. The *Home and Community Connections Model* (Nyberg & Manzone, 2022a, 2022b) is activated through a series of prompts. The selection and application of the *Home and Community Connection* prompts are not to be assumed by the classroom teacher alone. The response to the prompts is determined by the student within the context of their culture, interests, and lived experiences. This separates the teacher from making assumptions about the student's home or community. It also places control of the instructional experience in the hands of the student, which is necessary when engaging in authentic *Instructional Critical Action*. The teacher cannot be the only expert in the classroom who has the agency to engage in *Curricular Critical Reflection*. Delpit, in her seminal piece titled "The Silenced Dialogue" (1988), states that "to deny students their own expert knowledge *is* to disempower them" (p. 288). These prompts provide a tangible means for teachers to value, acknowledge, and integrate students, thereby giving agency for learners to inject their voices, choices, and identities into any classroom experience. The prompts that comprise the *Home and Community Connections Model* are defined on the next page in Table 15.3.

Engaging in *Curriculum Critical Reflection,* followed by *Instructional Critical Action* using the *Home and Community Connections Model,* is a fluid and dynamic process. It unfolds in real time as teachers and students reflect and take action to implement learning experiences on a daily basis. The results of utilizing *Curriculum Critical Reflection* to promote critical consciousness in the curriculum using the *Home and Community Connections* prompts provide tangible and immediate results that transfer to *Instructional Critical Action*. These results include, but are not limited to, amplified student voices, increased student engagement, and a transformation of teaching and learning (Kunnath & Jackson, 2019). Under this paradigm, teachers and students are collectively taking action that can be seen and felt in their own contexts and communities. Yet, curriculum modification using the *Home and Community Connections* prompts

Table 15.3.
The Home and Community Connections Prompts

Prompt Name and Visual Icon	Description of the *Home and Community Connections* Prompt
Communication Structures	This prompt refers to the **methods, means,** and **structures** that **families** and **communities use** to communicate. Structures of communication can include **verbal, nonverbal,** and **written** modalities and **impact** the way that students **send** and **receive messages.** This prompt examines how **different modes** of **communication vary** between **cultural groups** and impact **how** a **student participates** in any situation or context.
Cultural Elements	This prompt encompasses the **beliefs**, **rules**, **knowledge**, **rituals**, **collective identities**, and **memories** of a **family** or **group** of people. This prompt focuses on **valuing** and **recognizing** the cultural elements that make each student unique. Students can examine the **cultural elements** that create the **range of diversity** in the classroom and world, as well as **patterns of overlap between** and **across groups** of people.
Communal Philosophy	This prompt refers to the **intentional variables** a **family** or **community shares**. These variables can include **resources, interests, beliefs,** and **values**. This prompt acknowledges that various **communities** have **different philosophical orientations** that impact how they interact with the world. Students can **examine** their own **philosophical** beliefs and the **degree** to which they are **similar and/or different** from others.
Historical Perspective	This prompt refers to the **influence of time** on history, on the **culture**, **heritage**, **families**, and **people**. This prompt helps to **contextualize** the **treatment** of a **family**, **community**, or **group** of people **over time**. The **impact** of that **treatment** at the **individual**, **communal**, **national**, and **global levels must be examined**.
Social Development	This prompt refers to the relationship **individuals** have with the **world around them**. The concept of **multiple group memberships** is **critical** to the examination of this prompt. **Students** are simultaneously **members** of **multiple social groups**: peer groups, family groups, religious groups, sports teams, etc. Each **group contributes** to a different piece of **students' social** and **developmental identity**. This prompt also **examines** the **controversies** that arise when **different social groups** have **conflicting** and **competing points of view**.
Political Point of View	This prompt refers to the **political affiliations** and **orientations** of **students** and their **families.** This prompt recognizes that a **students' political perspective** is **impacted** and **influenced** by **multiple groups**: their familial group, their peer group, their social media group, etc. This prompt recognizes that how we **view** and **respond** to issues is **inextricably linked** to our **individual** and **familial** political **points of view.**

Table 15.3. continued

The Home and Community Connections Prompts

Artistic Contributions	This prompt refers to the **scope** and **influence** of the **artistic works** and **contributions** of **families** and **communities**. Art can take **any medium, form,** or **function.** This prompt is interested in examining the **art created** by **all people** within a **community**, not just as pieces hanging in museums.
Collective Action	This prompt refers to the **actions** taken by a **family** member or **community** in service of an **intended outcome** or **objective**. These actions can be in **response to** both **internal** and **external stimuli**. For example, a family or community can take collective action to help an ill member or to rally around an issue of social injustice experienced by many. This prompt examines **both the action taken** as well as **the motives or reasons** for that **action.**
Traditions Over Time	This prompt focuses on the **customs** and **beliefs passed down** over generations between **family** members and **community groups**. This prompt examines not only the customs of families, but the **symbolic or special meanings** of those **customs.** The **relationship** between **seminal** and **contemporary family traditions** is inherent in this prompt.
Linguistic Contributions	This prompt focuses on the **vernacular**, **syntax**, **words**, and **phrases** used by students and their families. This prompt **values** the **language**, **dialect**, and **expressions** indicative of a specific family or community. Language also refers to the **relationship** between the **home language** of the family or community and its **uses in various contexts.**
Thinking Process	This prompt refers to the **strategies** that **individuals** and **families** use to **solve problems**. The **integration** and **juxtaposition** of **new knowledge** with **previously learned understandings** is a major **focus** of this prompt. This prompt **examines** the conditions under which students and their families **synthesize** and **apply** knowledge and skills in **various contexts and situations**. This prompt highlights the idea that **different cultures** and **families solve problems** in **various ways.**

(Nyberg & Manzone, 2022a, 2022b)

is also projective. It creates the road map for future action and change. The learning experiences students and teachers create today form critically conscious thinkers of tomorrow. In this way, the prompts are used to *critically reflect* on the curriculum and engage in *Instructional Critical Action* to examine structural inequities of the past, address contemporary social issues, and mitigate against future dilemmas.

Instructional Critical Action: How to Take Action Using the Home and Community Connections Model

Curricular Critical Reflection for critical consciousness must be anchored in the assets and identities of students who have been historically underserved and systemically marginalized (Gay, 2002; Ladson-Billings, 1995; Paris, 2012). This paradigm demands that educators value, acknowledge, and integrate the personal and sociopolitical issues that impact students and affect the broader context of the community. Educators then use these issues as the basis for creating experiences that prompt students to question the world they live in, transform into agents of change, and critically confront systems of oppression and social injustice. The prompts of the *Home and Community Connections Model* provide teachers with a pedagogical springboard within an instructional experience that gives students voice and choice, affirms their responses, and provides for flexibility and change, enabling authentic *Instructional Critical Action* in the classroom.

There are three major access points where teachers can strategically and purposefully engage in *Instructional Critical Action* using the *Home and Community Connections* prompts. Engaging in *Instructional Critical Action* for critical consciousness in ways that leverage learners' cultural wealth and funds of knowledge can be integrated *before* the learning experience, *during* the learning experience, and *after* the learning experience (Van de Walle et al., 2018). Where we integrate and place our attention within an instructional experience conveys to students, families, and the community what we acknowledge and value. These access points provide teachers and students with specific places to reallocate and restructure experiences in authentic, culturally responsive, and sustainable ways that value, acknowledge, and integrate the assets and identities of each learner. Each access point is defined below. The authors have provided examples and guiding questions that teachers can use as inspiration to reframe the curriculum in their own classrooms, resulting in *Instructional Critical Action*.

Access Point #1: Instructional Critical Action *Before* the Instructional Experience

The purpose of this access point is to activate students' prior knowledge and create a pathway to participation for all learners. According to Kaplan (2018), this access point serves as a motivation; a means of "directing the intellectual activity" of the students as they participate in the lesson (p. 275). The *Home and Community Connections* prompts serve as a springboard at the start of the instructional experience to push personal boundaries, anchor the experience to the lives of learners, and expose connections to current events, community issues, and critical areas of social justice in the world. Students are more likely to participate in and derive meaning from an experience when connections to their lived experiences are formed at the onset (Bransford & Schwartz, 1999). Teachers must become advocates for pedagogical practices *before* the start of a lesson that honors, welcomes, and includes all learners.

There is not one approach to integrating the *Home and Community Connections* prompts at the start of an instructional experience. Figure 15.1 provides a few examples of how the prompts can be used as the catalyst for building critical consciousness, but they are in no way intended to form a complete list. However, the integration of any prompt at the start of the learning experience requires specific beliefs and criteria on the part of teachers. Teachers must address the Value, Acknowledge, and Integrate framework:

Value: Students' backgrounds, cultures, and experiences matter in the classroom and can be highlighted through community connections. The development of positive relationships and classroom climate impacts the learning process.

Acknowledge: Privilege and systems of power exist in society and teachers must address and mitigate this by introducing and dissecting themes of social justice that relate within and across a subject area.

Integrate: Students' perspectives and opinions hold as much value in a classroom as the teachers and can be integrated through direct connections to their homes and communities.

Figure 15.1.
Examples of Instructional Critical Action Before *the Learning Experience Using the Home and Community Connections Model*

Home and Community Connections Prompts	Instructional Critical Action and Questions *Before* the Learning Experience
Artistic Contributions	Show students an artwork from a culture or group of people who historically been excluded from the content standards. Ask students what they notice and wonder about the artwork and prompt them with the following questions: • How does this artwork and these *artistic contributions* connect with your home and community? • What feelings and emotions does this artwork elicit in you? What feelings do you think the artist is trying to convey in their *artistic contributions* to the community? • How does this artwork highlight the identity of the artist and their culture? How does this shape the *artist's contributions* in the community?
Social Development	Present learners with a concept or theme (e.g., power, conflict, equity) that connects to the content standards. Ask learners to think about these concepts in relationship to their own home and communities: • How does this concept make you feel in your *social group*, or community? • How does your *social group* impact what this concept might mean? Why might this concept mean different things in different contexts to different groups of people, or communities?
Cultural Elements	Engage learners in a virtual field trip to a cultural heritage site connected to a content standard. Ask learners to explore the site from various disciplinary perspectives: geography, sociology, economics, and psychology and prompt them with the following questions: • How are the identities, or *cultural elements*, of people evidenced in the site? • How has time impacted the *cultural elements* of this group of people? • How does the site highlight the *cultural elements* of land, people, and resources?

Access Point #2: Instructional Critical Action *During* the Instructional Experience

The purpose of this access point is to refocus and reshape the original curriculum so that it is examined through a lens of the student's home and community to activate critical consciousness. Like the stones in the base of a kaleidoscope, curriculum can be reexamined using the *Home and Community Connections* prompts *during* the body of a learning experience. The strategic placement of the prompts during the body of the instructional experience highlights students' perspectives and interests in the topic under study and creates opportunities to challenge the dominant narratives and perspectives in the curriculum. This is the place in the instructional experience where students begin to develop and refine critical consciousness, recognize the purpose of social justice, and start to grasp "its impact on their lives" (Boyd & Miller, 2020, p. 16). The more students "turn" the kaleidoscope via the various *Home and Community Connections* prompts, the more opportunities they have to reshape the core content through their own assets and funds of knowledge.

Integrating the *Home and Community Connections* prompts during the body of an instructional experience requires the analysis of two major variables:

the learners and the time frame for the experience. Student voice and choice are critical to participation and meaningful learning at this stage of the experience. Teachers can implement instructional strategies such as partner work, station rotations, and learning centers as options for students to engage with the prompts in a self-directed and authentic manner. The content should "come alive" for learners via the prompts at this stage of the experience. In addition, acknowledging the time frame and pacing of the unit is also important. The number of prompts teachers and students integrate into an instructional experience must be manageable and purposeful. The selection and application of the prompts should focus on deep, relevant exploration of nuanced areas of the content rather than surface-level, broad-stroke coverage. Figure 15.2 provides some examples of how the different prompts can be integrated during the body of an instructional experience in ways that directly build critical consciousness. This level of implementation requires that teachers:

Value: Extensions to the core content via students' home and community connections enhance rather than dissipate the original content standards.

Acknowledge: Students are capable of articulating how they best think and learn, and should have a voice and choice in the selection and application of the prompts.

Figure 15.2.

Examples of Instructional Critical Action During *the Learning Experience Using the* Home and Community Connections *Model*

Home and Community Connections Prompts	Instructional Critical Action and Questions *During* the Learning Experience
Historical Perspective	Show students a non-fiction text. Ask them the following questions during the learning experience: • What *historical perspective* needs to be included to understand this non-fiction text more? • Describe the history, or *historical perspective*, that your family or community has related to this topic? • Have there been instances where your family or community have *historically* experienced this topic before? What is their *historical perspective* on this topic?
Linguistic Contributions	Present learners with scientific phenomenon. Create connections between the language scientists use to describe the phenomenon by placing value on the language they use in their home and community by asking the following questions during the learning experience: • How would your family or community describe this phenomenon? • What specific words or phrases have people in your community used to discuss this phenomenon?
Thinking Process	Engage learners in a conversation during the writing process (in any content area). Ask your learners these questions during the writing process: • What steps do people in your family or in your community take during the *thinking or writing process*? How do they sort their ideas during their thinking process while writing? • What tools (e.g., pen, post it notes, computer) does your family or members from the community use during the *thinking or writing process*? • How do people in your family or community get feedback in their *thinking or writing process*? Do they share with others in the community? Do they get written or verbal feedback?

Integrate: Multiple means exist to reaching the same learning goals and objectives and connecting content to students' home and communities is a necessary practice in meeting these goals.

Access Point #3: Instructional Critical Action *After* the Instructional Experience

Critically conscious instructional experiences can be reframed so they focus not just on the application of skills and content in the classroom, but on the authentic transfer of knowledge to develop community project–based solutions. Static assessments that measure one moment in time can be replaced with dynamic projects and tasks that promote the transfer of knowledge and skills over time (Howell et al., 2019). Renzulli (2016) refers to this transfer as the "present use" of content and processes where learners are engaged in contextually situated problems directed towards "realistic and personalized goals" (p. 88). This is the place in a learning experience where students engage in civic action, function as agents of change in their own community, and produce expert-like work that impacts themselves and others. Students work in talent teams or alone to research community issues and design authentic products that offer solutions within their own sphere of influence. The *Home and Community Connections* prompts serve as doorways for individualized pathways of exploration for each learner within an instructional experience.

As students use the *Home and Community Connects* prompts after a learning experience to engage in community project-based solutions, they learn to break down barriers, challenge stereotypes, build relationships, and examine diverse perspectives. Extending the curriculum into authentic and contextually relevant projects that value the home and community pushes students beyond a superficial examination of social justice issues (Alexander & Murphy, 2020). As students develop solutions for their own communities, they become more invested in the communities, see themselves as agents of change, and develop the ability to critically engage in civic responsibility. Figure 15.3 provides some examples of the types of parallel pathways for exploration that can be created using the *Home and Community Connections* prompts. Creating authentic, experiential assessments to measure student learning requires that teachers believe:

Value: Student-generated questions are of equal (if not more) value than the teacher's questions.

Acknowledge: There are many and varied ways for students to demonstrate mastery of the content that differs from standardized assessments.

Integrate: Capitalizing on student interests related to their home and community at the conclusion of an instructional experience sustains learning and motivation.

Figure 15.3.

Examples of Instructional Critical Action After *the Instructional Experience Using the* Home and Community Connections *Model*

Home and Community Connections Prompts	Instructional Critical Action and Questions *After* the Learning Experience
Collective Action	Show students a primary source document that connects to a history content standard. Ask students to engage in the following assessment exercises: • How does the perspective from this primary source document reflect *collective action* by an individual or group? What historical events contributed to this *collective action*? • How can you connect what you just learned about this historical event to the *collective action* that is suggested in the primary source document? • Have members from your home or community engaged in similar *collective action*? What historical event prompted their *collective action*? How is it similar or different to what we just learned?
Traditions Over Time	Present learners with a fictional story. Ask learners to reflect on these questions after the story has been read: • Does this story reflect your home or community *traditions*? If not, how are yours different? • Why do you think the author chose to present *traditions* in this way? What is your family's purpose in sharing their *traditions* with others? How does this relate to how *traditions change over time*?
Communal Philosophy	Engage students with a math problem. Prompt them with the following questions after discussing the mathematical process: • Have a discussion with each of your family members- ask them their *philosophy* for solving the problem. Do they have different ways to solve this math problem? • How is your family member's *philosophy* regarding this mathematical process similar or different from the one we described in class? • Can you demonstrate your home and community's *philosophy* by solving this math problem in a different way?

There are only two types of educators—those who perpetuate the status quo and those who disrupt it. Engaging in *Curricular Critical Reflection* with the traditional curricular experiences using the *Home and Community Connections Model* requires disruptors that will subsequently engage in *Instructional Critical Action.* It requires educators who see themselves as more than technicians teaching content, but as agents of social change supporting the next generation and their home and community's perspective on empathy, justice, and power.

Conclusion

The need to engage in *Curriculum Critical Reflection* and *Instructional Critical Action* to build critical consciousness through the student's home and community is rooted in many things: a desire to challenge unjust educational structures, a need to respond to the identity and diversity of the students we teach, with emphasis on those who have been marginalized and oppressed, and a hope to create a critically conscious society for future generations. Reframing the curriculum using the prompts of the *Home and Community Connections Model* intentionally celebrates the assets and cultural wealth of the students sitting in our classrooms. The prompts provide educators across the grade levels with access points to leverage and uncover the talents of young people. Finally, the *Home and Community Connections Model* helps learners understand their intersecting identities, value diversity in others, and courageously speak out against violence, oppression, prejudice, and racism in their schools and communities.

Policies constructed at multiple levels of the education system impact inclusivity and student success in the classroom. In order to combat oppressive and destructive policies, Kilinc and Alvarado (2021) argue that teachers must become "critically conscious policymakers" in their classrooms (p. 489). Teachers must engage in the *Curricular Critical Reflection* now that creates the *Instructional Critical Action* that nurtures, builds, and sustains critically conscious learners for years to come. The authors hope that this chapter will provide a springboard for other educators as they:

Value: Create classroom spaces that value the student's home and community bell-to-bell, across all content areas.

Acknowledge: Directly address historical marginalization and erasure of cultures, racial groups, and languages in the education system.

Integrate: Authentically integrate the home and community into the curriculum and instructional experiences.

References

Alexander, A. S., & Murphy, E. R. (2020). "It started with this project": A mixed methods examination of a service learning project for preservice art educators. *Studies in Art Education, 61*(4), 312–329. DOI: 10.1080/00393541.2020.1820833

Boyd, A. S., & Miller, J. (2020). Let's give them something to talk (and act!) about: Privilege, racism, and oppression in the middle school classroom. *Voices from the Middle, 27*(3), 15–19. DOI: 10.58680/vm202030532

Bransford, J. D., & Schwartz, D. (1999). Rethinking transfer: A simple proposal with multiple implications. *Review of Research in Education, 24*(1), 61–100. DOI: 10.2307/1167267

Cintron, S. M., Wadlington, D., & ChenFeng, A. (2021). *Dismantling racism in mathematics instruction.* A Pathway to Equitable Math Instruction. https://equitablemath.org/

Delpit, L. D. (1988). The silenced dialogue: Power and pedagogy in educating other people's children. *Harvard Educational Review, 58*(3), 280–298. DOI: 10.17763/haer.58.3.c43481778r528qw4

Diemer, M. A., & Li, C. H. (2011). Critical consciousness development and political participation among marginalized youth. *Child Development, 82*(6), 1815–1833. https://doi-org.proxy.li.suu.edu:2443/10.1111/j.1467-8624.2011.01650.x

Flint, A. S., & Jaggers, W. (2021). You matter here: The impact of asset-based pedagogies on learning. *Theory Into Practice, 60*(3), 254–263. DOI: 10.1080/00405841.2021.1911483

Freire, P. (2000). *Pedagogy of the oppressed* (30th anniversary ed.). Continuum.

Gay, G. (2002). Preparing for culturally responsive teaching. *Journal of Teacher Education, 53*(2), 106–116. DOI: 10.1177/0022487102053002003

Howell, P. B., Cantrell, S. C., & Rintamaa, M. (2019). Setting the stage for action: Teaching social justice in the middle school classroom. *The Clearing House: A Journal of Educational Strategies, Issues and Ideas, 96*(6), 185–192. DOI: 10.1080/00098655.2019.1649630

Jack, N. (2020). *The pedagogy of consciousness: Pathways to education reform for urban youth culture.* Brill Sense.

Jagers, R. J., Rivas-Drake, D., & Williams, B. (2019). Transformative social and emotional learning (SEL): Toward SEL in service of educational equity and excellence. *Educational Psychologist, 54*(3), 162–184. DOI: 10.1080/00461520.2019.1623032

Kaplan, S. N. (2018). Differentiating with depth and complexity. In C. Callahan & H. L. Hertzberg-Davis (Eds.), *Fundamentals of gifted education: Considering multiple perspectives* (pp. 270–278). Routledge.

Kilinc, S., & Alvarado, S. (2021). Two dual language preschool teachers' critical consciousness of their roles as language policy makers. *Bilingual Research Journal, 44*(4), 485–503. DOI: 10.1080/15235882.2022.2043487

Kunnath, J. P., & Jackson, A. (2019). Developing student critical consciousness: Twitter as a tool to apply critical literacy in the English classroom. *Journal of Media Literacy Education, 11*(1), 52–74. DOI: 10.23860/JMLE-2019-11-1-3

Ladson-Billings, G. (1995). But that's just good teaching! The case for culturally relevant pedagogy. *Theory into Practice, 34*(4), 159–165. DOI: 10.1080/00405849509543675

Luter, D. G., Mitchell, A. M., & Taylor, H. L. (2017). Critical consciousness and schooling: The impact of the community as a classroom program on academic indicators. *Education Sciences, 7*(25), 2–23. DOI: 10.3390/educsci7010025

Nyberg, J., & Manzone, J. (2022a). The home and community connections model: Shifting the power from teacher differentiation to learner personalization. In R. Williams (Ed.), *Handbook of research on challenging deficit thinking for exceptional education improvement* (pp. 436–455). IGI Global Publishing.

Nyberg, J., & Manzone, J. (2022b). The home and community connections model: A strategy for creating inclusive classrooms. In J. Bell (Ed.), *New considerations and best practice for training special education teachers* (pp. 43–67). IGI Global Publishing.

Osorio, S. L. (2018). The vulnerable teacher: Working towards critical consciousness in a second grade bilingual classroom. *Association of Mexican American Educators Journal, 12*(1), 107–127. DOI: 10.24974/amae.12.1.390

Paris, D. (2012). Culturally sustaining pedagogy: A needed change in stance, terminology, and practice. *Educational Researcher, 41*(3), 93–97. DOI: 10.3102/0013189X12441244

Rapa, L. J., Boulding, C. W., & Jamil, F. M. (2022). (Re)examining the effects of open classroom climate on the critical consciousness of preadolescent and adolescent youth. *Applied Developmental Science, 26*(3), 471–487. DOI: 10.1080/10888691.2020.1861946

Renzulli, J. S. (2016). Freedom to teach: Using investigative learning to develop high potentials in young people. *Sobredotação, 15*(1), 75–95.

Seider, S., Kelly, L., Clark, S., Jennett, P., El-Amin, A., Graves, D., Soutter, M., Malhorta, S., & Cabral, M. (2020). Fostering the sociopolitical development of African American and Latinx adolescents to analyze and challenge racial and economic inequality. *Youth and Society, 52*(5), 756–794. DOI: 10.1177/0044118X18767783

Van de Walle, J., Karp, K. S., & Bay-Williams, J. M. (2018). *Elementary and middle school mathematics: Teaching developmentally.* Pearson.

Wegwert, J. (2011). LGBTQ youth and the hidden curriculum of citizenship education: A 'day of silence' in a suburban high school. *Counterpoints, 392,* 90–107.

Wegwert, J. (2023). The social context of education [PowerPoint slides]. Slide Share.

Westheimer, J., & Kahne, J. (2004). What kind of citizen? The policies of educating for democracy. *American Education Research Journal, 41,* 237–269. DOI: 10.3102/00028312041002237

Yosso, T. (2005). Whose culture has capital? A critical race theory discussion of community cultural wealth. *Race, Ethnicity and Education, 8,* 69–91. DOI: 10.1080/1361332052000341006

ABOUT THE AUTHORS

Greta Callahan was the President of the Minneapolis Federation of Teachers, Local 59 from 2020-2024. Greta has taught kindergarten in North Minneapolis for the last decade and was a finalist for Minnesota Teacher of the Year in 2017. Greta is a graduate of the Midwest Labor Leadership Initiative, has a bachelor's and master's degree from Augsburg University, is the Executive Vice President of the Minneapolis Regional Labor Federation, and sits on the Governing Board of Education Minnesota and the General Board of the Minnesota AFLCIO. Greta began her career in a charter school without a union, which is why she has dedicated her life to fighting for strong public schools. At the time of this publication, Greta decided to not seek a third term as president, but rather, run for a seat on the Minneapolis Public Schools' School Board, as her co-conspirator Marcia Howard is running for President of the Minneapolis Federation of Teachers. #powermoves

Janette Zahia Corcelius is a community organizer for the Minneapolis Federation of Teachers, Local 59. Before she started working for MFT 59, she was a music educator for 7 years and was a rank-and-file union member before becoming a union staffer. She taught in Fairfax County Public Schools (FCPS) and District of Columbia Public Schools (DCPS). She was an at-large board member of the Fairfax Education Association (FEA) where they organized to win back public sector collective bargaining, a founding member of the Virginia Caucus Of Rank-and-File Educators (VCORE), a national facilitator for National Educators United (NEU), and served as a member of the Democratic Socialists of America (DSA) National Labor Commission steering committee. She is an alumnus of Virginia Commonwealth University (VCU) where she received her Bachelor of Arts in Music. Clarinet is her primary instrument and music is still a source of joy. Janette enjoys reading, cooking, practicing yoga, and playing music in her free time.

Shiv R. Desai, PhD, is an Associate Professor in Teacher Education, Education Leadership, and Policy Department at the University of New Mexico (UNM). He is currently working with the Albuquerque Public Schools (APS)-UNM Ethnic Studies Education and Health Research Practice Partnership to study how ethnic studies teachers promote healing and wellness, engage in decolonizing practices, foster ancestral knowledge, and affirm students' identities. This research is also funded by the WT Grant Foundation and Hewlett Foundation to support a mixed-methods, cross-site study to examine whether and how ethnic studies courses mitigate academic and socioemotional inequalities experienced by BIPOC students. Dr. Desai's other research area focuses on a Youth Participatory Action Research (YPAR) project with LOUD (Leaders Organizing 2 Unite & Decriminalize). LOUD members—made up of allies, formerly incarcerated youth, and youth on probation—used YPAR to inform new policies to shape a more humanizing juvenile justice system. Dr. Desai's research draws upon critical race theory, critical literacy, and decolonizing/Indigenous methodologies. Dr. Desai was awarded the prestigious NAEd/Spencer Postdoctoral Fellowship in 2015, which supported his research in LOUD and examined key issues impacting the juvenile justice system. He also received the American Educational Research Association Early Career Award from Grassroots, Community Organization and Youth Activism Special Interest Group (SIG) in 2017. Dr. Desai was recently nominated for the UNM's New Teacher of the Year Award. Thus, Dr. Desai's scholarship, teaching, and service has been widely recognized for its advancement of social justice, equity, and critical education.

Katie Ehrlich is a special education teacher in Washington State. She is part of the Washington Education Association and Washington State Educators United. She served on the National Educators United Safe Return to Schools committee promoting health and safety during the time of COVID-19. Once the #OnlyWhenItsSafe campaign began, individual states held their own town halls to promote the campaign and take the lead in opening school buildings only once mitigation strategies were in place. Katie was a lead on this campaign in Washington State. She has also taught special education in a virtual setting in Fairfax County, Virginia, was a building union representative for the Fairfax County Public Schools Virtual Program for the 1 year of the program's existence, and served as a delegate of the Virginia Education Association Representative Assembly in Spring of 2022. She is in her 10th year of teaching in special education in various settings. She is currently going to school for a Master of Education.

Rebecca Garelli has been a professional educator for 19 years, focusing much of her career on teaching middle school math and science. She is also a lead organizer and co-founder of the grassroots organization, Arizona Educators United (AEU), and the Arizona #RedforEd teachers movement. Rebecca is also a former active member of the Chicago Teachers Union (CTU) for 11 years and participated in the historic 2012 strike. Upon moving to Arizona, she co-founded AEU and played an instrumental role in organizing the #RedforEd movement. Rebecca helped develop and successfully execute an 8-week organizing blitz through a detailed escalation plan that resulted in the organizing of 57,000 teachers statewide and the creation of a 2,000 volunteer network in over 1,200 school sites across the state. This massive organizing blitz resulted in a 6-day strike that was launched by a 75,000 person march to the Arizona Capitol through the streets of Phoenix, AZ and helped secure $434M in increased education funding.

Erin Hiebert is a former teacher and currently a Community Schools Organizer with the Arizona Education Association. NAU's Aspiring Educators program ignited Erin's passion for social justice work and labor organizing as she engaged regularly as a preservice teacher through AE, with various localized advocacy campaigns related to Arizona's school voucher expansion, school investment ballot initiatives, and school board elections.

Kimo Homer is a teacher in California. Drawn to organize by the #RedforEd movement, Homer actively worked as an aspiring educator with NAU AE in Flagstaff, at the state level with AEA, and nationally with the NEA.

Marcia Howard has been a teacher and union member since 1998, when the southern transplant and Marine Corps veteran moved to south Minneapolis. Originally from Arkansas, she bought a home near the high school where she still teaches. It was in 2020 that a former student of hers filmed the murder of George Floyd around the corner from that home and galvanized a teacher to become an ardent activist in a global social justice movement. Howard helps lead one of the longest running urban occupations in American history at what is now known as George Floyd Square. She has been joined and supported by union leaders and rank-and-file members while on leave to patrol the "autonomous zone" and after her return to the classroom. Following her involvement in the historic strike of the union in 2022, Marcia Howard was voted in as First Vice President under President Greta Callahan. In 2024, Marcia announced her candidacy for union President of the Minneapolis Federation of Teachers.

Denisha Jones is the Executive Director of Defending the Early Years. She is a former kindergarten teacher and preschool director who spent the past 20 years in teacher education. Denisha is an education justice advocate and activist working with various grassroots organizations to dismantle the neoliberal assault on public education. She is a part-time faculty member in the Art of Teaching program at Sarah Lawrence College and the School of Education at Howard University. Since 2017, she served on the steering committee for the national Black Lives Matter at School Week of Action. Her research interests include organizing activist research projects that examine grassroots movements to achieve racial justice in education, documenting the value of play as a tool for liberation with an emphasis on global approaches to play, and working with parents and educators to foster positive racial, ethnic, and cultural identity development in the early years. Her first co-edited book, *Black Lives Matter at School: An Uprising for Educational Justice,* was published in December 2020 by Haymarket Books.

Brianne Kramer, PhD, is an Associate Professor of Education in the College of Education and Human Development at Southern Utah University where she teaches Social Foundations of Education courses. Additionally, she coordinates the Educational Foundations and Policy major for the Master of Education and Master of Interdisciplinary Studies programs. Beginning her teaching career as a high school English teacher, she has been in the field of education for 20 years. She earned a PhD in Social Foundations of Education from the University of Toledo, and her research focuses on teacher workforce issues, diversity, equity, and inclusion, educational policy, and teacher activism. She has several peer-reviewed publications, has spoken at numerous conferences, and co-edited the 2022 book, *Children and Trauma: Critical Perspectives for Meeting the Needs of Diverse Educational Communities.* She also currently serves on the ACLU Utah Board of Directors and is a Contributing Scholar for the Research-to-Policy Collaboration housed at Pennsylvania State University.

Jeff Lang is a graduate of public schools and comes from a family of teachers, public servants, and union members. He worked for the Hawaii State Teachers Association organizing teachers on the Leeward Coast of Oahu before moving to the desert where he currently works as an organizer for the Arizona Education Association in the Phoenix Metropolitan area. He was also assigned as the staff lead to the AEA Aspiring Educators program and is proud of the work Aspiring Educators do in Arizona and across the country. He is a member of the Arizona Education Association Staff Organization, which is his staff union. He believes all workers deserve dignity and respect, which is why collective bargaining and union density is so important. He encourages the youth to join a union or to start one if there is none. Worker solidarity is imperative in the labor movement and young people are its future.

Rosemary Lee, PhD, is an activist and bilingual educator who has worked in higher ed, preK-12, and adult education in both urban and rural settings. A union activist, she has been a member of the United Teachers Los Angeles (UTLA), Bi-Lingual Education, and Human Rights committees, the Human, Civil and Women's Rights Committee of California Federation of Teachers (CFT), and on the picket line for UTLA and other unions over the years. Beginning with her doctoral research in Mexico, Rosemary has long been involved in international solidarity and working cooperatively across borders. She met the Trinational Coalition in Defense of Public Education at the WTO protest in Cancun in 2003 and has been a dedicated member ever since. As an internationalist and activist, her foci is on building coalitions and working in community-based popular education. She is deeply involved in collective research to counter transnational capitalism which is destroying humanity and the planet. Valuable input to the chapter was contributed by Maria de la Luz Arriaga, (UNAM, Mexico), Larry Kuehn, (BCTF, Canada), and Domenic Bellissimo (OTSSF/FEESO, Canada), founding members of the Trinational Coalition.

Christine Lemley (she, her) is a Professor of Bilingual Multicultural Education at Northern Arizona University. She draws on narrative inquiry and critical oral histories as a way to honor the power of stories. We have all been connected to the Aspiring Educators chapter at Northern Arizona University as students or advisors. As a bilingual, visually impaired mother-scholar from white, European, settler colonial heritage, Christine is committed to building relationships, respect, responsibility, and reciprocity with people, places, and ideas. Her research includes foci on social justice, equity, and inclusion, particularly critical oral history and stories from community members underrepresented by dominant systems and how these identities intersect. She uses critical oral history to address issues of power, structure, and agency to amplify unheard, or unlistened to, voices. She is committed to engaging diversity, equity, inclusion, justice (DEIJ) initiatives in her research, teaching, service, and everyday interactions.

Jessica Manzone is an Assistant Professor of Teaching in the College of Education at Northern Arizona University. She was a classroom teacher and instructional coach before entering higher education. Jessica currently serves as lead faculty for the Arizona Teacher Residency where she works to prepare graduate students for future careers serving their local communities. Jessica's research interests include curriculum and instruction for diverse gifted and advanced students. Jessica speaks at state, national, and international conferences on gifted education and provides demonstration lessons for school districts related to curriculum and instruction. Jessica is also the co-creator of the *Home and Community Connections Model*, which provides teachers with a means of modifying curriculum through a culturally sustaining lens. Her work has been featured at conferences and in multiple book chapters. Jessica is also the Co-PI on a U.S. Department of Education Innovation grant to study teacher recruitment and retention at both a state and national level.

Dana Morrison is an Associate Professor in the Social Foundations of Education at West Chester University of Pennsylvania. Her scholarship has focused on teacher organizing in Philadelphia, critical teacher education theory and practice, and debt financing and counter-organizing in public higher education. Her research in these areas has appeared in *Critical Education, Berkeley Review of Education, Studying Teacher Education*, and the *AAUP Journal of Academic Freedom*. Her forthcoming co-authored book with Barbara Madeloni, Eleni Schirmer, Sofya Aptekar, Jason Wozniak, Maria del Mar Rosa Rodriguez, Joanna Gonsalves, Tracey Berger, and Rich Levy untangles the complexity of debt financing in public higher education and provides theoretical and practical analysis for counter-organizing in postsecondary contexts. Dana has worked on collective efforts to support faculty who experience sexual or gender-based harassment, to extend the Black Lives Matter at School Week of Action throughout the Pennsylvania State System of Higher Education (PASSHE), and to research and organize against public university debt burdens in a nationwide debt reveal day.

Becky L. Noël Smith has been involved in the field of education since 2002. As a former public school teacher, a mother, a community organizer, and through her academic work, she advocates for democratic policies and practices in the public's schools. She now has the privilege of putting to use her teaching and learning experiences in her work with future teachers in the Department of Liberal Studies at California State University, Fresno. Her teaching is grounded in the tenets of social foundations, democratic pedagogy, and Deweyan inquiry, and her current writing projects focus on the aesthetic and moral dimensions of the craft of teaching and the persistent struggle to make public schools more humane. She worked with Save Our Schools March for 7 years on their many actions and conferences, she co-founded the Opt Out Florida Network, and she is a co-founder and active member of Uniting to Save Our Schools.

Michelle Novelli is an Associate Teaching Professor at Northern Arizona University. She is co-faculty advisor for Aspiring Educators NAU, the student affiliate of the Arizona Education Association, and coordinator for the PRAXIS dual certified special and elementary education program. Prior to working at NAU, Novelli taught inclusive education at a Title I elementary school in Flagstaff, Arizona. A California native, Novelli originally fought the calling to teach, succumbing to pressure to follow a career that wasn't in education, but eventually, she earned her teaching degree and started her career. A proud 24-year member of the National Education Association, Novelli has always believed in the power of unions and collective bargaining and works for a day when education has the recognition, compensation, and respect it deserves. Along with working to elevate and amplify the voices of beginning teachers, Novelli is assisting the Aspiring Educators at NAU in their fight for paid student teaching in Arizona.

Julia Nyberg is a Professor at Purdue University Global in the Department of Education. Dr. Nyberg was a K-6 classroom teacher and professional development expert in the United States and Asia before entering higher education. Dr. Nyberg's research focuses on curriculum and instructional design, artificial intelligence pedagogies, gifted and talented students, and curriculum strategies to value, integrate, and culturally sustain populations who have been marginalized in education. Dr. Nyberg speaks at state and national conferences and provides demonstration lessons for school districts related to her expertise in curriculum design, artificial intelligence pedagogies, and differentiated instruction. Dr. Nyberg served as the lead for the Diversity, Equity, and Inclusion Curriculum Guide and the Artificial Intelligence Curriculum Guide for Purdue University Global. Dr. Nyberg is the co-developer of the *Home and Community Connections Model*, an instructional strategy that integrates the student's family and community into the curriculum. Dr. Nyberg serves on numerous professional organizations, including the California Association for the Gifted and the National Black Student Achievement Association.

Natalia Ortiz (she/her/ella), a mother of two and a Chilena-Riqueña native New Yorker, was educated in the public schools of New York City and brings years of experience as a classroom teacher, university professor, racial equity practitioner, coach, mentor, organizer, writer, and facilitator. She is a former founding social studies teacher at a transfer high school located in Brooklyn, NY. She has coached professors with the implementation of writing and student-centered pedagogy as a Writing Across Curriculum Fellow at LaGuardia Community College. She has taught both undergraduate and graduate students in Social Studies Education as part of the Curriculum and Teaching program at Hunter College. She taught undergraduate students at Barnard College as a Term Assistant Professor in their Education Program, and currently, she is a Clinical Assistant Professor and the Director of the Office of School and Community Partnerships in the Department of Teaching and Learning at the NYU Steinhardt School of Culture, Education, and Human Development. In addition to higher education experience, Natalia served as the Director of Programs at the Center for Racial Justice in Education (CRJE) and as an Equity Transformation Specialist with Courageous Conversation working with educators in developing a racial equity practice. Along with her work in schools, academic institutions, and equity organizations, Natalia is a board member of the Education for Liberation Network, a national coalition of teachers, community activists, researchers, youth, and parents whose aim is to help improve the practice of education for liberation by bringing people together to learn from each other's experiences. She is also a core member of the New York Collective of Radical Educators (NYCoRE), a grassroots organization that fights for social justice inside and outside the classroom. Natalia is a passionate educator and parent who believes change is necessary and possible in order to ensure equity for all children in New York City. Natalia co-authored an article titled "Critical Professional Development: Centering the Social Justice Needs of Teachers" in the *International Journal of Critical Pedagogy* and is featured as one of the four teacher-activists in Keith Catone's book, *The Pedagogy of Teacher Activism*. She also has been invited to speak on panels, present papers/workshops, and give keynote addresses at academic institutions and conferences such as the American Education Research Association's Annual conference, Harvard Graduate School of Education's Alumni of Color Conference, and Teachers College, to name a few. Natalia received her bachelor's degree in Latin American Studies from Wesleyan University, her master's degree in Education from the Harvard Graduate School of Education, and her PhD in Urban Education at The CUNY Graduate Center. When Natalia is not educating, facilitating, or organizing, she is dancing, spending time with loved ones, traveling, and enjoying theater.

Stephanie Price has worked in the public schools as a speech-language pathologist for over a decade. She believes education is liberation and has been an advocate, activist, and leader in efforts to create meaningful and lasting change in public schools. During the 2018 Teacher Walkout in Oklahoma, she witnessed firsthand the transformative power of collective action and union solidarity. Motivated by this experience, Stephanie became a union leader in her former local, serving as chair for the racial and social justice committee. Her efforts focused on organizing initiatives aimed at advancing equity for Black and Brown students and educators. Stephanie's commitment to social justice extends beyond her local community; she served as a former member of the National Black Lives Matter at School steering committee and co-created National Educators United. Now residing in the Pacific Northwest, Stephanie continues to advocate for the rights of educators and marginalized communities and currently serves on her local's executive board. She remains dedicated to fostering inclusivity and empowerment within the education system.

Jennifer (Jenna) Queenan is a white, queer educator who joined NYCoRE when she moved to New York City in 2011, where she taught high school in Brooklyn for 7 years before starting a PhD in Urban Education at the CUNY Graduate Center. Her chapter is connected to her dissertation research on strategies used by radical educator collectives, like NYCoRE, in social movements.

Ivonne Rovira is one of the co-founders of Kentucky Educators United, and she was one of several organizers of the 2018 teacher march on Frankfort. She's a proud teacher, parent, writer, union member, breast-cancer survivor, and troublemaker in Louisville, KY. A native New Yorker, she has called Louisville her home for more than 35 years. Before answering the call of teaching, Ivonne worked for newspapers and The Associated Press. Somehow, she's still cheery and optimistic anyway. Ivonne was later the executive director of Common Cause/Kentucky, which works to take money out of politics and make government more accessible to its citizens. She is the mother of three children, all of whom turned out better than anyone could have expected, considering their mom. Ivonne's parents were Cuban immigrants, giving her an outsider's perspective on the promises and limitations of the American Dream. Ivonne is lucky enough to teach Spanish to the cutest kids in the world at Wilder Elementary School in Louisville. Before that, she taught at the Teenage Parent Program, an alternative school for pregnant and parenting teenage girls when it was still in its golden age, attracting visitors from across the country and even from France, Moldova, and MTV.

Pam Segura (she/her) is a political educator and former public high school teacher. She organizes with the New York Collective of Radical Educators (NYCoRE).

Jennifer Sink McCloud is an Associate Professor of Education at Roanoke College where she teaches and conducts research through a critical lens. She raises questions about power, privilege, and oppression in schools, society, and research settings. She is intrigued by questions that begin with "Why?" and "How?" Thus, she turns to qualitative interview, ethnographic, and autoethnographic approaches to research, as well as philosophical/theoretical explorations on difficult matters. Issues of research ethics and care frequently emerge in her publications. She has had the privilege to publish in journals such as *Qualitative Inquiry, Journal of Autoethnography, The High School Journal, Critical Education, Philosophical Studies in Education*, and *Intersections*. She is part of a multi-institutional group of founding research partners in the National Center for Research on Educator Diversity: Research Practice Partners (NCRED-RPP), a national grant-funded research consortium based in the University of Houston that is dedicated to increasing teacher diversity in PK-12 contexts. She holds a PhD in ESL & Multicultural Education from Virginia Tech.

Jesse Sharkey is a teacher in the Chicago Public Schools. He is one of the founders of the Caucus of Rank-and-File Educators and served as the vice president and president of the Chicago Teachers Union from 2010 until 2022. Sharkey grew up in rural Maine. He was raised by his mother, who was a poet and school teacher. He won a National Merit Scholarship and attended Brown University where he majored in modern American history. After graduating, he took an organizing job with the United Steelworkers in North Carolina and later worked for 1199 New England. Sharkey taught at Chicago Vocational Career Academy (CVCA). During his first year of teaching, he suffered a brain hemorrhage at school and was taken to the hospital. After a 12-hour surgery, he eventually recovered and returned to the classroom. After three years at CVCA, he transferred to Senn High School. In 2004, Sharkey began to take a more active role in the CTU and citywide activist politics when his school was slated to close as part of the Renaissance 2010 school reform initiative.

Lauren Ware Stark is an Assistant Professor in the Faculty of Education at the Université de Sherbrooke. She completed her PhD in Critical Policy Studies and the Social Foundations of Education at the University of Virginia. Her research explores the work of social justice educators both inside and outside of the classroom, highlighting their organizing in such organizations as the national United Caucuses of Rank-and-File Educators (UCORE) network. She has taught social foundations and methods courses at the University of Virginia, Bowdoin College, and the University of Maine at Augusta. She also spent over 8 years as a critical secondary English, French, and Humanities public schools educator, including serving as a union representative and Steering Committee member for the Social Equity Educators caucus in Seattle. Her research explores the work of social justice educators inside and outside of the classroom, drawing on her experience as a labor organizer and teacher activist. Her most recent projects contribute to scholarship on adult education, educator learning and knowledge production, social justice unionism, and teacher and student engagement in social movements.

Melissa Tomlinson (she/her), a special education teacher of 24 years in South Jersey, found her passion for being a public education advocate when she joined the Badass Teachers Association (BATs) in 2014. Fighting for educational equity and access to resources for all students, Melissa currently serves as the executive director of BATs. Since then she has expanded her own work as a social justice advocate and as a local union leader in the New Jersey Education Association (NJEA), serving on various committees at the county and state level, including as a representative of her county NJEA members on the NJEA State Executive Committee. Melissa is a co-founder of NJ21United, a caucus of NJEA that works to strengthen democracy and transparency within the union to better advocate for public schools, students, and communities within New Jersey, as well as a founding member of National Educators United. Most recently, Melissa began serving as the deputy director for the Atlantic County Queer Alliance, a 501(c)3 nonprofit organization devoted to building a foundation of community among South Jersey's LGBTQIA+ organizations and individuals.

Gerald Wood is an Associate Professor of Educational Foundations.

Index

D